WOMEN'S ISLAM

WOMEN'S ISLAM

Religious practice among women in today's Iran

Zahra Kamalkhani

Routledge
Taylor & Francis Group
LONDON AND NEW YORK

First published in 1998 by
Kegan Paul International

This edition first published in 2010 by
Routledge
2 Park Square, Milton Park, Abingdon, Oxfordshire OX14 4RN

Simultaneously published in the USA and Canada
by Routledge
711 Third Avenue, New York, NY 10017

First issued in paperback 2014

Routledge is an imprint of the Taylor & Francis Group, an informa business

© Zahra Kamalkhani, 1998

All rights reserved. No part of this book may be reprinted or reproduced or utilised in any form or by any electronic, mechanical, or other means, now known or hereafter invented, including photocopying and recording, or in any information storage or retrieval system, without permission in writing from the publishers.

British Library Cataloguing in Publication Data
A catalogue record for this book is available from the British Library

ISBN 978-0-710-30599-2 (hbk)

ISBN 978-1-138-86999-8 (pbk)

Publisher's Note

The publisher has gone to great lengths to ensure the quality of this reprint but points out that some imperfections in the original copies may be apparent. The publisher has made every effort to contact original copyright holders and would welcome correspondence from those they have been unable to trace.

CONTENTS

ACKNOWLEDGMENTS

This book is based on my Ph.D. thesis, and I am grateful to those who emotionally, financially, intellectually and practically have supported me on my way to complete this work. I am grateful to the Norwegian Research Council for Science and the Humanities (NAVF), for the doctoral and publication grant. The Social Science Faculty and The Department of Social Anthropology, University of Bergen for publication grants and providing me with office and research facilities.

I am grateful to Professor Reidar Grønhaug, for his advice, and support throughout my research work at University of Bergen, to Dr Shahla Haeri for her many constructive comments, to Professor Erika Friedl, and Dr. Fulya Atacan for critical reading of the earlier draft of the manuscript. My thanks go to several other colleagues, Senior Researcher Karin Ask, Dr Knut Vikor, Professor Leif Manger, Tor Skudal who suggested useful comments on an earlier draft of this work. I thank Professor Reidar Grønhaug, Kjell Soleim and Professor Alan Black for supporting me in my academic career.

My highest appreciation goes to my mother who gave me inspiration and for her company in the field and her emotional support. For his concern, I thank my husband, Dr Hoshang Lahooti, who shared with me the pleasure and uphill struggle of becoming an academic person in the host country in Norway. In an effort to express my love and hope for the future, I dedicate this book to my daughter Ghazal and my son Maziar.

ONE

INTRODUCTION

In this book I will focus on two socio-cultural domains – the family and religious activity in the lives of Iranian women. Women maintain the integrity of the household, while at the same time taking part in wider social activities. With this background I explore the religious practice among today's Shirazi women, its transcendental and pragmatic aspects, specifying women's performance in religious rituals.

At my father's home

The main reason for choosing my home city of Shiraz, in southwestern Iran, as a setting for my research was not simply a matter of research convenience.[1] I anticipated that the quest would be both emotionally and methodologically challenging. A combination of my education and experience in 'exotic' Europe made it possible for me to observe my home country with a new consciousness and comparative insight. Political insecurity, war and economic barriers had hindered such a visit until 1989.

The return to my father's home after ten years abroad was for me as dramatic an experience as it might be for a foreign visitor coming to Iran for the first time. I returned to my father's home as a married, educated daughter of the family. My position was such that I was independent, and yet my children and I were still under the protection of my parents. Soon after my arrival I found myself to be engaged in sets of relations which were important to my parents, relatives and acquaintances, and gradu-

[1]This is an accusation sometimes levelled at non-Western indigenous anthropologists as against Western social scientists studying their home communities.

ally I became incorporated into their everyday activities and concerns. These social relations included, among others, activities such as religious rituals and exchanges of visits.

The visiting pattern of my community was such that from the day of my arrival, close and distant relatives came to pay tribute to my family and to welcome me home. I was welcomed with gifts of flowers, or small Iranian handicrafts thought to be of interest to those living abroad, and even a tray of homemade bread baked by my childhood nanny. Then it was my duty to return their visits, whether in response to an invitation, or at my own initiative. For those who were closest to my family I brought some small gifts from abroad. A customary pattern of mutual visits, with or without gifts, kept a balance of reciprocity in social relations and value exchanges. I could not give a gift in return to all my relatives, but my mother, who often intervened to protect my social honour, made excuses, arguing that I was a student.

My original research proposal was not concerned with the study of women's religion, but soon I learned that women were engaged in important religious activity that until then had escaped my attention. On the second day of my arrival I participated in the annual memorial service (*sar-sāl*) of a close relative in which the entire Qur'ānic chapter of *anām* (Qur'ān: 6) was recited. One of the female preachers, who was a distant relative, was impressed by my interest and invited me to attend her Qu'rānic meetings further.

Subsequently I participated in several Qur'ānic meetings led by my distant relative. The meetings were usually held in a small room in a private home packed with up to twenty women, some bringing their school-age daughters and young sons as well. There I was informed about other religious meetings, and soon I became interested in the way these meetings were performed, interrelated, organised and led by women. Eventually I began to participate on a regular basis.

Coming from Europe to be a Qur'ānic student?

The women in my surroundings found my curiosity and regular questions on Islamic matters both admirable and puzzling. Some of my upper-middle and middle-class relatives, who were less involved in religious matters, were particularly puzzled by my interest in spending hours at religious meetings on hot summer days when the temperature often reached 42° C. Some thought that I should rather go window shopping with them, or visit relatives. By contrast others, who were engaged in religious activities and took part in religious meetings and Qur'ānic lessons, admired my interest and were willing to take me wherever they went.

Despite not sharing many of the views of my informants, the fact that I am an Iranian and have lived half of my life in Iran provided me with a guideline for pursuing my anthropological inquiries in a more native manner. I carried out my study independently of official authorities. I was able to come into contact with women with different degrees of religious beliefs and involvement, and I participated with them in as many social and religious events as possible. I expressed to the women I met daily a willingness to attend events to which I was invited, or which were open to the public.

I felt a series of rights and duties towards my relatives quite apart from my academic research plan. As a mother with two children aged 7 and 10, I experienced and shared some of the social constraints typical for Iranian mothers, such as spending a lot of time in crowded clinics, or queuing up to purchase parents' ration goods. However, having a mother and sisters nearby reduced my work with my children, enabling me to move more freely and with less worry. I also spent much of my free time visiting other families and female friends in social and religious events.

As a native Iranian anthropologist, and living in my father's home in the old part of the city, my observation and social involvement was not confined to one particular quarter of the town, but was extensive and widespread. I chose to adopt a flexible form of contact and to follow secular and religious events. By utilising both my own female relatives, as well as other lines of social contact, I was able to observe a variety of ritual situations, exploring the formulation of women's religious activity and family lives. Hence I was able to develop a model of their everyday life.

Participant observation

I started my anthropological observation from participating within a known social network of relatives, and gradually extended this to the unknown local neighbourhood, with whom I had daily social interaction, and extended my contact to their friends. I followed these women in different social and religious fields: such as private religious meetings, shrines, the mosques, funerals and visiting graveyards, as well as my relatives and family friends, evening window shopping, and wedding parties. Through such relations my observation and participation was not confined to one particular ritual, but was extended to a wide range of activities, which again generated broader social relations.

My observations were largely carried out in the densely populated part of the city, where most of the lower- and middle-class families live. This is also the part of town where many of the shrines and mosques are located, as well as the main bāzār. The background of the middle-class women varied. Some were semi-educated or educated housewives, whose husbands were well-off *hajji* merchants, shopkeepers, traders, civil servants, or educated engineers. Other women were religious experts, educated preachers, religious teachers, employees in the civil service, students, schoolgirls, or former wage workers.

To me, participant observation is not only a matter of acting as a native, but emotionally feeling as a native, sharing tasks and taking responsibility. My fieldwork was an experience of intense social involvement, of both observing and participating actively, renewing old relations with my relatives and friends, as well as fulfilling my rights and duties towards older relatives.

My participant observation was passive in the sense that I conducted my observation in the religious meetings (*rowżeh*), staying in the background for hours, reading whatever participants read, and listening to male and female preachers. My participation was active in the sense that my fieldwork involved me in deeper social, personal, and emotional relations, with mutual and continuous feelings of rights and obligations.

I could hardly remain formal in questioning those who were associated with me as relatives and friends; nor could I use a tape recorder, being aware that this might alienate and embarrass them. They often had a positive conception of life in Europe, and one woman expressing a slight envy of me said, 'You have neither the problem of high prices nor the hot summer weather in Iran.' Being identified as an expatriate Iranian was often the equivalent of being attributed with the prestigious status of 'well educated' or 'modern', liberated, well-off and secular. They generally believed that women in Europe were very concerned with their looks and clothing, and were surprised to hear that this was not necessarily so. I was surprised to see the amount of time and money the upper- and middle-class Iranian women spent on their social appearance, compared to the average Iranian immigrant women in Norway.

Collection of data

My data was collected mainly during my first fieldwork, especially during the six months of Ramaẓān, Shawwal, Dhul-Qa'adah, Ďhul-Hījjah, Muharam and Safar of the Islamic calendar (March-August 1989). My second fieldwork covered the months of Muharam, Safar and Rabi-ul-Awwal (June-August 1994). However, the data for my book as a whole is also a product of a longer social and deeper cultural engagement, and cannot be confined to my fieldwork period alone. Furthermore, my material was cross-checked through my continuous contact with some of my main female informants (e.g. letters and telephone calls), by reading local newspapers, and in 1995, returned to Iran on a short visit to attend the funeral of a close relative.

As an Iranian middle-class woman having one third of my life experience abroad, I knew very little about Arabic and Qur'ānic text and prayers. My knowledge on Iranian culture in general and Islam in particular gradually increased along with my graduate and post-graduate studies in anthropology. During my fieldwork in Iran, I often rewrote my notes in detail after returning home from the field. I did not always remember the whole speech given by a preacher, particularly if it involved Arabic and Qur'ānic verses. I was, therefore, fortunate to have my mother and several other female relatives accompanying me at the religious meetings. Their engagement was not due to me and my research, but was part of their own local social network. I checked my notes with them to ensure I had all the information and had understood the speeches correctly. They often told me not to be afraid to ask the preacher herself, as they appreciated the religious interest of educated young women. The Iranian political propaganda in the mass media often criticised expatriates who in one way or another were associated with the West, attacking them for creating a false Muslim identity, and for giving a negative picture of the political struggle of the country on their return abroad. In 1994 the security of the female religious arenas became endangered by several explosions in a shrine (e.g. July 1994 in the Shrine of Imām Reza in Mashhad). Security was tightened and women and their bags were checked by guards at the entrance. This development, along with the general and official view of the 'researcher' being synonymous with internal and external 'spies', made my work in the public arena difficult. It was always hard to know how to interact with the government officials as an Iranian expatriate, without giving the impression of being a 'foreign agent'.

In 1994 I returned to Iran for a second period of fieldwork, and since I only had a few months I had to be more specific about my tasks. I immediately started renewing my participation in the *rowżeh* meetings. I now felt better informed and more familiar with holy texts and ritual problems. I found that I was not the only one taking notes during religious meetings, and I saw several young participants, either students, or middle-class housewives, taking notes of sermons. Also some of my co-*rowżeh* goers took notes of the sermons and blessing verses (*do'ā*), in order to read them later on for increased efficacy.

The religious life of women

The anthropology of Islam, despite its wide range of studies and branches, has contributed little to the study of Muslim women's Islamic beliefs and practices in general, and to Iran in particular. Despite the fact that Iranian women have increasingly become an object of interdisciplinary research studies (since the Islamic political turmoil in Iran in the 1980s), they are often treated as an object of religio-political rhetorics (Thaiss 1978; Fischer 1980). Researchers have not paid enough attention to women's own account of Islamic thought and religious involvement.

It has not been as prestigious to study the sociology of Muslim women's religious practices and organisation, when compared to dominant themes such as women's status and position in the Muslim world, and we are only recently beginning to gain an understanding of the involvement of women in Islamic religion and practices in Muslim societies. Among the books and papers we may name are the unpublished Ph.D. thesis of Altorki (1977), Betteridge (1980), Beck (1980), Fernea and Fernea (1972), Friedl (1980), Haeri (1989), Jamzadeh and Mills (1986), with fieldwork prior to Iranian revolution in 1979; and from other parts of the Middle East, Bowen (1993), Holy (1991), Early (1993) and Buitelaar (1994), Starr (1992), Tapper and Tapper (1987), Tett (1994). These studies show that women are no less concerned than men with religious performance, piety and duties.

This book will argue that the participation and activity of Iranian women in the religious arena is neither muted, nor obscure; and that as a result of the Islamic development in Iran, the women's religious activity has become more visible, both in terms of control and involvement.

Islam and gender

The classical anthropologist's approach to the study of Muslim women reflects a view that women are excluded from public religion, and from participating fully in Islamic rituals carried out in and around mosques and theological schools. I will argue that although Iranian women may not play a leading role in the mosque, they do play an important religious role in other complex forms of organisation, such as the social network of the home and the exclusive female religious houses.

There are at least two problems confronting a student of Muslim society. First, one has often focused on the exotic institution of Islam and the visible religious space of the mosque and schools. Since Muslim women do not play leading roles in rituals at the mosque, and since they therefore have not been readily accessible and visible to the male observer, it has often been assumed that female religious activity and knowledge is non-existent. Second, Muslim women are hazily designated as the protectors of religion in the home without researchers even taking into account its Islamic core and organisational pattern (see also Dwyer 1978:585).

The space of the home has often been regarded by feminist symbolic anthropologists as the women's minimal institution and a muted analytical category for all internal purposes (cf. Nelson 1974; Yanagisako 1979). The public life, such as politics, economic productivity and religious activities, have in the tradition of Islamic studies been tied to male culture, while private matters are associated with female (Ortner 1974). Islam has often been represented as a conservative force and not subject to women's controls. Islam has commonly been interpreted as a sexual ideology of the Islamic patriarchy (Mernissi 1975; Afshar 1982) where women are submitted to patriarchal structures. The students of Muslim societies influenced by such a classical feminist approach often associate Muslim women with nature and uncontrolled passion, and men with culture and political, economic, and religious rationality ('aghal). I study the individual actors as participants in a number of different fields or arenas of connected activities, such as women's religious life and household activities and the construction of the social person with respect to these. I also highlight the effect of wider political, economic and religious developments upon the construction of the person. The social reality of the everyday life of a person is integrated with respect to different fields of organisation (Barth 1992; Grønhaug 1976).

Islamic knowledge: text or practice

The anthropological perspective on Islam has largely been influenced by the Western intellectual reasoning, where the textual authority is treated as superior knowledge (Lambek 1990:23). Furthermore, it has been a gendered knowledge with the male elite as available informants in Islamic society. Its analytical and methodological core is based according to a fixed knowledge of text, scripture and learned male informants.

In European academic thought men are considered to be prominent in Islamic organisation; it is they who perform culturally important Islamic rituals. As a result most writings about Islamic beliefs and practices concern male, not female, participants and experts. The anthropology of religion developed, like most of the anthropological sub-disciplines, in the study of non-literate and inclusive societies (Malinowski, 1954). However, many ethnographers fell into the classical trap and remained ignorant of the women's religious ritual activity. According to Weiner this includes Malinowski as well (1989:12). Among researchers in the anthropology of Islam, the image of Islam has remained a masculine one (Holy, 1991:44), most being limited to scientific reports about beliefs and practices which concerned male but not women as participants and Islamic experts.

The traditional dominance of the scripturalist and intellectual elite in general remain a determinant issue in the study of the process of reproduction of Islamic knowledge (see also Fernea and Fernea 1972:39; Eickelman 1980). This underlines the constitutive nature of the process for production of (Islamic) knowledge (Bourdieu and Passeron 1977). The above-mentioned scholars argue that the literature on Islam has long been dominated by the assumptions and methods of Orientalists and Islamic theologians, focusing on the presumed unity of orthodox beliefs and practices while dismissing popular Islam and thereby ignoring a systematic study of women's beliefs.

I believe that the issue of Islam in practice has much to do with a field of discourse in which a consideration of both moral order and ritual performance is necessary. Leoffler (1988) is one of the few anthropologists who take into account the Islam in practice in Iran. In this study the fieldwork mainly involves interviewing male Iranians from different social classes and professional categories, such as mullahs, craftsmen, students, teachers, peasants, etc. so as to study their actual Islamic beliefs. The study does not include women. Having better access to religious men than religious women appears to be a common methodological problem among Islamic students, both foreign and native. The sex of the anthropologist is an important factor in the development of a network of informants in the field. A native male ethnographer from the local university told me that he had made an effort to do a study on women's religious meetings, but he was only allowed to sit behind a curtain to observe one of his female relatives' religious meetings. His sphere of experience as a male anthropologist did not allow the extent of his knowledge to go beyond the curtain.

There is no doubt that the religious beliefs and practices of Muslim women are even more inaccessible to the non-native male outsider. This is mainly due to the culturally required segregation of sexes and gendered spaces. Due to the exclusion of women the male researcher has practically no access to the women's sphere of religious activity.

This may be one of the explanations to the different insights among male and female researchers. One may assume, therefore, that the general formulation of Islam and gender has had a male elite bias (Mernissi 1991a).[2]

The dominant role of the elite as informants in the scientific works of Islam

Much of the ethnography on the cosmology and rituals of Islam has emerged from educated male informants with the visible public role and ability to explain matters to Western experts.

Many of the local male and female religious teachers who tried to assist me in my study argued that I should focus upon the knowledge that could be drawn from recognised religious books and Islamic texts, or talk to prominent preachers, rather than spend time at women's religious meetings. They made an effort to assist me by putting forward what they thought to be politically and scientifically important and necessary for introducing Islam to Europeans and non-Muslims. They often dictated male concepts of Islam and ignored the importance of the religious practices and beliefs of the women.

A male religious teacher from a girls' high school gave me a list of recent religious publications on Islamic family laws, and the economic and sexual rights and duties of husbands and wives (Mutaheri 1975). These are popular topics that have emerged since the Islamic revolution, and about which there have been published a large number of books by high-ranking male theologians and authors. On another occasion, my father, a traditional local *hajji*, asked one of his friends, a former tailor from a high-ranking religious family, to bring me some of his rare religious books from the private library of his family. On yet another occasion a shopkeeper friend of my father brought me several copies of a well-known interpretation of the Qur'ān (*Tafsir-e-Nemoneh* by Makarem-e shirazi). This book was also recommended to me as an introductory text to interpretation of the Qur'ān by one of the newly graduated preachers of the Islamic school of Maktab-e ekhās (School of purity) in Shiraz.

In general, those who tried to assist me emphasised the import-

[2]Mernissi (1991a) has investigated the historical roots of dominant Muslim views towards women, and argues that they have more to do with existing patriarchal norms and roles of male elites than with Islamic theological foundations. She argues that the way women's rights have been interpreted through the *ḥadīth* has cultural and not religious doctrinal roots.

ance of particular texts or interpretations given by certain Islamic experts. Although I did not use these books and informants directly, their resources improved my theological and normative understanding of Islam.

In contrast to my male informants, who explicitly undermined the religious activity of women as less scientific and important, and as being superstitious, my female religious companions went beyond the textual and guided me with local names and addresses of female preachers whom they knew well or had heard of. They also informed me of forthcoming religious meetings held in private homes or at the city mosque, and brought me books of blessing verses and religious poetry. To them the religious meetings formed an important part of their Islamic beliefs, equally important as the religious activity of the men.

TWO

FEMALE RELIGIOUS MEETING: *ROWŻEH-E ZANĀNEH*

Introduction

In this chapter I will focus on *rowżeh* and *jaleseh*[3] (hereafter referred to simply as *rowżeh*), the religious meetings of women, and their interrelated activities. I will refer specifically to the following points: (1) the networks of religious organisation; (2) the symbolic nature of Islamic rituals; (3) the Islamic ideas and its content, and the transmission of Islamic knowledge.

The female religious meetings (*rowżeh*), in its various manifestations, is carried out in the space of a 'home'. It constitutes a woman's social and religious network. The mosque is for women only of a secondary importance, and does not constitute the only, or highest, area for collective religious authority. Women are not excluded from participating in mosques, and some organisational responsibility has recently been given to younger women. However, they do not perform the main rituals,[4] nor do they give any speeches.

The average female preachers and female ritual experts maintain significant Islamic authoritative positions at the female religious meetings staged in private homes. This latter position is in strong contrast to women's position in the mosque. Thus, to understand the religious meeting of women (*rowżeh*), one must

[3]These two terms are used interchangeably to refer to any religious meeting, although used with a slightly different form according to the time and occasion. The term *rowżeh* often refers to meeting during the holy months of Ramzāun and Muharam, while *jaleseh* refers to most Qur'ānic meetings throughout the year.

[4]After my fieldwork, I heard that once a week there was a religious meeting for women in charge of a female preacher in the Mosque of Jāmeh in Shiraz. On this day the mosque was closed to men.

consider it within an Islamic context of personal, communal and family rituals, that mainly focus on women and their religious organisational networks.

The Islamic knowledge of women is gender- and sphere-specific. The religious activity of women has been defined not only as an act of worship but as a complex of social events (Jamzadeh and Mills 1986; Betteridge 1980). The meetings are exclusively organised and headed by women and forbidden to men.[5] They also have a network of their own, thus endowing the home meetings with a mosque-like impression. The home religious meetings of women allow for a certain degree of material and spiritual exchange, through which they can adjust their position in relation to gender boundaries and family formations.

However, in my view these religious meetings also mediate everyday social and political events. The female religious meetings performed at 'home', include the arrangement of regular family religious rituals, Islamic teachings, recitings of the Qur'ān and other holy Shi'ī texts, speeches, and exegesis of the Qur'ān (*tafsīr*). The frequency of these religious meetings has increased since the Iranian revolution. The number of female participants has increased on special occasions, such as the daily *namāz* during the Ramaẓān (the month of fasting), the *'aid-e-fetr* (last day of Ramaẓān), and during visits by prominent male and female preachers from one of the holy cities.

The structure and organisation of women's religious meetings

The women's religious meeting, such as *rowżeh* and *jaleseh*, contain a series of complex rituals. The meetings are often arranged by women, mostly in private homes or in some public building, such as a religious school or a religiously endowed house (*husyneh*).

Rowżeh is a meritful and votive act of women. It may be arranged in the house of an individual family, or in a religiously endowed building. It is a particularly popular way of meeting one's religious obligations, of demonstrating one's faith, and of

[5]In the newly established religious schools, students (*talabe*) study together, or they may sit on separate benches and have different social spaces. There are three female schools in Shiraz. Maktab-e zahra and Maktab-e zainab are in charge of a female preacher; and one, Maktab-e ekhlas, is in charge of a male clergy. All three were considered to be communal properties (*byat-al-amval*).

obtaining blessings (*barakat*) for the entire family. Attendance is based on neighbourhood relations, family membership, acquaintance and friendship. These relationships form the basis of an individual's religious network.

The news of a *rowżeh* meeting is often spread by word of mouth to neighbours, relatives and friends. When women meet at a Qur'ānic meeting, they may invite each other to their own meetings, or to a common friend's meeting, or exchange information about other local rituals. This is part of their general exchange of information. Moreover, at the end of each meeting, the preacher will inform the audience about other meetings, and the particular preacher to be in charge.[6]

The organisation of female religious ritual such as *rowżeh* is a contribution towards the religious community, family unity, and a reflection of personal belief. Its performance is influenced by the broader political discourse. For example, the illness of the Imām Khomeini initiated some votive meetings in local places.

The *rowżeh* are not the only religious meetings arranged by women in order to fulfil specific vows. There are various forms of rituals, such as *khatmeh-anām* (reading the entire Chapter 6 of Qur'ān), ritual of gathering of *aḥyā* (night-watching), reciting the blessing verse of *Joshan-e kabir* (in *Mafātieh*), and Qur'ānic courses (*jales-e ghar'āt*). These religious meetings differ in the form of the rituals, and in the motives underlying the participation in the rituals. They are practised by women of various social and class backgrounds, and they may be arranged as independent ritual events, or sub-rituals, of organised religious meetings.

During the Ramaẓān of 1989, seven religious meetings (*rowżeh*) were held in my neighbourhood, each supervised by different preachers and seminary teachers. By the time of my second field trip in 1994, the number of meetings had increased in size, frequency, and number of young preachers.

In 1989 the number of participants would vary from meeting to meeting, depending on the house, the day it was held, and the form of the ritual. The attendance at a *rowżeh* during the month of Ramaẓān varied from 20 to 100. The largest meetings

[6]This is partly similar to the way in which the male preacher may inform his audience about a newly invited speaker, the location for the next gathering, and the address of a local arrangement. However, male and female communal gatherings may publicly advertise by putting an announcement at the entrance of the mosque.

were on the night meetings (*aḥyā*) held on the night of 21st of Ramaẓān (marking the death of the Imām Ali), and the meetings of *Tāsoā* and *Ashorā* (marking the wounding and martyrdom of the Imām Husain). Women were packed in several rooms, and even the yard outside was crowded on the particular day of *Arbain, Tasoā* and *Ashorā*. Generally the participants at home meetings were relatives, family friends, friends of relatives, friends of friends, neighbours, schoolgirls, strangers who were passing by the house, and followers of the preacher. Some of the participants attended different *rowżeh,* as is the case of the Qur'ānic teachers, middle-aged *hajji* women, students of Qur'ānic courses, older and widowed members of the community, regular *rowżeh* participants, and the preacher's followers.

The Shi'ī Islamic text

Reciting the Qur'ān and traditional Shi'ī holy texts, reading from the book of *mafātieh,* or poetic song (*noḥeh*), and explaining rules of purity and pollution according to the book of *halol-masal'eh/ resaleh* (solution to problems), are central parts of these rituals, and are often followed by Qur'ānic commentary (*tafsīr*).

Mafātieh is used as a book of blessing. It includes a series of verses appropriate for each particular day of the week (such as Fridays), for every single day of the month of Ramaẓān, and for holy days. It also includes blessing verses (*do'ā*) for particular circumstances, such as journeys, illness, requesting fertility and health, and the like. Some of the verses are believed to vary in their effects, depending on the time of day at which they are recited. Some are, for example, best said in the middle of the night and in the form of speaking to God (*monājāt*), or immediately after the morning prayer. To achieve a desired state, an individual may read *mafātieh* and follow its prescribed rituals. These recitations can be arranged as independent ritual events, or as sub-rituals of *rowżeh*-meeting.

Initiation of the meetings

Much of the female religious activity has its point of origin in the practice of making vows (*nazr*). Women often initiate a vow, or visit shrines and religious meetings, in situations of uncertainty; e.g. in case of illness, death, economic and social turbulence, indeterminacy or problematic political ties. Women are often the initiators of the vow, and carrying out such rituals is a central aspect of their religious life. The objective of the vow may be to achieve something for oneself or a close family member, whether as a merit for the dead, or as a benefit for the living. The organisation of a vow is complex in its content, and varies according to rituals and forms. Different vows generate different rituals of different communal services. They involve several kinds of religious thoughts, ritual exchanges, and social activities, and embrace the sphere of the family, the relative, and the local community. For example, a woman may vow that if a particular request is granted, or a personal or family difficulty is remedied, she will sponsor a specific kind of religious ceremony. By making a vow to perform an appropriate religious ritual, the women commit themselves to active religious participation and communal sharing.

The principal themes of votive rituals concern personal wishes and the wellbeing of relatives, the living or spirits of the dead. Family concerns dominate, such as the desire to cure sickness, to facilitate the marriage of a son or a daughter, to ensure the security of children residing abroad, to maintain or improve family health and welfare (particularly during military service and business crises), etc.

Different religious meetings

One of the most popular Qur'ānic meetings among Shirazi women is the ritual of *khatm-e anām* (religious meeting held to recite the entire Chapter 6 of Qur'ān), which may be carried out throughout the year, and on various religious and family occasions. The performance of *khatm-e anām* at home is somewhat similar for men and women, but the meetings of women are more frequently held and are more heavily attended. As an annual votive meeting, it may be arranged during the month of Ramaẓān, which is believed to have particular merit. The participants read the short or long verses one after the other at the request of the preacher or voluntarily. Another popular meeting is that of *kumail*, in which a chapter of *kumail*[7] is read,

[7]That is another popular *do'ā* from the book of *mafātieh*. It is said to be performed on Friday, *aid-e-fetr* and *aid-e-ghorbān*. It is about the 12th shi'ī imām Zamān whom is believed to have gone into occultation in AD 874.

and of *nodbeḥ*[8] in which a chapter of *nodbeḥ* is read (both from the Shi'ī book of *mafātieh*).[9]

The votive religious meetings are generally carried out throughout the whole year, but it is thought that the flow of blessings is greatest on holy days. Some religious meetings follow the Islamic lunar calendar, being performed on specific days (on Thursday or Friday) in the months of Muharam and Ramaẓān, or on an annual basis, commemorating such days as the martyrdom of Imām Hasan, Husain and Imām Ali. The dramatic rise in the prices of rice, meat and oil have meant that many can no longer make annual vows of meal in the name of *sofreh-Abul Fazl*, one of the Shi'ī martyrs, although this is often the favoured form of ritual within the family.

Saḥarī, eftari

Most religious meetings are open to the public, although invitations are common for some rituals, such as the *saḥarī* ritual of sharing and serving meal (meal in the middle of night with which a fast begins), or *eftarī* (meal in the evening ending a fast). The Qur'ānic verse about the day of destiny (*al-qadr*, Qur'ān; sūreh 97) or verses from the book of *mafātieh* (Joshan-e kabīr), are often recited during the night meeting on the 27–29 of month of Ramaẓān. In the case of rituals involving communal meals, an estimate of the number of guests is necessary to ensure that there is sufficient space and food for the participants. The number of participants is often said to be larger at the meetings involving meals.

Aḥyā

The ritual of *aḥyā* may be performed on 1–3 holy nights during the month of Ramaẓān. The men and women believe that on such a night the door of paradise is open and Allāh grants people

[8]*Nodbeh* is a popular *do'ā* of *mafātieh* and is often read in both male and female religious meetings on Thursday evenings or Friday mornings. It is performed for fulfilling one's wishes.

[9]*Mafātieh* is said to mean a key of paradise, a collection of blessing verses and the Prophet's speeches, collected by Imām Ali, and then by his other successors Imāms and finally by Abas-Qumi. This scriptural tradition seems not to be a legitimate source among the Sunni Muslims.

all they ask for. Those who wish to arrange a Qur'nic meeting at home in the month of Ramaẓān may also include such a ceremony. The period of *aḥyā* is one of commemorating the wounded, the sick, the death of the Imām Ali,[10] and the night of *ghadr,* when it is believed that the Qur'ān was revealed to the Prophet. The night of the 27th of Ramaẓān is usually the date when the *aḥyā* is performed at the local mosque, while the women also arrange the *aḥyā* on the nights of 19th, 21st, and 23rd of the month. These are the different days that the traditional and reliable Shi'ī *ravāyāt* (religious authors) claim that Ali was killed. The ritual of women is outlined in the reading of the *do'ā* of Joshan-e kabīr[11] (which names God in eleven hundred metaphoric names) and *abuhamzeh,* as well as in the men's ritual.

The men's ritual of *aḥyā,* is often held in a small local mosque, or in a private home. In a similar fashion as the women's *aḥyā,* the men's meeting includes the reading of a specific prayer selected from the Shi'ī book of *mafātieh* (i.e. most often the same chapter of Joshan-e kabīr), and the carrying out of the ritual of *monājāt* (speaking to God). Furthermore, the meeting will end with serving a meal in order to start the fast (*saḥarī*). The male hosts may themselves take the responsibility for serving a meal, although the food has been provided in advance by the wife or, as is the case of a big meal, by a male cook. In spite of these similarities, the religious meetings of women are larger in the number of participants than the equivalent male gatherings.

The *aḥyā* is a very well attended form of religious ritual, and those who have not attended more than a few meetings during the whole month of Ramaẓān may wish to participate in the mosque nearest to their home. In some large mosques and Islamic cultural centres the men occupy the larger hall next to the pulpit, while the women occupy a smaller hall, a balcony, or they sit outside in the yard where they can watch and hear the speeches of the preacher on TV.[12] Participation in the ritual of *aḥyā* means

[10]There is no fixed date and according to the different reports, these days of Ramaẓān are to be the most likely. This assumption was also observed by S. Altorki among the women of Ahl-e-balad in Saudi Arabia (1977: 133).

[11]A very popular *do'ā* of *mafātieh* that includes 1,100 names of God. This was often performed at *rowżeh* meetings and broadcast as a radio programme during the month of Ramaẓān at night.

[12]At some large mixed pre-revolutionary *rowżeh-khānī* held in the yard, women were often placed very close to the *minbar,* sitting on the ground; and men next to the wall sitting on chairs.

that women spend a whole night outside their home together with other female relatives or friends. This is not a sanctioned behaviour for women. The places open to women at night are local mosques, private homes, religious schools and shrines on the holy night.

Within the religious space, women may practise some behaviour that may otherwise be considered culturally shameful. During the holy months and days they can, for example, go out in the street at night, sit in a public place in the company of other women, and stay away the whole night in a shrine during the holy months and days. The latter is particularly true for the holy nights of Ashorā and Tāsoah. Some women participate in *rowżeh* meetings despite their husband's negative attitude. Among the elderly the negative attitude of the husbands is defined as 'typical male selfishness', rather than being a concern for them personally, or because of being a 'true' Muslim. On the contrary, the men argue that the women are not practising a 'true' Islam, because they neglect the family responsibility and annoy the husbands.

However, despite such an increasing attendance of women in public religious places today, I also got the impression that there were a larger number of female religious meetings in private houses than in the mosque.

Going to rowżeh

Whenever I and women accompanying me could not remember the address of the particular house where a *rowżeh* was to be held, we looked for flag signs and followed these. Neighbours would know that a religious meeting was to be held when flags were hung at the side, or on top of a house. The outward sign of *rowżeh* is a triangular flag in black or green. Such flags sometimes identifies the religious descent of the host, as was explained in terms of *'ams*,[13] *seyyid*,[14] and *sheikh*[15] by my female informants.

[13]*'Ams* are the majority of families which are not descended from the Prophet's family.

[14]*Seyyid* are families who are presumed to be descended from the Prophet's family. This link thought to be of at least three kinds; *seyyid-hoseyni*, *seyyid-e-muhamadi*, *seyyid-e-tabatabi*. The last category presumed link are closest, involving the descent of both through father and mother. The former are presumed to be linked through one of the parents.

[15]A *sheikh* is a student of religion at the religious school. He/she may be a descendent of the Prophet's family.

Symbolic colours, such as those associated with religious rank, are commonly displayed in the holy month of Muharam as a sign at local ceremonies. Green is the 'colour of Islam', and black represents mourning. In particular black represents a Shi'ī mourning based on the cosmology of ties between the martyrdom of Imām Husain and Imām Ali, as portrayed in the Karbalā tragedy.

It is considered the religious duty of the male and female initiators of the meeting to ensure the privacy for the guests in their house, and neglecting this is 'to risk buying the sin of others for oneself'. Thus, the hostess feels obliged to protect other women by preventing the male residents from hearing women's voices during the meeting. Small children often play the part of messengers between gender-segregated spheres. Pre-school boys, as well as girls, may attend the womens' religious gatherings in the company of their mother or a close female relative, such as a mother's sister or grandmother.

At the religious meetings in the religious school which I attended regularly during the month of Ramaẓān in 1989 and 1994, women often reacted negatively to a man entering or passing through the yard of the house without warning. The only occasion I saw a husband entering the hall where a female *rowẓeh* meeting in Ramaẓān was in progress, was in the house of the preacher Zaki. Her husband, a religious man and well-known clergy, entered. He often announced his arrival by loudly reciting an Arabic phrase,[16] *'yā-allāh'* (in God's name), warning the female guest *'nā-maḥram'*,[17] to do their veil. When his presence was discovered by women sitting close to the entrance, they shouted the news to the others in the room, so that they could cover their heads and avoid letting him hear the voice of women. He stayed out of sight of the women, remaining in his office where he apparently had some private consultations. Whenever the husband entered the house during the *rowżeh*, the participant reading the Qur'ān stopped, and the wife in charge of the Qur'ānic ritual took over the reading. This was considered legit-

[16]He repeated *yā-allāh* (in God's name). This is a term repeated as a man enters his own house or that of a kin, in case there are women present. Men use this phrase in different contexts, for example, upon entering a sister's house, in case she might not be properly dressed.

[17]This term may also be associated to non-kin category.

imate since the relationship was both *maḥram* and a religious one.

The progress of the *rowżeh* meeting

Women arrive at the *rowżeh* in a steady stream, one by one, or in groups of two or three. I was often accompanied by one of my co-*rowżeh* goers, or I would go alone. On entering a meeting the participants greet the preacher, who often responds by saying *salām khānom*, which is a polite expression used for highly respected women. In addition to Persian, the Arabic expression may also be used. In the more private Qur'ānic course participants get to know each other better, and often establish long-lasting friendly relationships. A mother or grandmother may bring their small children or nephews or find a place next to her prayer rug. On religious national holidays children and schoolgirls attend the meetings in greater numbers. The seating arrangement is informal, except for the seat of the preacher. The younger participants are warmly welcomed as full participants, and they are referred to as a resource for the future of Islam. In this regard they are expected to take the place of their elders. The practice of greeting first (*pīsh-salām*), even if the counterpart is younger, an enemy, or a child, reflects personal piety modelled after the behaviour of the Prophet Muhammad. Models of good behaviour and character for women include not only the women of the Prophet's family, but also the Prophet himself.

The women who arrived early usually took a place next to the wall, which has higher status and is more comfortable in the main room where the preacher performs the ritual. A *rowżeh* held on a holy day or during the religious months may become crowded to the extent that those sitting in the centre will face the preacher, apologising for turning their backs to the women sitting behind them. Close friends, or assistants of the hostess, may sit next to each other. A religiously distinguished guest is often offered a seat near the preacher, or a place against the wall. These women are identified as 'learned' women, they have Qur'ānic knowledge, or are students of Qur'ānic seminaries; or they are the best readers of the Qur'ān, being able to recite the grief songs (*noḥeh*) with melody, invoking one's emotion, which is said to reflect goodness of heart and give rise to great affection. The 'learned' women often contribute to the meeting by reading to others from a particular chapter in Qur'ān and blessing verses, or by acting as assistants in instructing rituals from the book of *halol-mas'aleh* (resolving or unravelling everyday problems).

As the reading of the Qur'ān proceeds the participants regularly correct each other, or the reader by asking her to repeat the entire verse. Such correction is not considered to be insulting, and the break does not undermine the quality of the verse.

The correction of such mistakes is not only a matter for the most learned, but is thought to be the responsibility of any 'learned' participant who happens to notice it first. Corrections may give rise to some debate as to what the correct reading is, but the passage will be re-read anyway. There are hardly any reciting mistakes that can escape the better learned participants. Sometimes a whole page can be read before the reader is interrupted and reminded of an earlier mistake. The procedure is then that the reader repeats the whole verse (*āyeh*) correctly. This functions in a friendly manner between members with different social backgrounds. The 'learned' women generally make fewer mistakes and have a Qur'ānic melody. They are able to answer some of the religious questions, and have a greater knowledge of prayers, purity, ablutions, *ḥalāl* (lawful) and *ḥarām* (forbidden). The longer a woman has been a student or regular participant of Qur'ānic seminaries, or religious gatherings, the higher her religious rank.

The part of the house used for various religious meetings is the best room in the house, i.e. the guest room or *salon* where distinguished guests, workmates of the husband, old friends, and other guests, such as distant relatives and male family members, might be served. On a daily basis it is more common for the women to gather in the living room or the kitchen, or on a summer evening in some corner of the yard on a bench, chair, or small carpet spread on the ground. Housework is carried on while chatting. Close female relatives who are less reserved often visit in the kitchen as a matter of convenience and friendship, while the hostess may continue her daily cooking and cleaning routines. The nearby sitting room may be used for chatting and serving tea.

Women stress respect by holding the religious meetings in the guest hall, which is often used for male visitors coming from a distance. The *salon* is called *mehmān-khāneh* (house of guests) for special male visits and family occasions. When this room is used for a women's religious gathering, the best utensils and cups are used, an extra *chādor* is provided for the preacher in case she is willing to change, and other items carefully selected from holy places during holy journeys are particularly displayed. The guest hall is decorated with the best furniture and other valuable items, including photographs of important events, such as funerals graduations, weddings, and trips abroad. For the women's meeting, however, most of these items are removed, since much space is required.

The yard is usually surrounded by a wall for privacy, and during the days of religious meetings a curtain might be hung in front of the entrance of the open door, to shield them from the views of passersby. However, inside the hall a loudspeaker may be used if a large number of participants are expected. The use of loudspeakers is a completely new phenomenon at female meetings, although they have long been used by male preachers in the mosques.[18]

Theological and family matters

Most marriage arrangements are initiated in different forms within the feminine atmosphere of secular and religious gatherings. Other popular places to seek for the ideal bride are at family parties, in group journeys, among neighbours, and occasionally at mixed evening language classes, or at the place of work.

The nomination of a particular girl may be taken one step further by sending a message to the girl's house, suggesting a possible visit. However, the use of a match-maker has become more common among families today, as compared to previously when boys and girls were more mixed and free to meet in the public arena.

This form of nomination of brides or grooms does not only apply to those who live in Iran, but also to sons or brothers resident abroad. Men often place the full responsibility for finding a suitable bride on their sister, mother or sister-in-law.

[18]In August 1989 my religious companion attended a large ceremony marking the fourth day of mourning for Imām Khomeini. She later told me how surprised she was that loudspeakers had been used in the yard during the session. However, care is always taken at female religious meetings to contain the sound to the sphere of the house.

Women generally have a wider range of information concerning other families and their female members, thus providing them with an important authoritative role in negotiating marriages. In selecting a suitable girl for a male relative, the women will consider a series of factors and qualities, some on the level of family and others concerning the girl herself. A girl's character is judged from her social network, social behaviour, modesty and beauty. Once I witnessed a well-educated man resident in Germany who when visiting home hoped to marry a suitable bride through the mediations of his mother and sister. He wanted a good-looking girl from a reasonably well-off family, who was modest (*najīb*), since he was disgusted by the behaviour of the Western women. On another occasion it was the mother who wished to find a proper bride for her son, insisting that she be modest, although she need not wear the old long-length veil (*chādor*), the Islamic suit (*manto*) would be sufficient. A desirable bride is generally a girl who is both modest and able to converse.

In the view of the recent Islamist families of the *ḥezbullāhi* (party of God), the idea of a modest bride has somewhat changed. In one case they chose a girl whose father worked as a *pāsdār* (revolutionary guard), and whose mother was a regular *rowżeh*-participant, as suitable for a religious man. A bride who is strictly veiled, fulfils the everyday public religious duties, and spends a lot of time at Qur'ānic seminaries and *rowżeh* meeting, is of no interest to higher-class and middle-class educated men, unless they have personal connections with one of the new Islamic ideological centres.

The *rowżeh* meetings are also arenas for female interaction where topics concerning women are elaborated upon, such as motherhood, family problems, children, friends, market prices, local events, match-making, and sometimes daily political events. They often evaluate each others' appearance, as well as their Qur'ānic voice and degree of faith.

These kind of dialogues prevail among friends and co-*rowżeh* goers during and after the meetings. The seminar teacher often prevents participants from disturbing the meetings and the holy ritual with personal matters. The educated preachers are often less tolerant to the whispering of participants than the ritual experts, and may stop participants immediately for their lack of interest and for insulting the honour of the day. Once the young and educated preacher Moradi at one of the regular well-attended Muharam meetings stopped her speech to criticise a woman who kept knitting while speaking to other women. She argued that the women were there to listen and to learn religious problems, and not to waste time gossiping.

The symbolic construction of home Islamic rituals

The seat of the presiding preacher is often distinguished by a small table on which there are copies of the books to be read during the meeting. These are the Qur'ān, the book of *mafātieh,* and the book of *halol-masā'el/resal'eh* (solutions to problems).[19]

The seat may be further decorated with a praying rug (*janmāz*) that has a picture of Mecca, or the Mosque of Al-aqṣā[20] on it. The use of a podium (*minbar*), which is popular among male preachers, has not been common among female preachers. But I observed the chair of *minbar* at the newly established communal religious halls (*husyneh*), where it was used by the educated preacher Moradi during her speeches. However, a normal chair, or a cushion, is the common order in private homes. Nevertheless, for some, such as the traditional seminar leader Nosrat, the chair she sat on did not have the same height as a *minbar* used in the mosque. She considered her religious mother as a pioneer in the use of *minbar* in female *rowżeh* meetings in the city of Shiraz.

The blessedness and the power of holy objects and holy words

Some objects qualify as *tabarrok* because they have been in a holy mosque or a shrine, or have passed through a sacred ritual in the course of a religious meeting, such as those held in the month of Ramaẓān, thus becoming objects of power. A *tabarrok* object, e.g. water, nuts, fruits, or medicine, having spiritual and healing power, and may be enjoyed collectively or taken home for private use by attendants.

Richard Kurin, referring to the structure of blessedness at a

[19]These are often available in Persian and are used as text books for teaching rituals. More recent books have been written by high-ranking religious leaders, particularly the Ayatollah-Khoi, and, since the Iranian revolution, the Imām Khomeini, whose speeches and essays have been collected.
[20]Mosque of Al-aqṣā in Jerusalam.

Muslim shrine in Pakistan, has made similar observations regarding the belief and the power of blessed objects, and the quality associated with some of the rituals. He says 'blessedness may become substantiated, or imbued within material objects or human beings, in the form of *tabarrak*' (1983:314).

However, some substances, not originally defined as holy, are transformed into religious objects through the process of a specific ritual. I witnessed such a process on the holy days at religious meetings.

During the entire month of Ramaẓān, some *rowżeh* participants brought a glass of seasonal rain water (*nīysān*)[21] with them. This water was placed in front of the preacher, and at the end of each Qur'ānic chapter the preacher would bless the water by blowing toward the glasses. The water was then thought to have gained healing power (*āb-e shafā*).

The cloth on the table in front of the female preacher may come from a holy pilgrimage, such as to Karbalā[22] and Moshhad. The importance of such things as gifts are not so much based on their material value or uniqueness, since they are not necessarily expensive and may be found locally, but rather on their emotional association with a holy place, a holy ritual, or with a spiritual person. The so-called blessed gifts may be given by friends and relatives returning from *ziārat*, or a pilgrimage journey. Among the common pilgrimage gifts a *hajji* woman may give to relatives is a veil (*chādor*), a piece of the clay of Karbalā (*mohr*), and prayer beads (*tasbīh*).

Ideally, things associated with rituals must be lawful (*halāl*), religiously pure (*ṭāher*, and not soiled by impurities such as urine or blood. The more religiously oriented the hostess is, the more explicit is her concern of lawfulness and purity. Thus, women may at times avoid small children since their urine would make them impure. Exotic pictures may be removed by the hostess as they may distract the concentration of participants. These are instructions given both by male and female preachers. Generally people tend to remove pictures, or cover them with a cloth, when performing their daily prayers (*namāz*). A number of blankets

[21]Rain drops collected in the month of April.

[22]An important pilgrimage place for Shi'ī Iranians which has been inaccessible since the Iranian revolution. Here the shi'ites 3rd Imām, Husain, was martyred in 680.

are spread on the floor and pillows are scattered about in order to make it more comfortable, and to prevent contact with any impure things. Pictures of the Prophet Muhammad,[23] the Imām Ali, and of the Imām Khomeni, or a related martyred soldier, are hung on the wall and decorated as a tribute.

Purity and impurity

The purity of *tāher* is opposed to the impurity of *najes*. The latter not only implies that things are wet, or urinated on, but also that they are associated with objects or items that have been in contact with an unclean substance (*najes*). A *hajji* hostess told me that not only the preacher's place, but the entire room, had to be *tāher* (religiously pure) and she took care that the small children did not touch any items with their unclean hands.

A woman who is accustomed to praying regularly, and who has not deliberately missed a single prayer throughout her life, is more conscious of practising rituals of purity and pollution in personal and family matters (housework, washing, cooking, and caring for her children). Polluting substances include urine, blood, wet hands, and persons who have neglected *wużū* (washing before prayer). Purity is not, however, a clearly defined practice among different categories of participants, such as between old and young.

My religious companions claimed to perform their ablutions whenever we entered *rowżeh* and mosques. They always reminded me to do so, suspecting that I might forget, or that I would not do it in the prescribed fashion. In preparing a religious meal, particular attention has to be paid to purity. For example, utensils have to be washed and rinsed three times and thereafter touched carefully. The efficacy of the religious ritual is not only considered to lie in the performance, but also in the desire and will that is involved.

[23]These pictures were often old prints and it seems to me that the printing of these picture has been forbidden since the Islamic revolution as an incorrect practice of Islam.

Cultural impurity of menstruation

There are both verbal and practical criteria for determining a person's religious purity. Menstrual periods are equated with impurity. During menstruation women are not barred from participating in religious meetings, but are prohibited from touching holy objects such as the Qur'ān. Menstrual women must act passively and observe some particular taboos. They should not read a line from the Qur'ān, enter the main part of a shrine, or carry out certain rituals such as prayers or fasting. In a newly established mosque, where pilgrims come from all over the province to pray and listen to sermons, a small balcony inside the mosque is reserved for menstruating women.

Buckly and Gottlieb (1988) described menstruation as being 'culturally impure and socially dangerous'. In the case of Iranian women menstruation is considered impure because of its association with religiously impure objects – blood and wetness – but not necessary sufficiently socially dangerous to exclude them from local and family religious events. There are no social sanctions preventing menstruating women from entering and participating in home religious meetings, the yard of a shrine or sitting in a specific balcony in the mosque. The new mosques in Iran have made a balcony for menstruating women, enabling them to attend the sessions and hear the preacher's sermons.[24] In practice this brought the menstrual condition of women to its minimum taboo profile in communal Islamic participation and learning.

The social danger of menstruation is effectively made clear in the form of a story told by the female preacher Zaki, as part of her Qur'ānic lessons and commentary on illegal sexual relations outside marriage (*zinā'*). The preacher described it as an example of a sexual taboo.

The story of 'Bokhton-nahs'

> Once a female servant had sexual intercourse with her married master during her *heyż* (menstruation). This was particularly sinful, being both an act of *zinā'*, as well as taboo. She became pregnant and gave birth to a child. She

[24]I saw the new balcony made for polluted women in mosque of il-Khāni in Shiraz in 1994. I am not aware if there is a similar balcony in the male sections.

> kept the child under an idol (*bot*) and visited him every day. After some time she noticed that the child was growing up strong despite the lack of food. One day she stayed there and watched him the whole day, in order to find out how this was possible. She saw a dog suckling him and then cleaning him with its tongue.[25] When the child became a toddler, she took him with her. The dog, who could not visit him there, beat itself to death. When the boy was seven years old he got a job as a wood cutter. He later became the head of a prison because of his physical strength. He forced all the prisoners to work instead of doing nothing. He sold their work privately and received payment in secret. The government soon learned about this and demanded that he share the income with them. Then he decided to initiate a riot in the town, telling the prisoners to kill anyone that came out of their houses. They did whatever he said.

In her *tafsīr* the preacher stressed that the sins of breaking the taboo of sexual intercourse, either during menstruation or through infidelity, produced a person socially and politically corrupt.

This story has multivocal meaning for women's negative social identity. It has implications regarding 'bad women and evil forces'. It conveys information about the prevailing moral code and what is expected of men and women in the social context. A sinful mother is a metaphor for future misfortune, and thus the cause of destruction and the rise of immorality in society. The child of a forbidden sexual relation (*zinā'*) is fostered by a dog and thereby identified as non-human, impure, untouchable, and an object of misfortune; as opposed to a child which imbibes high spiritual virtue through the mother's pure milk. Such folk tales, religious stories, and reports of *ḥadīth* function as important educational tools, spreading religious and moral knowledge, and making explicit the sanctions and kinds of punishment involved. Stories are often used by both male and female preachers in their recitations and sermons in order to express morality and the Muslim ethic.

It seems that motherhood, rather than other structural role

[25]Being fostered by a dog identified him as untouchable and the highest form of impurity, in contrast to the high spiritual virtue of being fed by a mother.

relations such as the wife, is the dominant idiom in the Islamic discourse on morality. For example, preachers often explain that women ought not to fast when breast-feeding, nor submit to their husbands' sexual demands. In such cases Islamic duty as a mother prevails over marital duty as a wife. The dominant female identity of motherhood was also evident in mass media educational programmes. Several times during my first fieldwork I heard Islamist women speakers addressing the question of the role of women in Islam, claiming to quote the words of Imām Khomeini on TV. Statements such as 'each woman gives birth to a man' and 'man ascends to heaven from the lap of a women' were common. Thus, in its verbal and ideological form, Muslim women take upon themselves the duty of being the guardians of the faith, and of reproducing 'true' Islamic believers.

The efficacy of holy words

The notion of blessedness (*tabarrok*) corresponds with central aspects of Islamic rituals. Many *rowżeh* goers believe that the prayers recited by preachers may endow nearby objects with powers.

It was on the second day of the Islamic month of Safar 1994 (July). After a few days of absence I renewed my participation in the regular *rowżeh* meetings in the *husyneh*. I arrived later than usual and I could not understand what brought so many participants to that meeting. There were several bags of sugar and sugar cubes near the preacher, and she and others blew at them at the end of each chapter. I guessed that these bags belonged to the participants, and that the day was a meritful day open for blessings. As the meeting was about to finish a woman sitting next to me expressed herself critically about those women who had earlier competed to place their bags of sugar as close to the preacher as possible. She said: 'Tell them what difference does it make to have your bag of sugar near the preacher or wherever you sit in the room, the important thing is to get the *ṣavāb* and you get it wherever you sit.' She thought it silly and fanatic the way other women requested blessings. Such fanatic behaviour was often labelled 'superstition' by the more secular women and men, or as witchcraft (*jādu*), a consequence of illiteracy and leading to acts of fooling themselves. Generally men tended to identify women's belief in blessings and their power as a specific act of women. I was told by a middle-aged husband who was in state of conflict with his wife, that the cause of his sudden illness must be some strange things that his wife had fed him with without his knowledge. Such claims are often made about a wife who comes from a religious family, has a religious mother, or who is personally involved in religious meetings, and is believed to have the power of *do'ā* and its blessing.

The belief in the efficacy of blessed objects was also reflected in the acts of a *hajji* man, who had a metal bracelet and ring on which various prayers such as *vaínyakād*[26] had been carved in astrological formula and signs. He used it as a *telesm* (an object of magic, talisman) to counteract spells cast by evil eyes, or in case of a sudden sickness.[27] *Telesms* often claimed to be inherited but I saw some with a short life for sale in the old bāzār. I also saw similar instruments with carved astrological formulae and songs, used by men and women during fortune-telling (*ramāli*) in shrines or outside on the street. They received money for their fortune-telling and they had both men and women as clients.

The women may take a little for their children, or someone who is ill, on the grounds that ritual Qur'ānic readings transform some food items into holy substances with the quality of *shafā* (to cure). These foodstuffs are thought to purify the heart, opening or clearing a channel in the person through which blessedness may flow.

Network of religious friendship and sisterhood: **ham-jalese'ī**

The religious meetings strengthen women's social networks, friendship relations and their religious knowledge. A typical example of a regular participant in religious rituals with a network of friendship was my co-*rowżeh* goer. She knew many of the women at the more customary Qur'ānic meetings in the local area. Wherever we went together she spent time greeting friends, talking to an acquaintance, or to a relative. Whenever she had a chance she introduced me as her relative living in Norway. This often brought me into contact with several social

[26]A short Qur'ānic verse called *non-va-ghalam*.

[27]My relative *hajji* told me that he had inherited these *telesm* from his mother's brother (*dachi* in Shirazi terms) who had seemingly been a sufi (*darvish/mashagh*). He believed his *telesm* consisted of sets of Qur'ānic verses joined together and written in some mathematical symbols on the silver plate of a ring and bracelet.

categories, such as those middle-class women who had relatives abroad and wanted to know more about Oslo and Sweden. The female participants at the regular *rowżeh* meetings may be middle-class housewives, upper-class religiously oriented women, working women, schoolgirls, *hajji* women, and students of a religious school. They were all active participants during the holy months and on religious national days.

In the present Islamic society of Iran, Islamic concerns cut across groupings based on age, class, marital status and education. I cannot say that there is more Islamic activity among the literate category than among the 'illiterate'. The illiterate may have little secular knowledge, but a lot of Qur'ānic knowledge. There is more mixing and flow of people across families and neighbours and that may be viewed beyond the classical differences of social class and generation. The view that the younger and higher-educated generation is becoming less religiously active is completely misleading in today's Islamic Iran. To me, therefore, Islamic belief and the initiation rituals cannot be rigidly determined by classical Marxist class definition, in which religion is seen as feature of the poor and illiterate.

The identity of religious sisterhood and friendship (*ham-jalese'i*) implies a series of rights and duties *vis-à-vis* others in the network. Religious meetings not only manifest relations of religious sisterhood, but also relations of friendship and community. Such a form of contact functions as a 'communitas' (cf. Turner 1974), in the sense that relationships and a feeling of belonging are spontaneously generated.

Participants in the meetings consisted of both kin and nonkin. For some their friendship has extended over a period of 15–20 years since their first pilgrimage to Mecca. This was particularly the case of my co-*rowżeh* goer and those with whom she had contact. The categories of participants may be divided according to those who are related to the hostess, to the preacher, or to any other participant. The network of friends established through participation in *rowżeh* (co-*rowżeh* participants) is for some restricted to the months of Ramaẓān and Muharam, during which the meetings are more frequent. These rituals sustain the links between women, and those participating call each other *ham-jales'i* (co-*rowżeh* participants).

Ham-jales'i friendships imply participation in others' family rituals as well as friendly contacts beyond the religious space.

Although some of my religious companions only met each other at the *rowżeh* meetings, they were informed, and expressed an interest, about each others' private lives. Once, when I attended a performance of the prayer[28] of *'aid-e fetr* with my mother in a nearby mosque, she introduced me to one of her religious friends saying: 'This is the daughter I said was coming to visit me after living ten years abroad.' Later, on our way home, my mother told me everything about her friend's broken marriage and her suffering and tolerance, etc.

This shows how local women meet at local events. To them I was considered a 'true' believer, who despite a secular education and living among non-Muslims in Europe, yet remained a good 'Muslim' by holding Islam as a theme of my interest.

Conclusion

In this chapter I have looked at the structural and organisational aspects of women's religious meetings. These meetings are both part of women's religious participation in public religious buildings and private home gatherings. Women's management of their religious lives signals their characters and highlights the important role they have in the family, as well as in the religious rituals where Islamic symbols and meaning give rise to a multiplicity of events. These ritual events continuously provide the means for women to achieve Islamic knowledge and a religious position, and actively to organise religious meetings and remain part of a broader social network.

[28]I was told that *ham-jales'i* women may hold a collective prayer such as at the *'aid-e fetr* at the *rowżeh* without the female preacher. A woman of *mojtāhed* religious rank may lead, not standing in front but in the line with the others.

THREE

RITUAL EXCHANGES AND MORALITY

Introduction

Analysing the everyday rituals, events and their metaphoric substances led me to examine further women's religious beliefs of vow- and merit-making. The vow is their principal religious activity involving ritual exchanges of *nazr* (vow, object of desire) and *nazri* (promised gift). In this chapter I shall explore vow-making as a form of ritual exchange, and as a principal religious activity mostly practised by women. I shall focus on two aspects of *nazr* and *nazri* exchanges: (1) the 'pious' gift exchange, and (2) its relationship to the socio-economic changes in Iran.

A woman may vow that if a particular request is granted, or a personal or a family problem is solved (*nazr*), she will in return promise to sponsor a specific religious meeting, serve a special meal, or offer some gift to a saint or the needy (*nazri*). The principal themes of vow are personal wishes and the well-being of their own parents, children and husband. Children's social and educational progress, in accordance with the ideal social mobility, are often the desired objects of family *nazr*. In general it is the women's own kinfolk and the members of their personal network who are subject to *nazr*. This may also include those in-laws with whom one has established a strong sisterhood and relation of friendship. The ritual of *nazr* is displayed in daily social affairs, in which women often take the initiative and play important roles in maintaining family rituals. Narges, the 45-year-old daughter of my religious companion, hoped to affect the behaviour of her husband (e.g. increase his affection toward her) by making several *nazr* at various shrines in the city. The religious meetings of women are clear examples of occasions where women, as religious actors, constitute the points of reference to pre-initiated vows.

The preparation of a special meal by women is usually arranged in conjunction with family events, such as an annual mourning ceremony, or with special events of the Islamic Shi'ī calendar, e.g. Arb'īn, Ashorā or Tāsoah, to increase its merit. Contributing to a public meal is a central symbol indicating the fulfilment of a vow. It indicates a private achievement and call for others to witness its fulfilment. There are a variety of religious meetings for the fulfilment of one's promised gift (*nazri*). Holding a religious meeting is thought to having merit for the initiators and the recipient.

Shi'ī cosmology and food feast

The Shirazi women understand merit-making and the fulfilments of vows as a series of food giving and food receiving. The things given are thought to bring benefits in this life, as well as in the other. One popular votive ritual meal (*sofreh*) arranged by Shirazi women is the meal named after Roqayeh, the 3-year-old daughter of the heroic 3rd Shi'ī Imām Husian. Roqayeh, being a female and a child, is generally recognised as a spiritual intercessor to whom one can make one's own vow effectively. Roqayeh was believed to be too young when her parents died. She lost her mother and died ambiguously when the Prophet's family and his followers (*muhājirūn*) migrated from Mecca to the city of Madineh in Saudi Arabia. She and her six-month-old brother Qāsem were innocently killed when struck in the throat by the arrow of an *'umayeh* soldier, who fought with the Imām Ali and his family over the caliphate. She is a symbol of innocence and victimisation. They were refugees, walking barefoot over sharp thorns and surviving on what they could find in the desert.

This story is one of the most frequently referred to examples of Muslim suffering, along with the story of Imām Husain, and has at its core a kaleidoscope of themes such as infancy, injustice, immaturity, innocence, pain, dispersion, dislocation, military power, inequality, dominance, social suffering and sacrifice. Roqayeh is a victim of tyranny and injustice and suffers a painful death at the hands of the male, the adult, the military, and the non-Muslim oppressors who forced her people to move from their home city. Roqayeh is often referred to as a symbol of physical weakness, loyalty, purity, suppression, sacrifice, and resistance against the power of 'non-Muslim' enemies. Her suffering and naivety is often a locus of the Muslim discourse of resistance against forceful and destructive powers.

The women's food feast in the name of Roqayeh may take place in a house, as part of a home religious meeting, or in a public religious place, such as at the female section in a mosque or a shrine.[29] In these fora one may invite others for a meal simply by spreading a small tablecloth on the floor. To reject votive food is believed to cause misfortune. A woman initiating a *sofreh-e Roqayeh* as part of a religious meeting may often sponsor the entire expenses. Those who participate in these ritual services are themselves believed to gain merit.

The Roqayeh food feast is less expensive than the elaborate and big religious meals of *sofreh-e abul fazl*. The latter is more popular among the upper middle class and business families. The former requires only cheese, bread and dates. It is not surprising that this feast-giving has become more popular now than before. The meal served at *sofreh-e Roqayeh* is less expensive and more pertinent to folk beliefs in the merit of 'pious' gift-giving. This is the kind of food-giving which might be served to participants on different religious occasions, such as on the day of the month of Ramaẓān as a meal for breaking fast and distributed during the month of Muharam breakfast.

Food offered as a promised gift (*nazri*) is believed to have a healing power and its merit is for those who shared in its consumption. The months of Ramaẓān or Muharam are popular for such meal services. I knew some *hajji* families in my childhood neighbourhood who for the last two or three generations cooked large portions of votive meals of *ash*[30] and rice. During my fieldwork I ate it once again when my mother went out on the day of Ashorā and brought us a bowl *nazrī* food. Women will often give a votive meal, or hold a Qur'ānic meeting, on the holy days or months corresponding either to the birth or martyrdom of Imam Ali and Husain, or days associated to other members of the Prophet's household, as this is believed to increase the merit of the vow.[31]

[29]Most mosques and shrines have two sections divided by a curtain.
[30]A stew made of vegetable, beans, rice and meat.
[31]The 9th and 10th of Muharam.

There are often ritual events that mobilise women to accompany a female neighbour, friend or relative to the house where votive meals are given. The social movement of women, and the fact that they are outside in the street late at night, is not problematic as long as they are involved in religious matters. Many of these houses were giving communal meals, making special services to male religious groups (*hei'at*)[32] who perform the ritual of street mourning of flagellation (*sineh-zanī*) during the 9th and 10th of the month of Muharam.

The Shi'ī Muslim ceremonies during the mourning month of Muharam are its powerful symbolic objects referring to the early Islamic camp of Imām Husain and his followers. They have become a locus of ritual performance and 'pious' gift-giving for women. The communal distribution of rose water (*golab*) during the memorial ceremony of Imām Husain, and the recitation of blessing verses (*ṣalvāt*,[33] blessings to the Prophet Mahammad and his family), are metaphors for the historical events in the land of Karbalā[34] where Imām Husain and his followers fought against enemies, suffered from thirst, and became martyred. The motif of water taken from the account of Husain's death and his act of martyrdom is a familiar theme among Shi'ī Muslims. In religiously orthodox families a *nazr* may be fulfilled by dressing a small boy or girl as a water-giver (*saqā*). Clothed in a long shawl tied with a green belt and a green tuft on the head, conveying a jug of water, they can often be seen marching outside in the streets alongside the flagellants during the Muharam rituals. The water-giver (*saqā*) represents the holy Imām Husain's son (Qāsem). Giving water or soft drinks is a medium for communal hospitality and blessing. It may also be served at the commemorative meeting for a family member.

[32]*Hei'at* are different professional and ethnic categories in formal religious organisations based on temporary or permanent membership. They are associated with localities *hei'at-i mahalli*: Imam Husain's self-sacrifice (*hei'ate-husaini*), Khomeini's self-sacrifice (*hei'ate-khomeini*), common occupation (*hei'ate-senfi*) (see Thaiss 1977). In 1989, I saw at least 50 types of *hei'at* and noted that non-Muslim, non-Shi'ī religious ethnic minorities, organised groups to support Shi'ī solidarity in the city of Shiraz.

[33]alāh-homah-saleh-alā-muhamad-va-aleh-muhamad.

[34]Imām Husain is a symbol of martyrdom, reproduced since the Iranian revolution most significantly in the military mobilisation during the revolutionary period and later in the war with Iraq (see also Thaiss 1978).

Gift of blessing to a dead relative

The preparation and public distribution of a meal for the sake of the dead is a ritual variation of gift-giving (*kheyrāt*). A gift to the dead may be offered in the form of meals and drinks distributed in the residence of the deceased, at a nearby mosque, or the graveyard. Its merit is believed to return to the dead in the hereafter.

Kheyrāt for the community is usually a meal or drink made of rose water or lime, eaten and drunk on the third day after the death of a relative, or during the specific Shi'ī Islamic days (Arba'in, Ashorā and Tāsoah). It will be distributed by a male relative, or by a woman in the female section of a mosque. Many local shopkeepers carry out such public services in nearby mosques during the holy month of Muharam,[35] or in front of the shop offering drinks to pedestrians. This is the kind of service one may receive during the month of Muharam. Distributing a communal gift of cold water (*āb-yakh*) and rose water (*golab*) to relieve the thirst in public places, such as in the yard of a shrine during the month of Muharam (*saqā khāneh*), or among participants in religious meetings, may be initiated as a form of votive service to the dead (*amvāt*). The distribution of rose water to wet the body or face during the intensive religious activities in the month of Ramaẓān, or at Muharam meetings has increased in significance. Serving drinks on such a day is a mediator of the account of the Karbalā tragedy and the myth of Imām Husain. It is claimed that Imām Husain died by the sword of his enemies while thirsty and in pain. Water and thirst is thus a metaphorical reference to the myth of the 3rd Shi'ī Muslim Imām Husain and to his dramatic martyrdom in the desert of Karbalā where he died in the battle.[36] The mourning ritual of Imām Husain is a parallel to the food feast ritual of Roqayeh symbolising sacrifice, pain, and suffering.

Giving a meal service is believed to please the dead and to ensure happiness for the spirit (*rūh*). The common meal to the dead consists of *ḥalvā* (a sweet delicacy made of dates), plain dates, or cold drinks, particularly on the first and the third days following the death, or occasionally on Friday evenings. Those

[35]Especially on the holy days of Tāsoah and Ashorā when the martyrdom of the Imām Husain is the dominant symbol in the religious discourse.
[36]For further study see also Thaiss 1978, Fischer 1989.

who have been served a votive meal or drinks are expected to send a blessing by saying the verse of *ṣalvāt* three times, or reciting the Qur'ānic verse of *alhamd* once and *qolhovallāh* three times.[37] This expresses a wish that the soul of the dead should find happiness. This ritual is amongst others initiated when the initiator observes a sign, or the dead relative appears in a dream and makes a request or a complaint, or on religious occasions such as the annual memorial marking a death when it is believed that dead kinfolk should be remembered in a Qur'ānic gathering at home.

Economic aspects of women's votive rituals

The economic means of a promised gift (*nazri*) is largely provided by those married with economic support from their husbands or those with sufficient saving.

Some vows are made on the assumption that by the time they have been fulfilled, one would have enough money to carry out the promised ritual. This was the case of my religious companion, Nezhat, who made a vow to end an official dispute over a piece of land. The land (*mashā'*)[38] was not officially registered and was owned collectively by several people who did not have the right to sell it in 1989. Five years later, at the time of my second fieldwork, she optimistically told me that they were promised a letter of permission for the right to sell. When I asked her how she could afford to fulfil such an expensive vow with her poor economy she said: 'God is great, hopefully, when my vow is fulfilled, I can sell the land immediately and be able to afford such a costly meal.'

A fulfilled wish is a reason for offering the promised gift. Thus, one may wait days, weeks and months until the wish has been fulfilled, and then the vow will be completed. A long-lasting vow that does not produce the desired results usually remains an experience seldom mentioned.

[37]Also recited in daily prayers.

[38]A large collectively owned piece of land.

'Pious' gift-giving in everyday exchanges

The religious act of giving gifts may take on various economic forms, such as supporting a particular social class and religious category recognised as needy (*mostaḥaq*), e.g. the poor, a religious descent (*seyyid*), a widow, orphans, or a family who have lost their main source of income.

Charity (*ṣadqeh*) is a form of gift-giving practised by both men and women that is believed to bring gifts of merit, benefit one's health and wealth, and to prevent misfortune. Charity (*ṣadqeh*) is also considered a mean to protect oneself, a beautiful daughter, or a grown-up son from jealousy and evil eyes (or 'salty eyes'). Contributions of cash to those in need might also be a kind of daily or weekly ritual to enhance one's identity as a moral person.

In the middle of the Muharam meeting in the *husyneh* in 1994 my religious companion, Nezhat, was asked by an elderly female acquaintance to give her annual contribution to orphans. Nezhat offered some money and excused herself for not having more at the time. Nezhat then asked me to do the same, arguing that the money would be used for two orphans of the same age as my children. She also suggested that I give some of my children's shoes and dresses to the orphans to make them happy. Nezhat meant that these acts would in return protect my children.

Misfortune is believed to come from a wide range of classified objects and social activities. I will give another example. Any possible social destruction is thought to be caused by the failure of fulfilling a vow. A wish which is fulfilled has to be repaid with the promised gift. Nezhat argued that her son, who died of cancer abroad, was a victim of jealousy, although she perfectly well knew the real cause. To Nezhat, her children's high social achievement at a time of great economic difficulties had increased the jealousy of those who wished the same good fortune for their own children, but lacked the financial means.

Charity is part of a moral economic system meant to accumulate merit against times of misfortune and prevent evil eyes, and votive services to the dead are performed to ensure a state of morality free from sins. A symbolic thought may give rise to the idea that one should put some coins in the hand of a poor beggar, as both of the religious companions often accompanying me did. This is a customary act of charity practised by different social categories. When my own children became ill my mother asked me to buy a Thermos for a widowed relative in order to improve their health. This form of alms-giving may also be understood in terms of money or objects passing from people of a higher social and economic status to people of a lower status, the former receiving blessings in return.

According to the general understanding those who are merciful to others will receive God's mercy. Charity is also a symbolic recognition of the higher status of the giver. Hence, the donation of money provides the giver with both merit and prestige. This economy of charity can in Crapanzano's terms be called illusorily 'pure', gifts underlining a hierarchy of purity. Women with well-off husbands are expected to make higher contributions in the religious meetings.

Sacrifice

There are several different forms of gifts for preventing misfortune. The slaughter of a lamb is a Muslim custom that is performed annually to mark a particular ritual, such as the day of sacrifice (*ghorbān*).[39] It is also practised by male and female pilgrims the first few years after their first pilgrimage to Mecca, or for example as a thanksgiving for surviving an accident, recovering from illness, or for settling a legal dispute between relatives. Another occasion is the marriage of a daughter or son, or the arrival of a son/daughter or son-in-law from a journey from a distant place. Such a form of thanksgiving, apart from its partial meritorious effect on those who once performed the compulsory *hajj* journey ritual, is also associated with a series of symbols and metaphors that can be classified as part of the ritual of exorcism and shielding against the evil forces which flow from others as a result of jealousy. The place of slaughter is usually indoors, often at the entrance of the home, but the distribution of meat is performed in the mosque so as to reach the poor (*foqarāh*).

In 1979 many of the families I knew sent a portion of the sacrificed meat (*gushteh-ghurbunī*) from a votive occasion to the

[39]Such a ritual is said to be universal for all Muslims, based on the Islamic calender. On festive occasions an animal must be sacrificed. However it is important to explore its local form of practice and the context.

house of a male or female relative, or a neighbour, with a higher social rank than themselves. An influential relative has more chance of receiving a leg of lamb. These relatives with whom I shared residence in 1989 were confident that they would receive several votive meals on the days of Arba'in, Tāsoah and Ashorā.[40] Lunch was not prepared as my relative consumed the *āsh* and *sholzard* (rice porridge with sugar and *zafrān*) brought to us early in the morning. This form of promised gift involving sacrificial distribution is initiated by men and women as a personal means of protecting themselves and their children. Those who initiated such an expensive votive meal were among the better-off families.

For example, my religious companion Shazdeh, a well-to-do 55-year-old woman, once asked her husband to slaughter a sheep after she had miraculously survived a traffic accident. The largest portion was distributed to the poor in the mosque. Nevertheless, the price of a sheep (2–5 thousand tomanes in 1989) meant that much of a poor family's monthly income would be required for such an offering. Hence, such rituals are only staged on special occasions such as the marriage of daughter, or the return of a son from military service.

The contributions made by women at religious meetings were often less than those made by women in mosques or at shrines,[41] where gold and jewellery, and often large sums of cash were generously offered to Khomeini's office (*sandogh-e imām*). The only religious meeting I participated in that was able to collect sufficient alms to purchase a place of residence for a needy woman was in the newly established *husyneh*. The giving of alms at shrines and holy mosques are made through high-ranking spiritual mediators, such as saints, the holy Imam, or a member of his family. If a vow is fulfilled a larger contribution in favor of the shrine and the community is made by means of goods and some form of voluntary work. The cash contribution at regular religious meetings is often considered to give merit and to protect one's family from misfortune and bad health. The higher the

[40]The two days of mourning are the 9th and 10th day of Muharam; the former for the night before the battle of Karbalā, the latter for the killing of the 3rd Shi'ī Imām Husain along with his remaining 72 followers.
[41]There is often a room behind the shrine's bars where pilgrims may drop a donation. There is a special day for collection and removal of the donations, which are recognised as belonging of the Imām and his community.

contribution, the more vital the object of vow and the holier is the mediator.

Making religious vows and counsels through the intercession of a spiritual person

A religious woman may choose to make her vow indirectly through the mediation of a male or female preacher of high religious character; for example a preacher, a *seyyid*, a spiritual person who received a religious mission in a dream, or in the form of a miracle. This was particularly true for the participant who came to the preacher Nosrat on a Thursday, wishing the intercession of the holy ancestor of Nosrat (a *seyyid* woman) to help her with social and economic problems. At the end of each religious meeting participants approached Nosrat, putting forward their wishes, and asking her kindly to initiate a religious vow on their behalf. The attendants each explained their wishes while Nosrat placed her hand on their head to give them her blessing. Those present wishing her to undertake a special ritual that mediates the five holy ones (*panjtan*) for them would make an appointment for a special day. Then Nosrat would perform special rituals in a room on the other side of the religious halls called 'room of the five holy ones'.[42]

The act of divination is often performed by ritual experts through the mediation of the Qur'ān or praying beads. This divination is made through a person believed to have a pure heart, or a blessed hand, such as a *saint*, a *seyyid*, or a preacher. A person may decide to carry out a divination if she or he is uncertain of a decision, such as whether to marry a daughter to an outsider, take a long journey, or to proceed with some business venture. The successful result of a good divination is proudly talked about to friends and relatives. Sometimes the ritual must be repeated three times before the desired answer is received. The ritual of divination is also used in other contexts, such as communicating with God (*monājāt*) during the ritual of night watching (*aḥyā*).

Let us consider the case of Narges, the daughter of my religious companion, who is childless. I knew her as one of my relatives

[42]The five holy persons are the Prophet Muhammad, Imām Ali, Imām Husain, Imām Hasan and Fatemeh-e Zahrā.

and we shared residence during my fieldwork. Her husband, after several years of conflict, married a young widow with whom he apparently was in love and hoped to have a child with. Narges, who found herself in a desperate situation, went to a sufi man[43] related to her mother's sister. He had a shop selling traditional herbs in town and he was also active in a *khānegāh* (the sufi house). She had heard that the sufi had recently received spiritual enlightenment, and had become the subject of a miracle (*nażar-kardeh*) of the eighth Shi'ī Imām (Imām Rezā),[44] whose shrine is in the city of Mashhad in northeastern Iran. He was then nominated to the position of honourable servant (*khādem*)[45] in this shrine. His new position was officially announced on the day he was sent an honourable meal by airplane from the shrine of Mashhad to his place of residence in Shiraz.[46] Narges went to him and implored him sincerely to use his spiritual powers and read a particular blessing to return her husband to her. All the women who consulted the sufi were convinced of his holiness, except his older sister. She was known as a woman with a large network of friends, of being manly in manner, physically strong, and not afraid to fight. His sister claimed to know her brother better than anybody else, and did not trust his recent claim of being blessed. She argued that he exaggerated the idea of *nażar-kardeh* in order to improve his reputation and his business. He had recently bought a large farm next to his house where he grew plants and fruits from which he made juice in a traditional way. He made his farm products available in the city market in a package labelled *101*.[47] Nevertheless, Narges firmly believed that her approach would be efficacious, since he had given her the correct answer when she had consulted him earlier on the prosperity of her marriage.

Narges went alone to him in his shop and asked him to bless her to ensure that her wish was fulfilled. She wished that the second wife would not become pregnant, which would not only bring shame to her husband by identifying the problem of childless as his infertility, but also make him return to her. Some time

[43]He was a member of the Ali-Allahi's sect of sufi in Shiraz.
[44]The 8th Imām of 12 Shi'ī Imāmis of Iran.
[45]Offering services in the name of Allāh or the saint for divine purposes is believed to make one receptive of blessedness (see also Kurin, 1983).
[46]The shrine of Imām Reza, the 8th Imām of Shi'ī Muslims
[47]Number 101 is metaphor for the sufi term *yāhoo*, which means the Imām Ali.

later a friend of a distant relative of the husband informed her that the second wife seemed to be having difficulty in becoming pregnant, and had made an appointment with a doctor. This news cheered Narges, knowing now that her husband was in trouble. She was convinced that having to take care of two households had turned her husband's life in to a mess.

After a while her husband returned to her through the mediation of an elderly relative, but he maintained two separate households, one for Narges and one for the second wife. Narges viewed her husband's return as a positive sign and she hoped the next stage would be the divorce of his second wife. During my second visit five years later I met Narges in her father's house where she lived without paying rent, but shared in other expenses. Her husband had made an agreement to visit her every two days. Narges planned several times to leave her husband for good and join her sister and brother abroad, thus ending the persistent pain. While waiting for her visa application to be considered, she asked a female preacher friend of her mother to perform an act of divination on the question of whether this journey would be a success or a failure. The answer was negative. This was soon confirmed by the news that her visa application had been rejected, despite all preparations. She viewed the negative response as evidence of her powerlessness and she would not consider a further attempt, believing that there must be some meta-relation between the authorities' rejection and the negative answer of the divination. Her logic was that by staying at home she would not only avoid the pain of being in a foreign society (*ʿghorbat*), but could continue to shame her husband and put more pressure on him by being in his sight. After realising all this, Narges welcomed the negative answer to her visa application.

This kind of counselling through holy texts, saints and persons is common among women in a situation of social crisis. Some may even travel together to distant cities in order to get in touch with a particular spiritual person, or to visit a particular shrine (see Chapter 4).

Conclusion

The act of making a vow generates various religious meetings and forms of gift-exchanges. Women's votive rituals and religious beliefs are multi-centric and intertwined with economic values and personality. By initiating the vow and fulfilling a promised gift Shirazi women take on a religious role in relation to the instruments of social and economic pressures and family ritual patterns.

The act of making a vow transforms a desired object into the promise of gift-giving, or into a form of credit as its merit. The women's acts of *nazr* seem to lead to an intimate experience embodied in the past and the present, and hopes for the future. A vow is a profound hope and a belief in the social control of misfortunes. It is an important religious forum in which to display the Islamic cosmology and broad ritual events.

Vows among Muslim Iranian women are associated with symbols and metaphors arising from everyday social difficulties, individual economic constraints. The act of a female vow parallels the male vow, in which a meal is provided to the people in the mosque during the holy days and nights of Ashorā and Tāsoah. The interconnected complexity of the personal act of vowing, the wish of fulfilment, and the giving of promises, provides a framework for a moral economy of exchange.

The spiritual quality of merit is a key concept in such complex socio-spiritual exchange activities. *Ṣavāb* is a 'pious' gift obtained through the exchange of ritual meals, alms-giving and religious work. Acts of *ṣavāb* are thought to open a channel of blessing between oneself and close family members. The ecology of a *ṣavāb* act and its concomitant merit raises the question of ritual themes and gift-giving as a moral economy of exchange.

Such an exchange of a distinctive culturally constructed quality (cf:Mauss 1954, Kopytoff 1986, Parry 1986:467) characterises the Muslim women's moral identity and ritual exchanges within the discourse of being a 'true' or worldly oriented person.

The above descriptions of *kheyrāt*, *ṣadqeh* and *sofreh* gift-giving represents multi-vocal metaphorical activities of Islamic rituals. Marcel Mauss (1954) maintained that it is in the nature of gift-giving to oblige receiving. He proposed that the act of gift-receiving is desired due to necessity, and has consequences for gift-giving as well. The classical tools of Mauss are appropriate for my analysis of *nazr* and *nazri* gift exchange.

FOUR

THE FEMALE PREACHER

Introduction

In this chapter I shall focus on the role of female preachers (*re'īs-e jaleseh*). I will explore their career development, their role in the transition of Islamic tradition, and their Islamic thinking in the context of political development.

Fischer's 1980 study of male Muslim preachers in shrines and the religious school in Qum and Antoun's (1989) study in a village in Jordan have been of great inspiration for me. The transmission of Islamic knowledge from the male preacher to the male participants is richly explored in these two studies. Up to now there has not been a single study of female Muslim preachers in any country. My interest in the role of female preachers began during my first record of fieldwork and developed into a topic of its own during my second. My relation to these preachers was limited to meeting them in their religious meetings (except for one), and could not be extended into their other spheres of social activities. Nevertheless, for some their place of work was also their place of residence and worship.

The girls' religious school

One of the first established formal Islamic girls' schools is the Maktabeh-Zahrā (school of Zahrā) in the city of Shiraz. The number of religious schools for girls with three or four years of studies has increased since the Iranian revolution.[48] In 1989

[48]According to a study by Paidar (1995) the highly regarded Qum seminary admitted more than 400 women between the ages of 16 to 20 with secondary school education. Further, according to the women's magazine survey of Zan-e ruz in 1985, the Religious Science Complex for women opened in Qum. This complex, known as the society of Zahrā (Jameat ol-Zahrā), accepted more than 500 female students in 1985 (1995:319).

students were trained by both male and female religious teachers. These schools also served as a place for various religious gatherings, such as the Qur'ānic classes held throughout the year, and women's religious gatherings during the holy month of Ramaẓān (see Chapter 2). The Qur'ānic classes took place in a classroom where students sit on a bench on one side of the classroom and a teacher on the other side. This is in contrast to the Qur'ānic seminaries where attendants often sit on the floor, around the room and with the back to the wall.

Maktab-e Zahrā was established in 1973. The preacher Mumeni is a 60-year-old woman who learned the Qur'ān from her religious parents, and received her education as a midwife in England in the 1970s. Some of the most famous female preachers in Shiraz today have been her students. As a midwife women of all classes, in particular lower- and middle-class, turn to her when they have problems with family planning, pregnancy, infertility or miscarriage. Her midwife office is on the first floor of the school, and usually there is a small queue of women waiting to see her. She also issues 'certificates of virginity' for girls who are going to be married. Non-premarital sexual relation is important in Muslim marriage contracts and such a certificate is traditionally a proof of a bride's virginity. The proof of virginity is equally important to the family of the groom receiving a virgin bride, as it is to the family of the bride giving away a virgin daughter. Recently the preacher Mumeni reduced her work at her surgery and undertook only important religious rituals and Qur'ānic reciting on important religious days of the Islamic calendar.[49]

Religious school gatherings are held in a large hall (*shabestān*), where a huge picture of Ayatollah Khomeini hangs next to a painting of the Prophet Muhammad. This indicates that the school recognises the authoritative religious role of both leaders. It was said that after the revolution attempts were made to close the school, but that the preacher Mumeni appealed to the office of Imām Khomeini, visiting him personally and receiving permission to continue her work. Together with several other female religious seminary teachers she arranged a large memorial service on the 7th and the 40th day to commemorate Khomeini's

[49]The annual Shi'ī days of mourning, Tāsoah and Ashorā, on which the 3rd Shi'ī Imām Husain was martyred in Karbalā.

death in July 1989. I was told by my religious companion that the meetings were crowded with his followers.

In 1989 the students came from various social classes, including children of well-to-do religious urban families and girls from surrounding counties. The school expanded to include a higher college of theology, Zeynabyeh (house of Imām Husain's sister), which was due to be opened in 1994.

The preacher Mumeni is a woman of excellent character and strong faith and her spiritual quality and organisational power are highly valued by her followers. Her daily acts of worship were not only confined to prayers classified as obligatory, but also included non-obligatory acts of prayers. Practising Islamic prayers to such an extent claimed her cumulative spiritual role in the eyes of her religious students. Once I went with my religious companion, a former student of hers, to visit Mumeni at her office at the school. I knocked at her door but there was no response. I thought she was not there. My religious companion, who knew her well, told me to wait as she was often busy praying. A few minutes later she opened the door, wearing her white scarf for praying, and invited us inside. When she learned that I lived abroad and was interested in studying women's performance of Islam, she started telling me about her life experiences abroad and how Muslim culture is undermined there. She explained the event that lead her to her religious life:

> I used to go with my father, and sometimes my mother, to *rowżeh* to read the Qur'ān. Then I was sent to England to study medicine. As a student I noticed that some of the Western students thought that Muslims do everything different, including giving birth. I was about to be engaged with an Egyptian classmate, but a few days before our engagement, I dreamt that a holy man gave me a ring. Then I realised that I was asked to devote my life to something else. Since then I have been married to my religion. I graduated as a midwife and returned home. I first had an office receiving female patients and soon I started to look for a larger place to establish a religious school. I moved to this house and built a section as a religious school for girls.

A recent study by Paidar (1995:308) has shown that social welfare activities, apart from Islamic and political activity, play a significant role among the religiously learned women. This is particularly true among the women of prominent Islamic clergy families. The organisation of religious educational activity is also common among the religious participants and Qur'ānic leaders in the city of Shiraz. This is largely contributed as part of one's religious promised gifts, charity and alms (see Chapter 3).

The female preachers

Table 4.1 shows the female preachers (*re'is-e jaleseh*) whom I met and listened to in separate religious meetings. They are ranked according to their religious knowledge and teaching tasks. They carry out religious rituals of *rowżeh,* hold Qur'ānic seminaries in their homes, and run two religious schools for girls. The categories are based on the level of religious knowledge and ritual tasks; of reciting Qur'ān, performing commentary (*tafsīr*), and ritual instructions. I divided them into categories according to their teaching task.

Table 4.1

Name	Teaching task Qur'ānic reciting	Commentary	Ritual lessons
Farah (*mujtāhed*)	yes	yes	on request (semi-retired)
Malyheh (student of Farah)	yes	yes	yes
Zaki	yes	yes	yes
Mumeni	yes	yes	on request
Mostafi	yes	yes	on request
Jahanifard	yes	yes	yes
Nosrat	yes	not yet	yes
Naderi	yes	not yet	yes
Gohar (student of Mumeni)	yes	not yet	yes
Borhan	yes	not yet	yes
Moradi (student of Mumeni)	yes	yes	on request

The female preacher and leaders of religious gatherings can be divided into two categories: those who offer Qur'ānic commentary may reach the religious rank of *mujtāhed* over years;

and those who act as Qur'ānic teachers and Qur'ānic seminary teachers, but need further religious education before they can offer commentary. Qur'ān teachers and ritual practitioners take charge of the narrative problems at religious meetings, pray and recite the greeting text of *ziārat* from the book of a collection of blessing verses, *mafātih*.

The female preachers are often unmarried, widowed graduates of Qur'ānic seminaries and classes, a religious school (*maktab*), a college (*hozeh*), or a theological faculty of a university (*alahyat*). The youngest female seminary teacher I met was approximately 25 years old and she could also perform *tafsīr*. She was a student of higher degree in the recently established girls' school, Maktab-e Ekhlās (school of purity). One of the oldest retired teachers, Farah, was over 80 years old, and had received her religious education at a religious school in the city of Najaf in Iraq.[50]

The religious rank of female preachers

There is often a flexibility of teaching task across ranks and one has always a chance of advancing from an ordinary Qur'ānic student to a higher rank *re'is-e jaleseh* of commenting on the Qur'ān. The majority of these preachers started their religious careers as Qur'ānic students and participants at local *rowżeh* meetings.

The teaching tasks of a female preacher depend upon her years of experience at local religious meetings, as well as formal knowledge of theology and the Qur'ān, and her ability to handle the Arabic language. The preachers who are fluent in Arabic, and who can both recite and interpret the Qur'ān, are identified as 'learned' (*'alem*) people. It is important to be able to read the Qur'ān fluently with a correct intonation. Those who learn the interpretation of Qur'ān, as well as being able to recite it, soon become eligible to undertake *tafsīr*. Such permission is usually given informally by a higher ranked Qur'ānic teacher. The number of those who obtain the high religious authoritative role of *mujtāhed*, a position equal to a religious school doctorate entitling them to make independent judgments, is limited tra-

[50]Mullahs (male preachers) are often reported to have been educated in the *atābat* (holy city of Najaf or Karbalā). Najaf is a shrine town and is the tomb of Ali ibn Abi Taleb, the cousin and son-in-law of the Prophet and the father of the martyred Husain.

ditionally and extended through the centre of religious learning section for women in Qum (*hawza-e 'lmī khāhrān*). Being a true *mujtāhed* is always defined by the originality of one's book of *resāleh*. One of the prominent female *mujtāhed* with a general recognition was Mrs Amin.

Female preachers are identified, categorised, and ranked according to their religious knowledge, religious inherited status, popularity, and to the number of followers whose wishes have been fulfilled at their meetings. Their Islamic knowledge is obtained from formal and informal training. I met several of the lower ranked Qur'ānic teachers and ritual experts in 1989. They commonly perform various religious rituals among families, such as ceremonies associated with memorial services and votive meetings (cf. Chapters 2 and 3).

Some of the orthodox followers spend a lot of time during the month of Ramaẓān accompanying a preacher from one meeting in the morning to another in the afternoon.[51] The women often spend more time on such religious activities during the month of Ramaẓān, as well as having less cooking responsibilities during the day due to fasting. The information about a coming meeting, the name of the host, the bus to be taken, or arrangements for renting a bus, are provided soon after prayer at the end of such meetings.

The ritual experts

There are some important differences between the role of a high-ranked female preacher (*re'is-e jaleseh*) and the ritual experts (*Qur'ān-khān, noneh-khān* and *mas'leh-gu*). The former has, for example, the authoritative role of interpreting the Qur'ān (*tafsīr*), while the latter has not. The ritual experts will often be the ones to chant or recite a few verses from the Qur'ān or a praying book, without necessarily being literate or familiar with the Arabic language. Hence, the low-ranked female ritual expert (*Qur'ān-khān*), is somebody able to read a few verses of the Qur'ān and

[51]Housewives, who have greater responsibilities in the home, are often excused from such commitments. For some women the month of Ramaẓān means an increase in housework since they may have to prepare separate meals for fasting family members twice a day, as well as three meals for those not fasting. Others with less responsibility feel freer to attend several meetings, coming home in time to prepare the evening meal to break the fast (*eftārī*).

who will chant (*do'ā*) at local shrines or in the female part of the mosque. I saw several of these women acting as regular readers at the main city shrine, which has recently been divided into a male and female part. Most mosques I saw or heard about in different cities in Iran are constructed with two distinctive halls (*shabestān*), where men and women sit separately. Despite this segregation, women actively attend religious ceremonies in the mosques where the male preachers dominate the organisation and religious transactions through sermons, speeches, and prayers.

Qur'an-khān, as a religious career, is often pursued by men and women of a lower social and religious rank, many whom are illiterate. They may also perform some of the sorrowful poetic songs in Persian about the female members of the Prophet's family during the tragedy of Karbalā, such as the *Hazrat-e Roqayeh* (believed to be the 3-year-old daughter of Imām Husain who lost her mother and died in a slum district in Sham) or the *Fatem-e Zahrā* (the Prophet's daughter). She also sang poems relating to the death of Imām Ali, Imām Husain and his two infant sons. Despite the low rank in the ritual hierarchy they are considered experts in some of the common mourning rituals and they receive a small amount of money from their listeners after each religious performance. Such small payments are considered to be alms (*ṣadqeh*), and are therefore believed to protect one from misfortune and illness.

Becoming a preacher

The female preachers obtain their knowledge of Arabic and theology from a learned preacher (male or female – *akhond*, *mujtāhed* or *'alem*), a Qur'ānic teacher in a religious school, and/or from religious relatives (father, husband, husband's father, mother). To obtain religious knowledge one has to learn Arabic syntax after completing primary and secondary schools or university (whether a religious or non-religious school). Furthermore, one has to study three or four years philosophy, logic, Islamic law (*feqh*), and Qur'ānic commentary. The most important distinction between the traditional preacher and the newly educated preacher is that the former obtain their knowledge by participating in Qur'ānic seminaries, while the latter obtain their positions through formal education at religious schools and colleges.

Case 1: Malyheh

Malyheh was one of my preacher informants. She was among the first who attended the Islamic girls' school in the early 1970s when I attended secondary school. At the time she often avoided participating in secular family parties, and if she did she always wore a scarf. She was labelled 'old-fashioned' by many of her educated relatives. She was one of the children who often accompanied their mothers to religious meetings, thus attending Qur'ānic courses from a very young age. In contrast to the fashion of the 1970s she and a few young educated women decided to wear veils and cover their hair and body. In contrast to her sisters and brothers she favoured reading the Qur'ān and attending the Islamic girls' school. At that time only a few schoolgirls wore *chādor* at my school. When I returned home after a decade abroad, I inquired about her. 'She has made much progress and has become an independent preacher,' I was told. Since the revolution she has been in charge of Qur'ānic courses and religious meetings, as well as having the authority to give Qur'ānic commentary (*tafsīr*).

On the second day of my arrival I participated in the third anniversary of commemorating the death of a male relative. There I met Malyheh in the company of another higher-ranking preacher in charge of Qur'ānic recitation. I had the opportunity to contact her and to meet her inside and outside the context of her religious meetings and Qur'ānic courses.

She was a part-time student of three prominent female preachers in the area, one of whom in 1989 was entitled to the higher rank of an independent Islamic interpreter (*mujtāhed*). She also spent a few years at the religious school Maktab-e Zahrā, where she received lessons in performing prayers and teaching the Qur'ān. Later she was in charge of various ritual occasions, such as reciting the entire verse of *anām* at the request of relatives, friends, and other co-seminary friends.

It took Malyheh all the years of her childhood to obtain the necessary informal and formal Islamic training and to obtain the necessary knowledge of the Qur'ān, *ḥadīth* and *sharīʿa*. As a graduate she was asked to be a missionary (*mobalegh*). She travelled to villages around Shiraz and arranged Qur'ānic courses, gave lessons on obligatory prayers and Qur'ānic recitation, and on ritual purity and impurity. During the war between Iran and Iraq she, along with other Qur'ān teachers, visited injured soldiers in the war zone to offer them sympathy and encouragement. Gradually Malyheh became more active in the local areas of Shiraz.

Malyheh did not want to marry and intended to live a life of celibacy with her old mother, who had always been a regular *rowżeh* participant. She had a network of relations with some other female preachers and they often met. She and many other young religious graduates were actively supporting the Islamic state propaganda (*Markazeh-Tablighateh-Islami*).

By 1989, when I met her again, she often received invitations to go to private homes. In 1994 she organised a Qur'ānic class of her own at the Islamic girls' school of Mumeni. She was often in charge of a series of family religious rituals inside and outside the city.

I attended several of Malyheh's Qur'ānic classes organised in private homes and in the Maktab-e Zahrā, where she had students of different ages (as young as 9–10 years and as old as 50–60 years old). She was also in charge of several religious seminars in private homes arranged through private initiatives. In June 1994, on a very hot mid-summer day, I attended one of her Qur'ānic classes at the school of Zahrā. Her students were sitting on a bench in contrast to the Qur'ānic seminaries in private homes where attendants often sit on the floor. In the middle of the lecture we were served lime drinks by one of the schoolgirls. First she read a verse from a chapter in the Qur'ān which was repeated by every student. I whispered in Malyheh's ear, asking her kindly not to ask me to read as I was not sure to be able to read as well as her students. I often compared my own knowledge of the Qur'ān and the prayers with other schoolgirls or housewives participating in her Qur'ānic-classes or *rowżeh* meetings. She seemed to consider my lack of Qur'ānic knowledge as an involuntary cultural loss resulting from my long residence in Europe. She gave a lecture on the question of Muslim death and re-birth. She recited first a Qur'ānic verse followed by the translation in Persian:

> We created you to die and we gave you death to give you

> a new birth. We have two kinds of deaths, one the normal one when we are laid in the grave. There we will become alive again to answer God's questions. Then we become putrid, until the day of judgment where Esrail breathes upon us and we become alive again. We will all die in the end, but first we have to accept it. It is like first diagnosing a disease and then trying to cure it. If for example we accept that we have the disease of jealously and hatred, then we can cure it, but if we deny it, we cannot cure it.

She read some more Arabic verses and interpreted them in the context of everyday individual experiences before ending her class that day.

Malyheh's religious network also extended to some of the preachers in other towns. Female preachers coming from Isfahan or Tehran were highly honoured, often being classified as the most learned Islamic commentators (*mufassir*). Through her I was able to stay informed about meetings in the town. News of sermons of a learned preacher drew the largest numbers of young women and students, as well as the regular *rowżeh* participants. It was often suggested to me by the less religiously active middle-class informants that in order to obtain correct information I should interview the high-ranking preachers, rather than relying upon the less educated ritual experts, or *rowżeh* participants.

Case II: Nosrat

Nosrat is one of the older preachers. She arranges *rowżeh* meetings in the house of her deceased father located in the slum of the city. I especially started participating in her meetings during my second fieldwork in 1994, as I was then more interested in studying female preachers. Nosrat comes from a highly religious family. She claims to have an ancestral *sayyid* reaching 18 generations back to the Imām Ali. The hall is decorated with pictures of her grandparents and her mother, while Imām Ali and Ayatollah Khomeini are exhibited on another wall, thereby providing a clear representation of her religious ancestry, her spiritual position, and her claim to descend from the Imām Ali from both her father's and mother's side. A bilateral *sayyid* title gave Nosrat a noble identity, suggesting a direct communion with saints of the past, and with the Imām Ali himself. Her meetings are renown for their ritual efficacy and miraculous stories. She often asks her clients to tell the audience about their experiences in her meetings and the way their wishes have been fulfilled. She will give the microphone to volunteers, who in detail will describe their miraculous experiences to the other participants. They describe religious vows pertaining to common problems such as complicated illnesses, childlessness, the social problems of children, success in education, the work of husbands. Very often they will break down in tears while telling their story. In the following I will give a few examples noted in a meeting during Muharam 1994 (July).

> *Case I* The preacher Nosrat pointed out a middle-aged woman among the participants at the meeting. Covered in a full-length veil she stood up and told her story: 'I used to come here as a child. After I married I became so engaged in other activities that I could not come here any more. Now I have an 18-year-old son who is addicted to opium. His father kicked him out of our home. My son left for Tehran and I started to come here everyday. We did not hear anything from my son for two months but then one day he gave us a call telling us that he was no longer addicted. Happily he returned home and his father slaughtered a lamb for him. At present he is in the military. I will soon pay my debt the 5,000 tomans to Mrs Nosrat.' She then burst into tears.

> *Case II* 'I started to come to this *rowżeh* and made a vow to recite *khatm-e anām* 14 times in order to get my wish fulfilled. At first I gave 500 tomans to Mrs Nosrat, because I could not afford more.[52] Then my wish was fulfilled. Today I was passing by and I entered to perform the prayer for Imām Ali. I was told it was performed yesterday. I became mad. I just saw a light (*nur*)[53] in the ceiling during

[52]The requested sum was 5,000, in the name of five members of Prophet Muhammad's family (*panjtan*).

[53]The audience at Nosrat's religious meetings believed that whenever she gave her religious song in the honour of Imām Ali, a bow of lights appeared in the ceiling in the hall. I saw a bow of light that gradually appeared on the ceiling of the hall at her meeting. I thought that it must have something to do with the extra reflection of the sun through the window on that particular time. My logical explanation of what they believed to be a miracle created some agreement and disagreement among my religious companions with whom I exchanged my view.

> the Nosrati meeting. I addressed the *imām-e zamān* [the 12th Shi'i imām], that you are always at my side and protecting me. Finally, after many months, my wish has been fulfilled, and I am shameful of not being able to pay all the promised money to Mrs Nosrat. I will pay my debt as soon as I can.'

The preacher addressed a third person to tell her story in her own language. Covered in a full-length veil she started up and talked about the absence of a young girl.

> *Case III* 'A young follower of Mrs Nosrat told me that for several years she had been trying to take the university entrance exams, but had failed. Then she resorted to Mrs Nosrat and started to pray. Afterward she passed the matriculation exam for medicine at the university. Since then she has not left Mrs Nosrat and takes part in her meetings whenever she can.'

The participants personally believe in Nosrat's power to perform miracles and that her spiritual house creates strong emotional feelings for the participants so that they become stronger believers.

In contrast to the educated preacher Malyheh, the traditional ritual expert Nosrat offers less Qur'ānic commentary to her participants. Instead she performs religious poetic songs and counsels her religious descendants to fulfil the wishes of the participants. She regularly reads the Qur'ānic verses of *anām,* recites prayers, and at the end initiates the participants' wishes. On the one hand she does not talk about Islamic veiling restrictedly like other preachers, and many schoolgirls sit and listen to her in their school uniforms and large scarves without being asked to wear the traditional veil or *chādor* over. In contrast, the woman attending Malyheh's meeting wore the full-length veil. One day when we were sitting and listening to the preacher Nosrat, two young schoolgirls entered the house. Before entering the main room they stopped at the yard, removed their scarves, and put on their *chādor,* as is the usual dress code at *rowżeh* meetings. Such an attitude is in many ways different to that of Mumeni, another educated preacher, who is a veteran of the first Islamic girls' school. She had no objection to me taking pictures, as the participants were fully veiled at the meetings. She also considered it important to communicate the Islamic message to a foreign viewer. At the end of this chapter I will present another newly educated preacher.

Dissemination of Islamic knowledge and learning

The production of Islamic knowledge within the family is not the only source of transmission of religious knowledge, but it has extended the series of formal Islamic educational institutions. Today the practice of memorising the Qur'ān and its meaning is also encouraged for children at Islamic state national schools.

As I have explained the recent learning of the Qur'ān is not confined to the religious leader (*re'īs-e jaleseh*) alone. In the case of Hinduism the male priest (guru of the Brahman caste) alone has access to a holy text, having been taught by his own ancestors and having the right to continue their practice (Ortner 1989). In the case of Iranian Muslims religious knowledge is generated through a process of learning, both through religious networks and at school.

Traditionally illiterate women learn and memorise the holy text by participating in religious meetings where verses of the Qur'ān are recited and chanted. Only seldom do they ask questions concerning the actual meaning of the holy text. As I have shown earlier, the normal procedure in such a meeting is that the women read two or three verses each, followed by a commentary by the preacher. Some of the verses, both in the mosque and at *rowżeh* meetings, are read loudly, or chanted without all of the participants having the text in front of them. In this way even the illiterate can learn to recite and memorise the verses without being able to read the text.

Restructuring of Islamic learning

The socio-political reforms initiated by the Islamic state included not only a new state bureaucratic system, with a recruitment policy training the 'true' Muslim, but also an educational reform that attempted to juxtapose modern science and Islamic knowledge. In the past Qur'ānic knowledge (*savād-e Qur'ānī*) and school knowledge (science) were explicitly separate fields of organising knowledge. Students might not learn the very basic religious norms, the elementary rituals[54] and ideological pillars[55] of Islam. Religious and scientific knowledge were meant to be complementary in relation to each other.

In Iran political and socio-religious changes have reshaped the school curriculum and the educational system, mixing secular and religious subjects. Qur'ānic classes in the post-revolutionary period brought together men and women of different backgrounds, placing more emphasis than before on reading Qur'ān and its commentary. In the new school curriculum it is obligatory to teach the Qur'ān and prayers. Such knowledge has become a pre-condition for gaining access to jobs, higher education and social recognition. The reforms require the teaching of religious knowledge, socio-political issues, and 'approved' behavioural norms.[56] In turn, such an approved education has increased the options in job markets. Such an institutionalised form of knowledge has required the transformation of the former religiously conservative education.

The school books are important in transmitting religious values and in creating an awareness of political ends: the ideal characteristic of an Islamic state and the Shi'ī image of martyrdom and Islamic revolution. The relation between religion and the school system seems to reflect what Bourdieu terms 'reproduction', giving birth to a new framework of cultural meaning and social differences (Bourdieu and Passeron 1977:5–6). According to Bourdieu religion and education constitute a 'field' of forces comparable in their functioning to magnetic fields. This view corresponds to the former secular Iranian state policy with religious conservative education, and the present Islamic state where religion and education is integrated. The intermediation of these two forms of knowledge (the religious and the secular) constitutes a powerful aspect in the identity of many Iranian Islamic intellectuals today. The post-revolutionary Iran manipulates the content of the educational curriculum and text books to transmit 'legitimate' state political views and Islamic cultural models.

[54]Five obligatory elements of worship; *namāz, rowżeh, khomes, hajj, zakāt*.
[55]Five pillars of Shi'ī Islam; *tohīd, nabovvat, imāmat, 'adl* and *qiyāmat*.
[56]Mehran (1991) suggests that the date of the complete rewriting of elementary and secondary school text books was 1981–2. The major changes in the content of social studies text books indicates a new socialisation as Muslim citizens.

The spirituality and intellectuality of the religious leader

The piety of a religious leader is believed to be a source of popularity by the followers. This is believed to stem from one's holiness, of having a strong faith and a high Islamic knowledge. The shiny face of a religious leader without make-up is considered by the followers to be a result of regular worship, purity of thought (*nīyat*), and to be a manifestation of her inner self (*batin*). Describing such a preacher, a woman who had known this particular preacher for years said she was 'a woman of this world and here after'. The preacher Naderi, who enjoyed economic prosperity and an increasing popularity, was considered by many to be an example of a woman with a pure heart. The simplicity of her dress and lack of ornaments identified her as non-materialistic. Moreover, the preacher's dedicated religious worship (*ebadat*) signified a high social status to her followers and female acquaintances.

In contrast to this status a preacher often took the chance to present herself as being humble by repeatedly referring to herself as a person with high religious position, but also having to take into consideration daily moral behaviour if she would be called a 'true Muslim'. This is an area where a Muslim's act of everyday prayers is judged by its purity of intention and not by authoritative role and the numbers of times it is performed. The value of faith is manifested in the quality of a person's entire social relation as a 'true Muslim'. Such a view is often adopted by newly educated preachers in order to oppose other preachers whom they consider not to be practising the true faith.

Having an effective voice, and being fluent in speech and on Qur'ānic commentary, are some of the qualities by which a high-ranking preacher is identified. Once my religious companion, Nezhat, took me to a *rowżeh* meeting where she had become a regular participant since my first fieldwork in 1989. She was impressed with the preacher's commentary and explained that there was an important difference between the preachers who describe Islam in a fearful manner, and those (like her favourite preacher) who focus on its relevance to everyday aspects of life. I soon discovered that the more a preacher redefined the religious norms in terms of practical and everyday common sense, the younger and more educated were the participants.

The newly educated preacher

In 1994 there was a new female religious hall, the House of Husain. I had been familiar with the house since I was a schoolgirl owing to its religious arrangements. But only recently the house became entirely devoted to the community although the owner still sponsored the full cost of its religious meetings. The property upon which the religious hall was built was given as religious endowment to the community (*vaqf*) by its *hajji* owner, a religiously oriented elderly woman from a well-off business family, with a long tradition of sponsoring communal meetings. The *hajji* owner used to live there before and had given annual meetings for years.

The preacher Moradi represents another category of religious leader. She graduated from the school of theology and had experience in organising educational and religious activities in the post-revolutionary period. On the second day of the month of Safar I attended meetings at the House of Husain where the preacher Moradi, a former student of Mumeni, and two other ritual experts were giving daily lessons and holding speeches. The meetings started from seven in the morning and lasted until noon, when the women went home to their families. The preacher Moradi, a young and high-ranking seminary teacher, held sermons every day during the two holy months of Muharam and Safar. Before I entered the house I could very clearly hear the voice of the preacher reciting and singing the sorrowful song (*noheh*) Al-Yasin in honour of Imām Mahdi: the awaited messianic figure believed to be the 12th Shi'ī Imām who went into hiding in AD 874.[57] Later on I discovered that the song was the popular greeting text (*ziyārat-nāmeh*) performed by the religious student Gohar. Her loud performance was very surprising to me as it was generally not acceptable for women to broadcast their voices in public, and in particular to men. Although the use of loudspeakers has been common at large religious meetings since the revolution, it has generally not been acceptable for women to broadcast their voices.

When the meeting ended I got the chance to approach the religious student Gohar, who had performed the sorrowful song. She was a young student in her final year at a new Islamic

[57]The Iranian *Ithnā ashariyya* Muslims believe in twelve Imāms the last of whom is al-Mahdi.

girls' school. I expressed my surprise that her loud and effective performance could be heard outside by the pedestrians (i.e. men). She said her religious mission is more important on such a holy day than the restriction on her voice as a woman. A few days later at the *husyneh* I approached a religious student selling religious cassettes of male clergy and Islamic books, and to my surprise I was able to buy the greeting song of Al-Yasin performed the other day by preacher Gohar. That was the first time I heard a recorded voice of a female preacher.

The differences between the newly educated religious leaders such as Moradi and her former teacher Mumeni, was that the former adopted a stronger feminist standpoint within an Islamic context than the latter. Not only do they place priority on the woman's religious duty as mother and wife, but also on taking an active role as a Muslim, independent of other social forces, conscious of international politics rather than being submissive and ignorant. This category of preachers is not only popular among the younger generation of Islamic intellectuals, but they are in better contact with the high-ranked moderate *ʿulama*.[58]

Islamic alternatives to higher social mobility

Since the revolution the admission of women to theological schools has grown and a religious authoritative role of women has emerged as a result.

When comparing my fieldwork in 1989 to 1994, there was not only a clear increase in the number of educated female preachers and religious meetings, but also a rearticulation of the sex differences among newly educated preachers. The latter had often obtained a higher degree in Islamic knowledge by, for example, writing an Islamic thesis (*resāleh*) at one of the new Islamic girls' schools in Shiraz, or through corresponding studies at theology school in Qum. By 1994, the female preachers could mobilise many followers, even more than the average male preacher of an average religious rank (*akhānd*) in the local mosque. Islamic education is important in integrating women into higher-rank Islamic circles and theological debates.

[58]In July 1994 I heard about a highly educated woman who was teaching the readings of the Qur'ān with correct pronunciation, and that all those specially interested in being students could register through the office of the leader of Friday prayer (*imām-e jomeh*).

The most significant aspect of the religious authoritative role of women lies in their capacity to carry out Qur'ānic exegesis and act as leaders of prayer (*pīsh-nāmaz*) at female religious gatherings on special days. There were many occasions when the preacher in charge of *rowżeh* meetings performed a short prayer of *namāz* as she led the prayers. The procedure was that she would recite loudly while we placed our foreheads on a piece of clay presumably from Karbalā (*mohr*). While sitting with several women I asked them about the role of female preachers in performing communal prayers. I was interested to find out if they had observed any female preachers performing communal prayers despite the general Islamic prohibition against this. Not only did they know several learned preachers performing communal prayers, but they also had contrasting views. One said, 'Whoever can read the verses of communal prayers correctly and in the right tones, can take a seat in front of the others and perform the communal prayer.' A school teacher objected to this view and insisted that this communal ritual role could not be performed by women. The third, my religious companion, insisted on asking a more educated clergy friend, but believed that it sometimes was possible for a female preacher to perform such prayers in private female gatherings.

Later, I put the same question to a recent graduate of the new Islamic girls' college. She smiled and said: 'Some *'ulama* say yes and some *'ulama* say no.' She told me of the male *'ulama* who objected, including Ayatollah Khomeini, and the high religious scholars who were positive, such as the prominent Ayatollah Araki. Later on this question raised a discussion among some of my friends and relatives with wide religious experience. Their comments led me to believe that there were different Islamic understandings and practices than what the official Islam suggests.

Nevertheless, one thing was clear: female preachers perform occasional communal prayers on special occasions at female religious meeting held at home, or in the *husyneh*. Furthermore, there exists both a liberal and more conservative view on the subject of women's engagement among the clergy. For example, on the day of *'aid-e fitr*, when celebrating the end of the fast month, the preacher Zaki did not take a prestigious and authoritative position in front like that of the male preachers at the communal prayers, but stood instead in line with the others.

However, this did not mean that women preferred to attend the communal prayer led by male preachers at the mosques. To them the amount of promissable merit is the same. On the contrary, many learned preachers perform the prayer on the last day of Ramaẓān in the company of other 'learned' female preachers and religious companions.

The economic position of the female preachers

By arranging Qur'ānic classes teachers gain social respect, as well as earning an independent income. Teaching Qur'ānic lessons independently represents an alternative career option for Qur'ānic teachers, both bringing them income and moral status. It is generally the case that these self-employed women earn as much, and sometimes more, than teachers and civil servants in the official sector of the Islamic state. A Qur'ānic teacher or ritual expert with a little knowledge of the Arabic language can support herself with the money earned from local religious seminaries and classes. The amount of money paid to a female preacher for each meeting is based on informal agreements and varies according to her rank, the occasion, the time spent on rituals, and the generosity of the hostess and the class. The amount may vary from a few hundred tomans to several thousand.[59] Moreover, the preachers may often participate in several meetings during a day, particularly in the month of Ramaẓān. The fee is paid privately in an envelope. The emphasis is on spiritual aspects, morality, and the objective of the meeting. Therefore, money becomes just a reward.

To have some elementary Qur'ānic knowledge, or to be fluent in reading a few popular chapters, such as the verse of *anām* or the blessing verse of *komyl,* has encouraged religious-oriented housewives to arrange meetings of their own. This has provided a number of lower-class women with an opportunity to earn money in the neighbourhood. The interest in such informal jobs has increased greatly among housewives, particularly those with grown-up children, and who have some Qur'ānic knowledge and education. In today's Islamic Iran it has become increasingly

[59]In 1989 one US dollar was equivalued to 115 tomans, while in 1994 the official rate was 240 tomans to one dollar. In 1989 the minimum income of a primary school teacher was between 400 and 10,000 tomans.

common for preachers to give private lessons in the Qur'ān to school pupils, university students, housewives, and older women. The improved economic position of ritual experts is the result of the increased local demand for religious meetings.

More recently this kind of Islamic female career and education has increased across social categories, and have also been adopted by more upper-class Islamic women. The Islamic elite women are more officially integrated into the state Islamic organisation and are protected by the leader of the Friday prayer (*imām-e jom'eh*), who is one of the highest local authorities in the Islamic state. The relative of my religious companion was a *hajji* woman who, apart from the *rowżeh* meetings, often accompanied me to several other family parties. There she often met friends and relatives who knew many of the seminary leaders in the local area. Once we went together on a visit to the house of her preacher friend, a distant relative and a former fellow student at a Qur'ānic class. They were teacher and student, but knew each other as classmates. Although no fee was specified, she was going to offer the honorary annual fee as a gift of celebrating the Iranian New Year. This was the time for paying and receiving visits. The money was put in an open envelop, and when the preacher left the room to bring us tea, her student left it on the shelf and served us drinks (*sharbat*) and homemade sweets. On her return the preacher immediately noticed the envelope, and as matter of courtesy (*tārof*[60]) she pretended to refuse to accept it. However, her student kept repeating that the gift was not worthy of her work. Finally the preacher accepted it, still without opening it. This shows an ideal of being humble and of not being concerned with material affairs, particularly *vis-à-vis* those with whom one has an established relation. This attitude may not be practised to the same degree by all members of the community. It is rational to differentiate the degrees of morality and friendship, and as in the above case, to highlight spirituality and the importance of money as a gift.

It has also been a common tendency among the recent Islamic elite to take care of the interest of intellectuals and the younger generation, such as school children and pupils. Ideologically this

[60]A spoken interaction form that deliberately rejects an offer despite one's real desire.

category want to locate the Islamic norms in their everyday praxis.

The preachers Mumeni, Moradi and Nosrat are single and own the houses that are devoted to female Islamic meetings. The economic contributions they receive are in terms of alms (*zakāt*), or other forms of private donation made by people who have made a religious vow to contribute to the arrangement. For example, sugar, tea, lemon juice and boxes of sweets were often brought to the meetings of Nosrat, the contributors wanting them to be served to the other participants. In her *rowżeh* meetings there are always several religious servants (*khādem*) responsible for collecting alms, and serving tea and drinks. Often the amount of money collected at the meetings of Nosrat are greater than at the meetings of Mumeni and Moradi. Nosrat frequently reminded the participants to donate alms on behalf of themselves and their families.[61] Many women believe in alms as a protection against misfortune and unexpected events (see Chapter 3). Those responsible for collecting the money make careful notes of the cash donations, giving a few sugar cubes in return, while reading spells, reciting the Qur'ān, and blessing the participants by blowing at them. My religious companion at Mumeni's meetings once came with me to a meeting headed by Nosrat. In the middle of the meeting she asked one of the servants to give her some of the blessed sugar that was piled in a big shiny green bowl in front of Nosrat. She paid some money, picked up a few of the sugar cubes, and put them in a small paper. Although my companion was a religiously oriented woman she was surprised to be charged for the rituals of Nosrat. There is no doubt that Nosrat fully covered the expenses of her communal meetings through the contributions of her participants. Nosrat often requested the support of her participants in terms of alms and charity, and once she started her meeting by accusing those who insinuated that she was robbing them by demanding too much money. She argued that, 'Your donations, no matter how small, will help the existence of this meeting. It is not going to be spent on myself, but will cover for the services you receive. Last time we bought an air conditioner and now we need a water cooler.'

That day money was collected for buying a water cooler to be

[61]*Zakāt* a form of tax for agricultural production, compensation payment of breaking religious norms, health insurance and community support.

installed for the use of the participants. It was also a common practice by participants to give money at the end of a meeting, as part of a religious tax (*zakāt*) to receive blessings for their health. My religious companion suggested that I pay for my children and myself a year in advance, as I would be away. She herself paid a substantial amount of money in religious taxes every year in order to keep her husband's increasing capital under the protection of the holy Imām.

At the house of Husain there were three different religious leaders of different ranks who made speeches and were in charge of rituals. The amount received as donations was often reported during the religious meetings. In one case a ritual expert listed the following amount of money and jewellery collected that day: 20,000 tomans in cash, a bracelet worth 41,000 tomans, two rings each worth 11 and 15,000 tomans, and a bracelet worth 11,000 tomans. The intention was to collect money to accommodate the family of a poor woman. The more prosperous families were expected to make the highest donations. She blessed the participants by saying that God will fulfil all their wishes, even those who have paid only one or two tomans.

Conclusion

The few studies on religious activities and ritual experts (Betteridge 1980, Starr 1992) only indicate the way in which religious careers may bring economic and social prosperity to women. In present-day Iran religion attracts the newly educated and the young middle class, as well as the elderly women. It not only brings economic and social prosperity, but also Islamic political choice to women.

Ever since the Iranian revolution in 1978 the Islamic state has supported this form of Islamic learning as part of the process of instituting a religious tradition and reconstructing secular education. There are no sanctions against the participation of women in the field of Islamic education. However, there is a limit to women's religious leadership and they are excluded from the male-dominated leaderships of mosque.

At the time of my first fieldwork in Iran in 1989, it was evident that the education of boys and girls had become a locus for the transmission of cultural traditionalism and the Islamic cultural revolution. The aim of the Islamic state has been to disseminate religious knowledge across the differences of gender, generation and class. Women have become more visible in the religious field, and their religious and family duties have increased systematically as a result of the Islamisation of the various levels of education, and through the large number of mosques, shrines and female religious meetings and Qur'ānic classes with strong educational potential.

Many housewives of the traditional religious families actualise their Qur'ānic knowledge by rapidly achieving a competence in prayers and Qur'ānic lessons, thereby enabling many of them to act as the ritual experts in charge of various occasions within the family and local community. Many women are able through such traditional religious activities to make inroads into Islamic politics and ideological discourses.

Middle East ethnographic studies have largely ignored the formal and informal religious activities of women. They focus on the Islamic elite culture of men with discursive traditional linkages to the Qur'ān, *ḥadīth*, mosques, religious schools and their scriptural interpretations. The female preachers obtain their knowledge of Islam through formal religious education, such as the newly established girls' schools, and by having access to religious texts and ritual instructions. They were once ordinary religious participants and students of the Qur'ānic seminaries at home. The family and personal experience in everyday life is also an important source of informal knowledge that can be transferred in religious activities. This has provided several categories of women with an economic and social alternative, enabling them to remain autonomous and powerful within the female domain and across the segregated gender boundary. Today's free access to Islamic texts makes a considerable religious mobility possible. Many of the local preachers today expand their religious position from being a participant to an organiser of religious rituals, or a leader of Qur'ānic seminaries. The religious authority of a woman is still, however, confined within a female religious network, and does not reach into the religious organisation of the mosque. Once I heard a high-ranking religious woman give a talk to soldiers on the importance of their struggle for Islam. Through higher religious knowledge women are able to extend their social power. This kind of public Islamic mission of a high-ranking female preacher has under the Islamic state led to a growth of a female Islamist elite. In my view this is an area that has gained political and modern dimensions as they contribute actively to the building of the contemporary Muslim nation.

Finally, in two areas the Islamic education and practices of women are comparable to that of men. First, the Islamic learning and practices of women are traditionally integrated within the social system of the family and its rituals. As for the men, their religious practice is extensively associated with formal ritual assemblies. Second, the training of female religious leaders is a matter of social modernity in the way in which it articulates with the Islamic state's political project and the ideology of becoming a politically conscious Muslim. Therefore, through religious careers women get better access to social and political mobility with no traditional and Islamic state obstacles.

FIVE

THE CONCEPT OF MARTYRS AND ITS SYMBOLIC APPLICATION

In this chapter I shall focus on the significance of women's public rituals and symbols involving death (see also Chapter 6) and the way in which rituals involving death have been politicised under the Islamic Republic. The Islamic state requested various rituals to be offered to the deaths of those characterised as 'martyrs' and as political conspirators (*monāfeqin*) since the Iranian revolution in 1979. The local and state positions involve divergent ideas about the religio-political meaning of death and its social consequences.

The idiom of martyrdom (*shāhadat* – defending the faith against corrupting influences) is best portrayed through the 3rd Shi'ī Imām's martyrdom, Imām Husain's death in the fight in Karbalā in AD 680. Imām Husain is also called Seyyid al-Shahadā, the Lord of Martyrs. This characteristic re-emerged and reconstructed a new local image and concept of Islamic national salvation. The religious idiom of Shi'ī martyrdom has effectively been transformed into a revolutionary ideology, first for a mass social change and political mobilisation in opposing the regime of the Shāh (cf. Fischer 1980, Hegland 1983, Thaiss 1977), and later in the mass religious military recruitment during the war between Iran and Iraq (1980–8).

Having a relative killed in the Iran and Iraq war, demands an expected respect and public recognition, as is made evident in neighbourhood ritual events. Being the mother or sister of a martyr is thus a new public identity, implying social respect, political participation and Islamic commitment. The Shi'ī Imām Husain is a common theme in speeches given by preachers at the Qur'ānic meetings held by women, as well as the speeches of male preachers in the mosque.

Political nature of Islamic rituals

Before I elaborate further on the Islamic political content in the symbols of funeral rituals and martyrdom, I will present the case of a mother of a martyr, with whom I made an informal interview. The case represents an example of a voluntary soldier (*basījī*) from a lower middle-class urban family, who joined the mass Islamic military mobilisation (*jihad*) during the Iran–Iraq war in 1985–6.

A mother of a martyr

Nayreh is 60 years old. She has worked as a maid for several families, including my father in her youth, and was now known as the 'mother of a martyr'. She comes from a lower-class family that migrated from a village near Shiraz in the late 1960s, and now lives in a poor neighbourhood.[62] When her sons grew up and her husband got a mini-bus, she stopped working as a maid. In 1977 her husband bought some cheap land in the lower part of the town and built a house. First they built one room, but after their oldest son's marriage they built another one. Having three grown-up sons and a house of their own was a lot to be proud of before the Iranian revolution.

Nayreh was among the first visitors who came to see me upon my arrival at my parents' home. She brought a large tray of homemade bread as a gift to welcome me. My first impression of her was that she looked unusually old for a woman of her age. She kept drawing my attention to her teeth and to her hair,

[62]The social and political recognition received by families of martyrs has remained the ideal for children from families with limited social and economic means. Other motivating factors, such as religious passion, family morality, and the desire to join the movement with friends, were also more powerful among the lower classes than among higher and middle-class urban families. There is also the fact that better-off parents could afford to send their sons abroad. There is no study available on the social and class categories of martyrs. My data on this subject was obtained through my personal participation and observation in various local arenas, rather than through statistical techniques and surveys. I was able to conclude that the numbers of martyrs, particularly those classified as *basījī*, was larger among the lower social classes in Shiraz. The most explicit evidence of such a distinction was the greater number of martyrs' pictures displayed in the lower part of town which contained the older and poorer-standard buildings. The structural explanation for this feature may be sought in the socio-economic advantages promised to the *basījī*. 15–30,000 tomans paid in advance, job advancement and improved social status.

most of which had fallen out during the four years following her son's death.

Her martyred son was killed a year after joining Iran's mobilisation force (*basījī*) in 1986. After his death her oldest son got a job through the martyrs' foundation (*jihad*), but apart from that she was reluctant to request other benefits available to the families of martyrs. Such benefits would in her opinion represent an acceptance of money in exchange for her son's blood, two values that to her were unexchangeable. After her youngest son safely returned from military service, they were encouraged to appeal once again to the martyrs' foundation to get a job for him as well. Like the families of other martyrs, Nayreh visited her son's tomb almost every Thursday evening and Friday morning. The day she had promised to take me to the cemetery, her husband fell ill, so I was accompanied by another woman who had known her son well and knew where his grave was. Nayreh was among the occasional religious participants who was illiterate and had no Qur'ānic knowledge. Whenever I asked her to which *rowżeh* she went, she would say, no, 'I do not like these women going to *rowżeh* and coming back home sitting and talking about their neighbours for hours.' She was not a religious person as such. Her oldest son, however, whose political and moral status had been promoted to that of a martyr's brother, became the Imām of their own local mosque.

Nayreh told me the story of her son's martyrdom, and of his courageous life once when she came to visit me at home.

> *Image of a martyr*[63] 'One day when my son Shāh-Husain came home after playing football, he stood in front of the mirror combing his hair. I noticed his foot was injured. I asked him if he had a fight with somebody? Reluctantly he answered "no". I asked him again. He said: "You might be afraid if I showed you something." I said proudly: "Not at all. How could a woman like me who has lived in many places, and stayed outside the home until late at night, be scared of anything." I assured him that I was not frightened of anything except God. Then, he put his hand in his pocket and pulled out a dagger. He said when he fell down the hill the other day, his hand had reached into the sand and

[63]I present the case without editing as an example for its political rhetorical concepts.

touched the dagger. [This event was believed to be a message from the 12th Imām by the mother.] The dagger had no handle, so the next day he took it to a man in the neighbourhood and asked him to make a handle and a sheath. When he returned home, he said the dagger must have belonged to Imām Husain's brother (*Abūllfazal*). "I will send it back to the *imām-e zamān*" [the 12th Imām who is believed to be in a state of occultation for more than eleven centuries, only to return in the society of the unjust as messiah]. [Nayreh understood that to her son the dagger represented a message of becoming a good Muslim.] A few months later he joined the army and was sent to the front to fight against Iraqi troops. After a month's training, during which he learned how to shoot, he was sent to the mountains for parachute training.'

'I was there to watch his training every Friday. Once when I was there waiting for him to finish, I noticed three young women sitting next to me. They whispered to their sons to leave the area, and I heard them say, "We know what to do next." They had explosives in their bags. I knew they wanted to place these among the mothers in the audience, so I went to the guard without saying a word to the others. I asked him to let me in the building to see my son immediately. I asked permission to go inside, so as to inform the officer of the women's intention. I did not get permission, but I insisted and threatened: "Either you let me in or I'll kill myself." The guard let me enter but I was stopped by the next guard. I insisted, saying I had an urgent message for my son. Later on they called him over the loudspeaker. He was shocked at my presence. He was accompanied by a guard. I asked the officer to come with me quietly, and told my son to surround the area quickly with the help of the others. At first, the officer was reluctant to listen to me, but I assured him that I would show him something very important. We went out together but the women had moved. Finally, they were found and accused of planning sabotage. Apparently those women were hanged the next day. They wanted to kill our children, but not their own. My son used to remind me that I'd done my religious duty and he admired me for doing so. He kept reminding me of being a pure, tidy and clean mother: "You don't like to clean your dishes where other people wash their polluted (*najes*) clothes; to disregard such things, is like the act of a non-Muslim and non-believer (*kāfar*). So, we must fight with non-believers in the war," he said. He joined *basījī* only a few days after he learned that two of his friends had been killed in the war zone.

'A few days before I had learned that my son was martyred. He had sent us a telegram saying that he would be visiting us soon, but we waited for a few days without anything happening. That particular day I was visiting my oldest son's daughter, who was very ill in hospital. I was in a bad mood the whole day. I had an argument with the hospital staff, accusing them of treating the patients in the hospital like savages. I saw my granddaughter lying naked in bed without a sheet to cover her. Other patients did not dare to say anything. I told one of the nurses: "If my grandchild was to lay down on the floor who then would be blamed for such an impurity (*nejasat*)." I saw many unused sheets in the cupboard. I took out some and distributed them among the patients. In return, the parents wished me a long life. I criticised the nurse and told her, "Look, the king [referring to the former Iranian king] might truly have taken all the gold out of Iran, but not the hospital sheets." [Nayreh was known to be straightforward in expressing her political opinions.] At lunch I was happily asked to share food with the patients, and as I was about to put a spoonful of food in my month I saw my oldest son approaching, accompanied by a man from my neighbourhood. My son went to his daughter and kissed her, while his companion came to me, calling me by my oldest son's name, mother of Husain, as a matter of respect. Later I learned that he knew about my son's death, but pretended to know nothing. He asked me to return home. He said: "It seems you had a fight with a neighbour the other day, so the authorities want to talk to you." I said, "I have not harmed anybody, I have acted piously all my life." Finally, when we got back home, I saw many women, including our nearest neighbour who had lost her son not too long ago. I greeted her, but she responded in an ignorant manner. She was sitting at the entrance of her house and kept crying. The man who had fetched me came into our house and took all of my son's pictures off the wall. I didn't notice when the man left. The man needed the pictures for the funeral ceremony and for the decoration in front of the *pāsdārs'* car, which was to carry the corpse to the martyrs' home. I asked him why he wanted those pictures. He said: "The pictures might break here." I said that I had not broken them for years. [She now realized that some misfortune had befallen her son.] I was confused, not knowing whether or not some misfortune had happened. I was flabbergasted when a green bird flew in and circled around me and touched my heart. [The bird was thought to be the son communicating through one's broken heart.] It flew back and forth and I had a feeling that somebody was telling me "go", "go forward". [The son's spirit encouraging her and wanting her to be patient and face the reality of his death.] When I stepped out into the street I saw my son's picture hanging on the front of the police car from the martyr centre, which was driving slowly up our lane. Some women of the neighbourhood were riding in it.[64] Then I knew everything. I started crying and biting myself so hard that I lost all my teeth. [She showed me her teeth and her hair whenever she spoke about her son's death and her suffering. The loss of one's teeth in a dream indicates a death event and loss of a close family member.]

'On the burial day at the graveyard, the other women tied my hands to prevent me from hitting myself. They were scared that I would harm myself. As they took my son's corpse to the washing room [the Muslim ritual of last ablution], I promised the *pāsdār* not to cause any harm to myself if he would let me see my son for one last time. The *pāsdār* consoled me and said, "Look, mother, you should not grieve so much, but be thankful that your son died in a condition in which his body is not smashed into pieces. Imagine those martyr's mothers who have to suffer not only the death of their sons, but also see their mutilated bodies. Your son died by a single bullet which entered from one side and came out from the other" [a less painful death

[64]During the funerals of martyrs, the families of the martyrs sat in the front seat of the Islamic police's car next to high political and religious authorities.

for a religious duty. This was not a relief to her at all as she persisted in seeing him for last time.']

'The *pāsdār* let me enter the washing room. I saw my son's wide-shouldered corpse laid out [sign of his masculinity and the ideal of manliness]. His face was surprisingly wide, as big and round as a moon in shape [a metaphor equating shininess with a spiritual person – a rite of passage from the state of ordinary to an exceptionally blessed one]. I got his hand in my arms and started to kiss him [touching a corpse is taboo and demands spiritual purification of ablution according to Islam].[65] As they tried to stop me, my hand struck the stone beneath the corpse. Then the guard sent me outside and I could only catch a glance of my son as his corpse was carried to the grave.

'My son was so good, and so was his funeral. The funeral was crowded; it started with a big march from the main street across the city toward the graveyard, a distance of several kilometres. The following night my close neighbour and friend dreamed of my son. She saw a huge vineyard of green grapes with many branches and big flowers, growing at the corner of my house. She went closer to see if the flowers were my son [such flowers in the middle of a grape vine were often explained to me by other listeners as a metaphor for her son]. The next day a few mothers of martyrs visited me and brought me a bunch of flowers – the flowers which my neighbour had dreamt of. On the third and seventh day of his funeral, the other mothers of martyrs came to pay me their tributes with bunches of flowers. They paid me their respect for having a brave and honourable son who sacrificed himself for the nation.'

A few days later Nayreh invited me and my family to her house. After having lunch her eldest son excused himself and went to carry out the Friday ritual in the nearby mosque. The other members of my family and I could hear his voice praying over the loudspeaker, and his mother proudly drew our attention to

[65]Women are often reluctant and fearful to touch the body of the deceased, the exception being corpses of very close relatives and corpses which have a holy sign, i.e. corpses which look as if the deceased is sleeping, or have a 'special light' in the face, and so on. However, the common view seemed to be an emphasis on the polluting effect of corpses.

it. 'He has just been nominated as imām of the mosque to lead the Friday ritual of reciting the *du'ā* verse of Komyl' (from *mafātieh*). The mother admired him and was clearly proud of his success. In spite of losing a son, she often thanked God for providing a higher social status for the other. He also acts as a counsel in the neighbourhood and people come to him for advice in cases of family conflicts, or for some other local matters (electrical work, etc). Nayreh's third son joined the military following the initiation of obligatory duty in 1987. He feared a similar fate to that of his dead brother. He asked one of his friends to shoot him in the leg in order to have an excuse to be sent back home before his life would be more seriously endangered.

Although it was often the case that the mother of martyrs became more religiously active and initiated regularly *rowżeh* meetings at home, this was not the case with Nayreh. Nayreh's eldest son became instead more active in the local mosque and with the Islamic police. The new official Islamic institution has created new social categories. Martyrdom was perpetuated by the ideological discourse of the Islamic authorities (i.e. the privileged), and its symbolism defined the martyr as a sacred person and as a first-class citizen under the Islamic Republic.

The cemetery

Many aspects of life situations and the local place of traditional religious rituals have become the locus of diverse ideological differences and Islamic political turmoil by means of political control and social changes.

The Shi'ī Muslim burial ritual is such that after the corpse has been laid in the grave, a few stones are placed at some distance from the corpse. The *lahn*-stone is apparently the last one and is placed under the head. The right cheek must touch the soil, and a stick should be placed under the right arm to help the deceased stand up on the day of resurrection. Then the grave is ready to be filled with clay. After one or two days it will be covered with stones upon which the person's name, the names of the father and mother, the dates of birth and death, and, in case of a tragic accident, sometimes a meaningful poem about death are traditionally engraved. The mortuary has a washing room with a few broad stones for washing the corpse, filling some orifices of the body and draping it in the cloth of *kafanī*. The person undertaking this task is the 'corpse-washer' (*mordeh-shor*) (see also Chapter 6, 'The passage of the dead').

The funeral of martyrs, the graveyard, and religious meetings are among the situations that have become major ritual occasions in which the knowledge of Islam in its plural term 'islams' are played out. Different categories of people, without denying their Muslim identity, reflect and project different views of what is the 'correct' and what is the 'false' way of practising Islam.

Women, as mothers, sisters and wives, may become part of the prestigious category of the dead martyr's family. The family of the martyr is honoured by hanging pictures of the martyrs in the nearest mosque, or by giving family members priority in applications for a place at school or university, and/or access to work in the local area. In this way the family gains both a high status and actual economic rewards.

In the Islamic Republic the politics of death have changed the traditional articulation of the cemetery, where a funeral ritual used to be performed for all deceased equally. The cemetery has acquired political dimensions and has become an arena for religious discourses. Since the Iran–Iraq war cemeteries have been changed into three sections: one for the war casualty martyrs, which is crowded and where the Qur'ān is regularly recited; one for those who died in conflict with Islamic police, categorised as hypocrites (*monāfeqin*), which is free, dry and isolated land; and one for members of the general public who have died of natural causes, in which one may buy a plot in advance.

The graveyards of martyrs are identified by a range of religious symbols which signify their high spiritual status and their honourable deaths. The graveyard is decorated with Islamic flags. Their graves are shaded on the top, decorated with green plants, a verse of Qur'ān, a large well-framed picture, and a text commemorating the martyr's name, age, the name of his last battle, and the time and location of his death.[66]

The opposite religious symbols apply to the political opposition of the Islamic state. In the political rhetorics of the Islamic Republic, those who have died in counter revolutionary clashes with the Islamic police are identified as hypocrites (*monāfeqin*)

[66]The last battle which led to one's death was named after the early Islamic battles in the town of Karbalā in Iraq in AD 640.

and as being punished by the Islamic Republic and are therefore denied a proper traditional Islamic ritual burial.[67] In contrast to the 'pious' death of martyrs, the graves of those categorised as '*monāfeqin*' are isolated in the cemetery, or located in a dry, 'naked' and dusty field. They are thus deprived of communal blessings such as the ritual of ablution and praying. The cemetery of unnamed *monāfeqin* are distinguishable also by the size of the mound.[68] They are buried in graves which are not permitted to be covered by a stone. The grave stone is believed to reduce the pain of longing and loss of the dead soul of the deceased.

In Shi'ī Iranian tradition the grave stone is placed on the top of the muddy grave during the funeral ritual of the third day when the ceremony takes place at the cemetery, followed by a ritual meal and a women's Qur'ānic meeting at home. Mourning and ritual visiting of the grave sites of the deceased *monāfeqin* was apparently forbidden by the Islamic Republic. They were treated as 'non-believers'.

In contrast, the local funerals of most martyrs of the war were distinguished by public and collective rituals expressing great honour. They were attended by local shopkeepers, religious leaders, the Friday Imāms, and officials of the Islamic Republic. I was told that women also attended such funerals together with family, relatives and friends of the deceased. In this way, the ideal political and social order created a ritually innovative perception of funeral sessions. This symbolic discourse of social power promised religious honour, and a gift of eternal blessing to attendants.

Participation in the public funeral ceremonies of martyrs did not, however, mean that everyone felt the same political loyalty towards the Islamic state. Many talked about it as a matter of enforced rules that were applied to the state employers and bazaris which had an important functional role in local life. They had a need to protect their job's prosperity and their businesses in the context of the Islamic Republic bureaucratic organisation. Thus, the funerals of local youths were transformed from private family rituals into the realm of political discourse, and were used

[67]Ablution is understood by Shi'ī Muslims to purify the dead and decrease the torment of the grave.

[68]I was told that the 'naked' scene of the cemetery created the symbolic meaning of the desert of Karbalā and one's innocence. However, the cemetery for *monāfeqin* has since been demolished and turned into an ordinary cemetery in 1994.

in the demarcation of a particular legitimate political and Islamic ideology.

The following case is that of a so-called *monāfeqin* family, who were forced to abandon the death ritual, but continued to fight for the right to hold a proper funeral ritual. Aftab, a well-to-do middle-aged *hajji* woman, told me how her son had been executed in 1983 because he was a member of the forbidden political party *Mojahedīn-Khalq*.[69] The father had visited his son the day before his execution, and had been promised that he would be released soon. The next morning the family was shocked to hear the son's name on the radio among a list of the executed. The day after the corpse was delivered to his relatives. In spite of the strict rules regarding such funeral rituals, the mother managed to perform a proper burial ceremony. After a series of arguments with the authorities it was finally agreed that he could be buried in the ordinary graveyard. At first, however, the family were not permitted to place a stone on the grave, but one day they were allowed to go ahead without any objections. Hence, the grave was not only covered and named, but also had a symbolically meaningful poem about dying in defence of one's political view carved on it. The symbolic meaning, which metaphorically opposed the state political language, was allowed to remain on the grave in 1983.

In order further to honour and publicly acknowledge the martyrs of the war, their names were given to streets and schools. Since the victory over the Shāh in 1979 and up until 1989, the names of many streets have been changed several times: from names commemorating historical persons and events associated with the Pahlavi dynasty to names associated with the struggle of the Mujaheddin (Islamic political 'leftist'), to names of the heroes of the revolutionary members of the Islamic Republic party, and to names of martyrs of the Iran–Iraq war.

Preachers in the Qur'ānic meetings explore the ideology of martyrdom in the Islamic context. They commonly request the attendants to send blessings to a range of spiritual figures, including war casualties and Islamic fighters. On the 21st of the month of Ramaẓān in 1989 the preacher Zaki performed a mourning song to mark the day Imām Ali was assassinated.

[69]An Iranian Muslim guerrilla group based in Iraq. The group is opposed to both the return of monarchy to Iran and to the present Islamic government.

The hall of her house was packed. The female preacher, as was customary, started her performance by reading the Qur'ān from where they had left off the previous day. After she had finished the entire verse of the day, she took a folded paper out of her bag and passed it to one of the religiously learned women sitting next to her. It contained a mournful song about the Imām Ali, and she asked the woman, who had a sorrowful voice, to recite it for the others. The woman put on her glasses and started to read it in a loud mournful lamentation. She performed it in an improvised style, often changing unrhythmic words to create the proper melody.

The religious narrative song on injuring the Imām Ali: *'noḥeh-żarbat-khordan-Ali'*[70]

I am the servant of the all-graceful Ali.
Waiting for my Lord to come
desire to see him has filled my head.
Oh Ali, Ali, Ali.
I have come from the eternal God
I have come to visit my lord, Ali,
sad, I've come with a voice of honour.
Oh Ali, Ali, Ali.
I've come from Habasheh[71] and Zangbar
to visit the King of kings, conqueror of my heart
all the kings are humble in his house.
Oh, Ali, Ali, Ali.
Open the door as I am growing sorrowful
to be in the service of my lord
to see the king of my honour.
Oh, Ali, the Ali, Ali.
Sorrowful and tearful Ziynab
told the Ghambar to be a little patient
till the Ali recovers.
Oh, Ali, the Ali, Ali.
The sorrowful Ziynab, my daughter,

[70]The *noḥeh* is a traditional form of religious poetry which uses idioms and melody and resembles the religious passion play of Ta'azīeh, which is traditionally performed mainly by male actors in public places. There are several forms of *noḥeh* that praise the holy Shi'ī Islamic figures.
[71]Abyssinia or Ethiopia.

it is far to gain the presence of Qambar.
Oh, Ali, Ali, Ali.
As he, Qambar, entered and saw the martyr
she screamed oh-Ali and collapsed on the floor.

The *noḥeh* song reached its climax in the dramatic death of Imām Alī. At this stage people responded by crying, or covering their faces and chanting, while some, like myself, sat in silence, being more eager to observe the others. This was among the powerful songs that moved many of the participants to tears, and that metaphorically and metonomically has a paradigmatic emotional tone reflecting the tragic experiences of many in today's Iran (Good and Good 1988:43).

When the song ended a woman sitting at some distance from me was crying loudly and bitterly, her face covered by a black *chādor*. The other participants stopped weeping and fell silent. Following the reading, the preacher continued her speech in a sorrowful voice. The preacher Zaki, who apparently knew the woman and her family, requested the participants to send her blessings, and wish for happiness on the souls of her children. I asked a woman nearby what had happened to her children. She whispered that two of them, as well as her son-in-law, had been executed recently, despite the promise of the authorities that they would be released by the Persian New Year (Ramaẓān/21 March 1989).

Thus the martyrdom of members of other forbidden Islamic political parties often received strong sympathy from the average local woman, as a matter of motherhood, sisterhood and religious friendship. Such a common view of martyrdom was more often the case among the average women and the neutral female preachers, than among those affiliated with the Islamic Republic such as *ḥezbullāhi*. The latter applied to the identity of martyr only for those who died in defending the legitimacy of the Islamic state and not those opposing it.

The mother who has lost a young male child becomes the image of Karbalā's women; i.e. Ziynab the sister of Imām Husain and Imām Hasan, or Fatim-e Zahrā the mother of Imam Husain. Aspects such as dying in the land of enemies, dying in pain, or in battle for one's beliefs, are the kind of Islamic idioms equated with social suffering and the individual's struggle against hardships. Emotional aspects of such a *noḥeh* ritual and the powerful religious poetry involved are made manifest in the symbolic structure and idioms referring to the graphic experience of suffering and sacrifice. A woman recognised as *da'gh-dīdeh* – suffering from a heart-wrenching death – is one who has lost a dear member of her family, most notably her child.

The participants' tears express personal suffering in the context of public events and its symbols, as embodied and signified in the songs of lamentation. This kind of process can be explained in Obeyesekere's terms. He suggests that personal symbols must be related to the everyday life experience of the individual and to the larger institutional context in which they are embedded (1981:13). The individual is integrated into the group via a set of personal symbols, which facilitate expression in the course of a cultural idiom. Psychologically speaking, these are the moments which may create strong emotional meaning for participants, since their private feeling of suffering may employ the symbolic representation of the story.

Martyrs: first-class citizens

Post-revolutionary ideology has systematically integrated the active Muslims into the executive, educational and social welfare sectors. One example is the way in which the families of the martyrs – the sisters, wives and brothers – are privileged over the average citizens in today's political economy. The first-class citizens are the pro-Islamic state Mujaheddin families (families who have lost a close relative as a martyr), those who have participated in the fighting and survived, and voluntary soldiers. A second category include those missing in military action, the injured and the disabled from the war with Iraq, prisoners of war, and refugees from the war. A third category are those who are associated with the new state offices *jāhade sāsandegī* (institute for reconstruction) and the Islamic police (*pāsdār*), etc. The latter constitute a new kind of social identity characteristic of the post-revolutionary ideology that defines who is to be given priority to state jobs and admittance to universities (cf. Habibi, 1989:31). Consequently, university qualifications and expertise are of secondary importance when applying for a job. A job application must be accompanied by letters of recommendation from three high-ranking religious persons from the local area. The higher the rank of these persons, and the more extensive one's Islamic knowledge and activity the better are the chances of getting a state office job. In order to gain access to a state office job, one of my female informants needed a letter of recommendation from two revolutionary guards. Fortunately she had a brother-in-law who was a revolutionary guard and a sister-in-law who worked as a prison warden. Furthermore, inquiries are made in the neighbourhood regarding the applicant's participation in religious activities. The final stage is the oral exam where the applicant is questioned about Islamic history and ritual. It is expected that the applicant knows the 'correct' version. In the case of my informant she passed this exam, as she had been fully prepared for such an interrogation.

Many young secondary school graduates, both male and female, view the study of religious ideology as an important factor in improving their chance of gaining a place at the university, or to be successful in getting a job. However, the increased sexual segregation in the social sphere has meant that there is a new niche for women to control other women as part of their Islamic faith and duty toward the community.

Conclusion

In this chapter I have examined the symbolic nature of the present political features of Islamic martyrdom. The current political classificatory terms are not simply reproduced in linguistic terms, but are themselves rules that produce a distinctive political culture of privileged and authoritarian categories with concomitant social consequences (see also Turner 1983:16). The social and spiritual identities are reproduced and institutionalised not only for the living Muslims, but also for the symbolic nature of the dead under the Islamic Republic.

SIX

THE PASSAGE OF THE DEAD

John R. Bowen (1993) correctly described the Islamic rituals of death as being a long process that requires much from the living. Among the Gayo Muslim the living and the dead continue to have a lot to say and do for each other after death (1993:252).

In the next section I shall take into account the Shirazi women's mortuary ritual and their communication with the dead, before discussing the political symbol of death and burial ceremonies. The mortuary rituals performed by women are publicly instructive in three ways. The first is the inclusion of Iranian Muslim women in public rituals; the second concerns the ritual exchanges; and the third deals with women's identity among friends and kin.

Female mortuary rituals: from death to burial

It was during my second fieldwork among the Shirazi that I participated in the funeral rites of one of the serious *rowżeh* goers. It was on a Friday during the Muharam religious meetings of 1994. The rituals started from the day before the funeral at the local *rowżeh* meeting at *husyneh*. On that day, at the end of her speech, preacher Moradi requested a prayer for a patient who was in a critical condition. The patient was the mother of a religious female student who sold Islamic books in the yard at *husyneh*. The next day, entering the meeting and sitting on the podium (*minbar*), the preacher announced the sad news of the death of the patient, and apologised for cancelling her sermon and other religious work in order to attend the funeral. She invited others to go with her to gain religious merit (*ajr*). The funeral procession was to start from the hospital, from where the deceased was to be accompanied by friends and relatives to the graveyard. Many of those present followed the preacher to the funeral. The hostess, realising that the meeting was about to end, came out of the kitchen where she usually sat with the others who carried out the ritual services, sincerely asked the audience to stay and to continue the meeting. One woman sitting near the podium took the initiative and started reciting verses from the Qur'ān. I asked two of my companions whether they wanted to join the funeral or not. One said that since it is Friday it is good to do so. The other said that she would like to go since she could then also visit her sister's grave. They both thought I had better go with them since I had not visited the graveyard during my second visit home.

The three of us drove to the morgue, where male and female deceased were segregated in distinctive halls. As we went into the women's compartment, the washing room was already packed with other people. Some were familiar faces, such as *rowżeh* participants and a Qur'ānic teacher whom I had met in other Qur'ānic seminaries and at *husyneh*. All attended in the mourning dress code of black, and even we who came directly from *husyneh* meeting were in black *chādor*. Children were often kept away from the funeral rituals and in particular the morgue. The room was full of black-dressed mourners surrounding the corpse of an old woman laid on a high slab of stone. Those attending a funeral are expected to maintain a sad expression and to appear less decorative, so as to express their sympathy and share the grief of the deceased's close family (*sāheb-e ʿazā*). The dead woman's friends and relatives mostly stood at the head of the deceased. Her daughter, her older sister, and her religious friends were all gathered to her right. With a melodious and skilful voice they recited Qur'ānic verses together. A female funeral specialist was washing the deceased. She had a handkerchief around her mouth, two long thick gloves, and a pair of boots on her feet. She cleaned the deceased with a hard cloth, the same as is used by women in public bath houses. She gave her the last bath to purify her, and to remove earthly pollutions. Funeral specialists belong to an outcast category because of their physical contact with corpses and dirt, hair and blood. For this reason the mourners took a proper distance from the corpse, and only a few actually touched the deceased.

The funeral experts worked under the watchful eyes of the

many religiously learned women. Preacher Momeni stood in the middle of the group of religious students continuously reciting verses by heart. She repeatedly corrected the ritual of washing and praying, so that the rituals would be carried out step by step, and reminded the audience not to greet, give courtesy, or hug each other, as this would be improper (*makroh*) at such a moment. This view was challenged by my companions who are quite knowledgeable regarding such rituals. Preacher Momeni had a small plastic bag in her hand and asked us to give donations for the deceased. For the religious women the presence of the preacher is the key to salvation and preservation from the fire. The corpse-washer sincerely requested that we give a religious donation to her, saying she had five orphaned children. Meanwhile, the corpse-washer insisted that we follow the ritual of washing without interruption or instructions. She made sure that water was poured all over the corpse. The final act of washing was with some leaves of the lotus tree (*konar*) and camphor, and some water mixed with the dust of Karbalā (*ab e-torbat*). The latter was pressed under the tongue of the deceased. There were also a few branches of a palm tree to be placed under the deceased's arms. It is believed that the deceased will use them as a crutch to stand up on the day of resurrection.

A friend of the deceased loudly chided the mourners urging them not just to stay quiet and watch, but to pray to God for the wellbeing of the deceased, arguing that this would help the spirit of the deceased to be calmed. The already prepared winding sheet, cut into several pieces, was passed to the corpse-washer by a relative of the deceased. She wrapped the deceased with some pieces of the sheet, praising it for its holiness and said it was a fine garment from Mecca. There were seven pieces altogether, each was for a specific part; a headscarf, two wrapped around her wrists, three around the private parts, and one around the breast. I asked a woman next to me how many pieces the Muslim shroud contains? She looked at me with critical eyes. 'Don't you know?' she said. I felt ashamed for not knowing my religion well enough. I turned to my religious companion who was a relative and asked her the same question. She said seven pieces, each of which is associated with a particular part of the woman's body. Later on, when I told the above story to some other young women, they admitted that they were equally ignorant of many of the details concerning religious rituals. They knew about the seven pieces of the Muslim shroud, but not the other details. The conservative expectations of some religiously oriented women that as a Muslim one must be familiar with the basic rituals, did not fit with reality other than for those who were intensively involved in religious meetings, or who had taken some Qur'ānic courses. Having been dressed in the shroud the deceased was laid in a one-size-fit-all coffin used for both men and women. We went out of the morgue and joined the male mourners who were waiting for the women to join them outside. At that moment men and women were joined in the performing of a common ritual, although men moved to the front and women to the back. The coffin was placed in front of the crowd. The menstruating women remained outside the line of prayers. The two units of prayers for the dead ended and a man started a sorrowful song of Imām Husain, accompanied by a melodious chest-beating (*syneh-zanī*). Then some men took the coffin on their shoulders and headed towards the graveyard followed by the women. The session lasted an hour. We then left the family of mourners since my companion wanted to visit the grave of her relatives.

After the burial the relatives of the deceased begin the ritual of expressing grief (*ʿazādārī*), as well as preparing ritual meals and performing other religious duties believed to benefit the dead in her after-life. Such rituals are often held in the home of the bereaved on the first, third, seventh and fortieth day after the burial, as well as after the fourth month and ten days, and twelfth month. The mourning ceremony is arranged by the close kin of the dead person who are experiencing the state of separation and who are expressing most grief. A close relative, most often the biological mother, wife or sister, may cry profusely and continuously, whereas the father or brother usually cry silently while taking care of the services. Two or more families may be involved, and by sharing their sorrow they may overcome any conflicts they have experienced. This is the typical manner in which broken relations are resumed among Iranian families. The mourner's aim is to pay personal tribute to the dead and to share the sorrow of its 'owner' in their formal language. Sending the deceased blessings by reciting the Qur'ān is an act of merit (*ṣavāb*) by which one symbolically protects oneself and one's family from similar misfortune.

Visiting may in the beginning take place on specific days on a regular basis. Then it is reduced to a monthly basis, and thereafter once a year. Women are more active in carrying out rituals correctly, particularly when the deceased is a close female relative. However, ritual knowledge varies among the participants. The regular gathering of relatives around the grave of their loved ones, follows offering blessing by reading a Qur'ānic passage (the Alhamd once and the verse of Oolhovallah (Qur'ān sūreh 303) three times. They communicate with the dead by buying jugs of water that are emptied on the grave in order to cleanse the dust from the grave stone; and the drawing of lines on the grave stone is believed to open a window into the grave through which one may see and communicate with the deceased. The recitations are often whispered or read loudly by both men and women at the funeral, or when visiting a grave. The verses are in Arabic, but some Persian words blown towards the grave are added. There is a common belief that recitations generate religious merit, and participants will ask God to transmit that merit to the spirit of the deceased.

There are some ritual activities performed for dead relatives on a regular basis. For example, bringing and distributing home-made sweets or green plants at each visit, and giving money to the grave-keeper to wash the grave, water the flowers, and cut the grass around it. The grave is often decorated with green leaves. These are laid on the grave stone and may be used to sweep off the dust. The initiative of 'refreshing' the grave by washing off the dust, watering the plants, and cutting the grass surrounding it, express feelings of care and concern for the comfort of the deceased in the after-life. Ideally, carrying out a perfect ritual is assumed to generate mutual merit for the deceased and her living relatives, where the latter receive protection.

Meal to the dead

The offering of meals (*kheyrāt*) and drinks to the public and those mourning is carried out on the first, third, seventh and fortieth day after the funeral. By preparing a Friday evening meal of *ḥalvā*, a woman is not only offering merit to the spirit of the dead relative, but she is also fulfilling a duty, or asking for forgiveness. This ritual may be carried out regularly, or on occasions when the initiator dreams and gets the feeling that the dead relative is requesting something, or at annual anniversaries when dead family members are expected to be remembered. Dreaming about a dead relative invokes the idea of renewing an offering ritual which has been neglected due to housework and family hardships. One may also offer money to the poor in the street for the sake of a dead relative and wish happiness for his/her soul. One important feature of the votive gifts of food to a dead spirit is similar to another communal votive meal gift, namely the expectation of the protection of the family from misfortune.

The offerings of a *ḥalvā* is a communal consumption in a public place, such as a mosque, a cemetery, or in front of a shop. In return, the recipient is expected to recite the specific Qur'anic verse for the merit of the dead person. In other words, by eating food for the dead, one expresses sympathy and shares the sorrow of the relatives categorised as the 'owners' of the sorrow (*sāheb-eh ʿazā*).

Friday mornings and Thursday evenings are among the most blessed times for visiting the deceased. Visitors give blessings to the dead person by drawing a line on the grave and reciting some Qur'ānic verses. On one hand death is believed to be a passive state, from which it is not possible to return to perform neglected religious and kinship duties. On the other hand the dead are considered to be conscious and able to witness things done for them by those with whom they were most closely associated as friends or kin. Communication with the dead is said to take place in dreams. I was told by some women a story in which a mother claimed to see her deceased son as a shadow or image in a nearby yard, under trees, or on a corner of the room. Such claims are particularly common immediately after a death, when the religious rituals of mourning and the recitation of verses from the Qur'ān may last for several hours a day in the home of the bereaved.

A religious debt may be fulfilled by a living relative such as a mother, father, brother, sister, daughter or son, or by a religious person specifically engaged for the occasion. I know of a woman who paid a certain sum in alms to a *sayyid* (presumed descendants of the Prophet) to perform a number of obligatory prayers, or to fast or travel to Mecca on behalf of the deceased.[72] This is

[72]Previously it would cost only 30,000 tomans to travel to Mecca. In 1989 the average cost was 120,000 tomans, and by 1994 the price had doubled.

a form of exchange where religious worship becomes a thing one can 'buy' through the mediation of a spiritual person. Instead of arranging the third anniversary of her son's death, my religious companion used the same money to pay a religious man to perform the obligatory prayers on her son's behalf. She thought she in this way raised even more merit for him.

Everyday realisation of *ākhirat*

The reality of death is made evident every day in tragic accidents and the regular news of the death of a relative or a neighbour. The pictures of 'martyrs' of the Iran–Iraq war, and the suffering of their relatives makes death an everyday reality. The imminence of death is said to be a reason to 'collect' pious acts in this world.

The moral acts are commonly referred to in daily social interaction. One day I was in a taxi, in which the driver and five other persons were sitting tightly packed to make room for even more passengers. As one of the passengers got out of the taxi the driver accused him of being a selfish man, concerned only with this world and not with the realisation of after-life (*ākhirat*), since the passenger was occupying a lot of space and not making room for more passengers. He pointed out to the driver that life these days is getting shorter and shorter, so he should think about the after-life soon; and that his economy depended upon the tolerance of his customers.

Purity of intention is believed to be a necessary virtue for fulfilling individual wishes. One Friday night I was with a young woman who was about to divorce her husband. She had some religious vow to initiate at the main local shrine. The shrine is often crowded on such a day and pilgrims push forward to touch the bars of the shrine, whispering silent appeals. As we watched a woman pulled her *chādor* over her face, crying bitterly and whispering forgiveness (*alʿaf, alʿaf*). My companion commented on her being truly desperate and broken-hearted.

Realising the significance of the after-life (*ākhirat*) is an ideal stage of personal cognition in which one pays less attention to the material world. The practice of being less worldly-oriented and having a pure intention is considered a means by which a person gains a spiritual position. The symbols of pious acts are not only made manifest at religious meetings where one learns spiritual acts, but are communicative aspects in daily events. The ability to control oneself in favour of others encompasses much of Islamic morality and identity management.

Acknowledging death by preparing one's white shroud

The white shroud,[73] is often purchased on pilgrimages to Mecca, or to the shrine of Imām Rezā in Mashhad. As women grow older their recognition of proximity to death increases, particularly in these days of social insecurity. During the Iranian revolution, and at the start of the Iran–Iraq war of 1980, the white shroud was used symbolically in organised demonstrations. It signified the willingness of the masses to die and to receive the honour of martyrdom as reward for voluntary joining military service. Moreover, the resurgence in the value placed on the martyrdom of the Imām Husain was symbolised in aspects of rituals and in the form of mass protest (Hegland 1983). Thus, these symbols were not only made manifest at the religious meetings, but were also used as communicative aspects in daily events.

One day at a meeting in the month of Ramaẓān presumed to be particularly meritorious, the preacher Zaki read the Qur'ānic verses of *al-bashir, al-nameh,* and *forghan* (Qur'ān:sūreh 25), which are thought to have particular grace. For several hours she read the verses, one after the other, with several breaks to offer salutations to the Prophet Muhammad, as well as interpretations of certain passages. In the middle of her reading the preacher stopped in order to help a woman sitting nearby to find the right place of a verse. The woman next to me passed me a folded white cloth and asked me to sign it where she indicated. The white cloth belonged to another woman who wished to circulate it among some of the attendants. The woman was one of the participants that I had become friendly with at the *rowżeh,* and she considered me to be her religious companion (*ham-jales'i*). She found a place next to me and asked about the health of my mother, whom she knew well. Whenever a particular verse finished, she blew on the shroud as many other women did with things they brought with them. This is believed to bring particular merit. That particular day was considered to have a

[73]Men's and women's *kafanī* (shroud) are slightly different in the number of pieces to cover parts of the body.

special effect and to be the best day to appeal for God's forgiveness. The sight of the shroud shocked me at first because of its association with the dead, but it seemed quite acceptable to her. She smiled and talked easily about death. My shock was not only a matter of my lack of experience with such a ritual, but rather of my cultural unfamiliarity with its metaphoric meaning. My own mother has always kept a shroud purchased in Mecca in a cupboard close at hand in case it is needed.

The smiling young woman who owned the shroud asked for my signature, indicating that she considered me, like the others who were regular *rowżeh*-participants, as one of the forty faithful women whose signatures were needed to transform the shroud into a sacred object. It is locally believed that these persons will act as mediators on the day of resurrection, entering into a dialogue with God to ask forgiveness for the deceased. I signed the shroud and passed it to the women on my other side. By calling me *bā-imān*, thus considering me a good Muslim, she ascribed to me a high status I doubted was applicable to me, since this meant a person who performs the obligatory prayers, and regularly veils. Nevertheless, the compliment made me feel good. The transformation of the shroud from an ordinary garment to a sacred object through others' blessing is considered to reduce the degree of a person's worldly sin and to increase one's blessedness in the life after death.

Purchasing a burial plot

The recognition of *ākhirat* is signified in various symbolic ways, such as by buying plots in the cemetery, preferably near relatives such as a husband, brother or mother. The grave may remain empty for years, but one is reminded of *ākhirat* when visiting the graves of other relatives on Fridays.

In 1989 I went with my mother to visit the graves of my own relatives who had died during my absence. She led me from grave to grave, and it made me sad to see the male pictures at the top of the grave stones and remember them as they had been when I said farewell ten years before. She smiled at my sadness, and pointing at the two empty plots side by side she said, 'Fortunately your father and I were quick to buy these two graves before they became scarce in this area.' The graves she considered best were situated close to my dead uncle and his wife, who 'unfortunately had not got a place near to their son and daughter'. I looked uneasily at her and changed the subject. She believed that one should have a strong heart and not fear death if one has performed meritful acts (*ṣavāb*).

Lesson on *ākhirat* in the tradition of the Prophet

The preacher Zaki, during the daily *rowżeh* meetings, often prevented a normative interpretation of *ākhirat,* and accused those who disregarded them as having a 'weak' faith. By recounting *ḥadīth*[74] Zaki legitimised and reproduced meaning in the context of the social reality today. Zaki conveyed an ethical lesson to her followers by linking a *ḥadīth* with everyday socio-political conditions. She included the following *ḥadīth* with a ritual of Qur'ānic reading during the month of Ramaẓān:

> Once a woman, who regularly visited the mosque, did not turn up for several days. The others who noticed her absence became worried and went to her house to inquire. There they found her half burned and lying in bed. They asked her what had happened. She said: 'I was asleep when I saw *ākhirat*. I was questioned and I had not many meritful acts to be protected with. Then I faced the flames [of hell]. But I invoked Imām Ali's mediation. I was suddenly pulled out of the fire of Hell. The fire still marks my back.'

It is believed that the family of the Prophet, including his daughter Fatimeh, her husband Ali, and their two children Hasan and Husain (the blessed five), can be used as mediators to facilitate the flow of blessings. When the *ḥadīth* finished, some of the participants were astonished by the events described and expressed their fears by whispering 'we seek refuge in God' (*panah-bar-khodā*). They loudly besieged mediation of the blessed Prophet's family and wished for a better 'record of one's deeds' for themselves than the woman in the *ḥadīth*.

I did not know which book of *ḥadīth* the preacher used, as she seemed to know them all by heart. Nevertheless, I noticed that the *ḥadīth* cited was carefully selected. The *ḥadīths* used by preachers with a more traditional knowledge and view of religion differed from those chosen by younger, more learned

[74]*Ḥadīth* is the Prophet's tradition, i.e. his sayings and deeds.

and liberated preachers. For example, when one preacher was speaking about the attributes of the Prophet's wife (Hazrat-e Khadījeh) as she was about to die, she stressed that the wife was without a shroud (*kafanī*), expressing her material poverty. Thus, she borrowed a robe (*ʿabā*) from Khadija's husband (the Prophet). Another preacher, sitting next to the one undertaking the interpretation, apologised politely and corrected this statement, saying that, in fact, the *kafanī* referred to in the *ḥadīth* had been sent to her by the angel Gabriel from paradise.

The preacher linked local events to authoritative Islamic texts. Thus the *ḥadīth* provided the scriptural support of one's exegesis, although sometimes from differing sources. The wife of the Prophet was widely recognised as a tradeswoman[75] who enjoyed high social status as the honourable wife of the Prophet. By dying 'without' a 'shroud' the preachers stressed the ideal of humanity. The lifestyle of the Prophet's family, which was without luxury, is recommended to participants.

Different sources and understandings of the Prophet's tradition might create some disagreement on Islamic issues and its forms of practice. The disagreement was part of the discourse between different preachers, both male and female, on the degree a woman should cover herself.

The kind of statements exemplified in the above *ḥadīth*, regarding the punishment of the failure to uphold proper norms and morality, were used as pedagogical techniques. The ideal morality for a good Muslim does not lie in accumulating wealth, property and gold, but in sharing with others. Giving a share of one's gains to others is thought not only to give a feeling of satisfaction, but also to cause one's wealth to double and to last longer. Sharing with others, giving alms to those in need, and avoiding causing others distress ('breaking their hearts'), are considered social acts which have implications for one's moral health as well as one's material wealth. The one who accumulates all the golden coins for him/herself alone and exhibits them to stimulate the jealousy of others will be punished in the life after death.

The typical definition of *ākhirat* given by the preacher Zaki

[75]Hazrat-e Khadījeh is known to have been a rich woman trader among the Quraish tribe, where she owned a large inherited property from her father.

during the month of Ramaẓān was expressed in the following manner:

> '*Ākhirat* is an after-life, the place and time of final judgment where worldly behaviour and thought will be rewarded or punished. The resurrection day is the day when all the dead, old and young alike, will rise up from their graves and receive a statement of their worldly (*nāmeh-aʿamāl*) behaviour. The judgment is based on all the personal worldly acts, both known and unknown to us. It is a time when one must explain one's acts both good and bad. The reason for life in this world is the existence of a world after death. If the world was going to end here, then everyone might commit every sin without anticipating later punishment. True believers in the after-life are not interested in today's material conditions, nor do they fall in love with this world.'

On another occasion she said:

> 'This world is the channel to the next one, and nothing reaches its final existence in this world. Those who consider only this world and enjoy the luxury of the present, forgetting the after-life, will be severely punished, since deliberate exhibition of part of the body, wearing a loose hair cover, and displaying naked arms, feet, or neck, are considered sinful acts, and matters of greatest concern. These acts will receive the hardest punishment. One may be hanged by a single hair; or the part of the body which has been exhibited willingly in this world to a forbidden male, will be burned.'

In the context of these sermons, political issues were expressed metaphorically, or were given explicit meaning through regular spiritual lessons. The economic condition of families, and the crisis facing many of them, was among the issues formulated in the theme of the realisation of *ākhirat*.

The ritual of forgiveness: *aʿraf*

Being in a state of 'broken-heartedness' (*dil-shikasteh*) is thought to facilitate a powerful 'conversation' with God, and to be an effective moment to set forth wishes and appeals for forgiveness. The conversation of the participants with God take the form of pledges and appeals to the Imām Ali and his wife Fātemeh (two Muslim ideals of masculinity and femininity), who are considered to be highly honoured by God as good Muslims, and to have seats in heaven to mediate (*vāseteh*) between God and his people.

The chants at the end part of the religious meetings are requests to God for pardon of sins, known as *al'af*. These often form part of the female religious meetings on the specific holy days. The most significant days for performing rituals, which are also the best attended, are the two days of Ashorā and Tāsoah in the month of Muharam: and the three days marking the wounding and death of Imām Ali in the month of Ramaẓān. Those attending such meetings believed the 'gates' of paradise are open and this is the time when one's vow is promised to be fulfilled.

On the fifth day of a votive Qur'ānic course (the one which I followed for the whole month of Ramaẓān in 1989), the Qur'ānic lessons reached the verse of penance (Qur'ān: sūreh 9, *al-tobeh*). This verse was read without the regular introductory verse of 'In the name of God the merciful and the compassionate'. The verse is said to be one of the few which does not start with such a greeting. One of the participants questioned this deviation, and the preacher replied that since this verse is about those who are so sinful that God's anger is aroused, they do not deserve a verse which could bring them merit and forgiveness. The woman next to me, one of the regular *rowżeh* participants, who seemed to have heard the verse more often than the others, suggested to the women next to her that the power in such a case is very strong. The Qur'ānic teacher illustrated this with the story of a group of very sinful people who were heading for *jahannam* (hell) to meet their fate. As they reached the entrance of hell, one of them read the greeting verse of 'In the name of God the merciful and the compassionate'. Suddenly God offered them merit and pardoned them, realising that by naming him they were after all aware of his existence.

On a Thursday meeting on the 21 of Ramaẓān (7 May 1989), verses of *al-'ūd* were read. Thursday is the day on which this particular Qur'ānic chapter is thought to be best performed by the religiously informed women. The ritual reading of the verse of *al-'ūd*, from beginning to end, is done by the preacher. Participants often consider it a day full of merit, auspicious for asking favours (*hājat*) of God; and it was thought to be doubly effective for participants in fulfilling their wishes, since it fell on the day commemorating the martyrdom of the Imām Ali in the month of Ramaẓān.

The ritual started after the reading of a sorrow song (*noḥeh*) in honour of Imām Ali (see text of the poet in Chapter 5), which made most of the women cry. At the end of the *noḥeh* there followed a period of silence, considered by the preacher to be a moment when one's heart is 'broken' and cleaned of sin: i.e. a state of innocence (*bī-gonāh*) required for mediating personal appeals of forgiveness.

Then the preacher repeatedly threatened her listeners to acknowledge the existence of *ākhirat*:

> 'Think of the moment when your corpse will lie beside the road; the moment you leave the material world and enter the after-life; the moment you are laid in the grave. Imagine the moment that the grave stone of *lahn* is placed over your face. God, we swear by you, and by the sign/light of Muhammad, and the Imām Ali to mediate for us [at this point the audience offers a *ṣalvāt*].
>
> 'Think as we are about to be placed on the washing stone in the mortuary, when our coffin is placed on the ground [after leaving the residence], we will look briefly at ourselves. We will be able to see everybody, we will see the other side of our coffin, we will see ourselves among the others. We will see everything, but lack the ability to say anything. So long as we are alive we are capable of doing things meritful for our *ākhirat*; later there is nothing we can do, as we will be dead.'

This was an explanation of the liminal period following death. The soul of the deceased is gradually separated from the world of the living and passes over into the world of the dead, where their sin will hopefully be forgiven and they will be brought to paradise.

Following the ritual of *al'af*, the preacher puts the Qur'ān on her head. She holds it with one hand and orders the *rowżeh* participants to bow their heads to the right side, an expression of being innocent. The preacher raises her hand over her head, spreads her fingers toward the ceiling, and asks the participants to face the direction of God's house Mecca (*qebleh*). The act of placing the Qur'ān on her head signifies its high spiritual status compared to the material surroundings. Most of the participants pulled their *chādor* down to cover their faces; others stretched their hands over their heads and left their faces uncovered while reciting a verse of forgiveness (*al'af*). To the preacher this orders a feeling of penitence (*nadel*). With a husky voice and tears in her eyes, the preacher took the position of mediator and said: 'Now, our hearts are broken.' Then she continued the lamentations (*monājāt*) believing all the participants to be possessed with a pure heart, open to the flow of blessing:

> 'We are all going to ask forgiveness, God's forgiveness. We call to God, God, we have come to you without any means except the Qur'ān, loudly reciting oh God, forgive, forgive (*al'af, al'af, al'af*).'

The lamentations and the image of the after-life are structured on the individual's moral attitude of the broken heart. A state of broken heart is a state of feeling depressed, of disappointment, and powerlessness, and is thought to be the proper time for a conversation with God. Appeals are whispered individually and in silence, while the desire for forgiveness (*al'af*) is expressed loudly and collectively. The conversation between a person and God (*khodā-yeh-khod-rāz-va-niyāz-kardan*) is a type of interpersonal discourse (*monājāt*) and is a private form of worship.

However, the ritual of forgiveness (*al'af*) and the reliance on the mediation of a spiritual person was often not only the final part of religious ritual, but was also included in a special form on the holy days. I observed it in rituals of night watching, marking the death of Imām Ali on the 21 of Ramaẓān. This ritual was called conversation with God (*monājāt*) and was the most emotional ritual I observed. The sacred attributes of Imām Ali as mediator represent powerful symbols at religious meetings, as is also the case during the annual ceremonies involving the significant religious manifestation of Imām Husain.

The Imām Husain, and the symbolic manifestations in ritual involving him, have been considered an important part of Shi'i cosmology and ritual by social scientists (e.g. Thaiss 1977:78).

Conclusion

The Muslim ritual of the dead is a lengthy event, performed both by men and women. The public funeral rituals are not exclusively male and women often play an active role in public places, as well as in the family rituals at home. I have in this chapter shown how female mortuary rituals are organised and symbolically constructed among women.

Today, there are also close connections between Islamic revolutionary ideology and the ritual of dead. An anti-Islamic state activity is the source of an evil deed and in contrast a pro-Islamic state activity stands for a spiritual merit in the after-life.

SEVEN

WOMEN MAKING THE PILGRIMAGE

The local and international shrines

It is in the older part of Shiraz, where the less economically advanced people live, that the main shrines and the famous mosques (both old and new) are located. The Shrine of Seyyīd Mir-Ahmad, or Shah-i chirāgh, are the main shrines in Shiraz, and are visited by pilgrims of various classes and rural and urban settings. The other public religious arena available to women includes the local shrines and several mosques. One local shrine is Astāneh where the saint Seyyīd-Alaidin-Husain is believed to be buried. It is believed that he is a relative of Seyyīd Mir-Ahmad and his brother Imām Reza, the former buried in Shiraz and the latter in the northern city Mashhad. Each shrine has its own visitation prayer. The prayer of visitation, known as the *ziyārat-Nāmah,* often hangs at the shrine entrance and may be recited by those who can read the holy text. The other public religious house is *takyeh,* where a spiritually inspired person is believed to be buried. In these religious centres mourning ceremonies and vows are performed and initiated. Some private houses are also considered particularly spiritual, because various signs indicate that visitors have experienced miracles (*mojizih*) there. There are several other religious houses that are not so popular among the upper middle-class women, who generally prefer to travel to distant shrines and mosques such as the prominent mosque in Qum, the shrine of Zeiynab in Syria, or to Mecca.[76] On average, a woman from a religiously oriented busi-

[76]The pilgrimages to Mecca are of two kinds: the religiously obligatory one *hajj-e tamatto,* and the voluntary minor pilgrimage, *hajj-e 'umreh.* Although the latter can be performed any time of the year, it is usually carried out during the two months of Zī-al'eqdeh and Zī-al haj.

ness family performs 1 to 3 pilgrimages to Mecca during her lifetime, in addition to several yearly visits to local shrines and holy mosques.

For the villagers living near the city of Shiraz it is more common to visit a local shrine in the town.[77] For example, each Tuesday evening the yard of the Astāneh shrine is packed with women and their families, coming from different parts of the city and sub-districts to fulfil their vows and to cook and distribute communal meals.[78]

The main part of the shrine, the central yard where the tomb is situated, is often the most crowded. People congregate around the holy grave while whispering their vows in order to obtain particular merit. A woman may cling to the bars of the tomb and pull the full length of the veil over her face, while crying bitterly as if her heart is broken, repeatedly asking for 'forgiveness' (*alʿaf, alʿaf*). Such bitter weeping is not, however, the only form of spiritual expression. Keeping silent is another one. Once Narges sat with me in one corner whispering words. Then, as we decided to leave, she went to circle the main tomb in a line with the other participants as part of the ritual of completing the visit.

At the main local shrines the act of kissing the bars of the tomb is part of completing a ritual. Women often address the saint in this manner, asking for his mediation, while whispering their wishes. Some sit in silence, others perform a prayer, recite verses of the Qur'ān, or merely listen to a sorrowful song. Still others may distribute some nuts or sweets as a sign that their vows have been granted. Pilgrims leave the holy grave and walk backwards toward the exit door. This act of avoiding turning one's back to the face of another is a sign of respect, and can also be observed in daily relations with a senior friend or relative.

[77]The Shrine of Seyyid-Mir-Mohamad, literary Shah-e Chirāgh, brother of the Imām Reza, is the popular pilgrimage place in the south of the province. See the studies by Fischer and Abedi (1990) in the village of Yazd, and Hegland (1986) in the village of Ali-abad in south and southeastern Iran.

[78]Friday nights are believed to be the most meritorious time for visiting the main local shrine (Shah-e Chirāgh), and making wishes. Narges, a former tax officer and my religious companion, used to visit the shrine either alone or in the company of her husband.

Gender dynamics of pilgrimage

Shirazi middle-class women may perform both religious and social visits at a religious house. Such social and religious visits represent important aspects of the free social movement of women, and are taken more seriously by women than by men (see also Betteridge 1993). Meanwhile, the secular visit of kinfolk is based on mutual visits and gift exchanges according to the type of social relation, age, family events and kin ties. The religious visit to a mosque or a shrine in another town, or even to Mecca, is performed individually or in groups.

Nancy Tapper (1990) has written about religious and secular forms of visits among Muslim women in a provincial town in southwestern Turkey. She describes their arts of visiting saints as a sacred journey, while the social visiting of seniors is referred to as a secular journey. The former visit is specified as an individual act performed by the more 'traditional' women (Tapper 1990: 252, 1983:76), while the secular visit is a family act (most often in the company of their husband) carried out by different categories of women.

In contemporary Islamic Iran the religious practices of *ziārat* involve different aspects. Although I agree with Tapper that the above two visiting patterns are an effective way of gaining social mobility among Muslim women, I believe that the religious or sacred journey is not limited to traditional or lower-class Iranian women.

My understanding of women's pleasure of *ziārat* and *hajj* is compatible with that of Carol Delaney (1990). She opposes the view that the pilgrimage is merely a spiritual experience and suggests that 'sacred' and 'secular' are two aspects of a single event, and are integrated into the social domains. She also opposes the view that Muslim behaviour in the form of 'sacred' and 'secular' are two different phenomena.

There are many social situations in which a woman may feel motivated to initiate a vow at a mosque or at a nearby shrine. Women may not only vow to make a pilgrimage, but may also vow to stay there for one or more nights. Women coming from rural areas,[79] are often with their husbands or other family

[79]See also Mary E. Hegland (1986) for a description of the part played by the city of Shiraz in the lives of villagers. She mentioned that women and families could take public transport for shopping, visiting, or making pilgrimages to Shiraz shrines.

members as part of their vow of making on *ziārat*. In large shrines, such as the tomb of Imām Khomeini in the Behesht-e Zahra cemetery south of Tehran, the shrine of Imām Reza in the city of Mashhad, or in the Astāneh in the city of Shiraz, there are often places to rest and cook.

Urban Shirazi women often travel in twos or threes – for example two sisters, a mother and a daughter, an aunt and a niece, two neighbours, or two fellow religious participants (see Chapter 2). Two or three who have known each other for years as Qur'ānic students may also travel together. The holy places, such as the main shrine or the Astāneh, are the kinds of religious places a Shirazi woman on particularly holy nights may stay the night alone, or with other female friends. Sometimes their husbands sit separately in the male section, particularly at the time of *aḥyā* (all-night watch and praying), or during the month of fasting when religious activity increases both for men and women. Some women come alone and stay in the shrine the whole night; for example village women, or those who seek to use the shrine as a place of refuge from their restrictive husbands and family problems.

This use of the public religious places as a free arena for women contrasts strongly with the highly constrained social mobility of women in secular places where sitting alone in a restaurant, or walking in a park, give rise to the stigmatised identity of being an available woman. This means that the acts of women in the religious sphere can be considered supportive: that is, women can stay away from home, make friends, and move freely, without being constrained by the sanctions that surround them in the secular social spheres (see also Chapter 3). I was surprised to learn that Vida, a young acquaintance of mine, left her husband as a result of a conflict, and went with another woman friend to the Astāneh, thus wishing to punish him, as well as to protest against her mother-in-law's support of him. She did not want to go to her mother's house, being afraid she might be blamed and asked to make a compromise. Such behaviour can, however, be met with strong reactions. She may, for example, be accused of having sexual desires outside the marriage. In another case a middle-aged woman sought refuge in a shrine where she believed it would take her husband some time to find her and convince her to return home. The act of leaving her husband's house in this manner was meant as a warning to his bad behaviour and ultimately as a threat of divorce.

Many wish to travel to distant shrines where, according to local women, the likelihood of a vow being fulfilled is greater.[80] It is also believed that the longer and harder the *ziārat* is, the more pious it is, and the greater the likelihood of the vow's fulfilment. The degree of difficulty is measured against the hardships experienced by the Imām Husain and his followers in the city of Karbalā. The longer the distance travelled, the higher the prestige, and the greater is the relatives' expectations that she will return with presents.

Women may go on pilgrimage individually. Nezhat, my religious companion, made her first *hajj* journey in the company of her first Qurā'ic teacher thirty years ago. Her second journey was from London where her son was living at the time. Half of the way she was guided by her secular sister-in-law, and the rest she managed by contacting one of the Iranian pilgrimage agencies in Mecca.

For a journey to the holy city of Mashhad, married women are more likely to persuade their husbands to join them, or ask their concession for travelling alone. Even in the orthodox and strongly segregated families, in which husband and wife seldom travel together on secular holidays, the husband may make a concession and travel with his wife, or pay for her expenses. A wife planning a religious journey in the company of other women may be away from her household for some time. She will therefore make sure that a close female relative, such as an older daughter, her own sister, or a sister of her husband, can take over her responsibilities in her absence.

The pleasure of these journeys can be summarised in the following three points: (1) performing religious duties, (2) bringing merit to the family; and (3) creating an alternative social network. Thus, travelling to the city of Mashhad to visit the shrine of Imām Reza is a journey for women's friends and their family.

[80]The mosque of *jamī* near Isfahan and shrine of the 8th Imām, Imām Reza in Mashhad are among the popular places visited by Shiraz middle- and lower-class women travelling with their husbands, or in company of other women.

The ritual of returning from pilgrimage

A pilgrim expects to receive a special welcome on her return, and may herself bring some small gifts from the holy town to distribute among family and friends. Already the first day after her return she may receive visitors. On her return she will be referred to as a woman of higher religious experience (*hajji-khānom*). The *ziārat* or *hajj* gifts are usually simple items valued for their 'goodness', such as a prayer stone symbolising the clay of Karbalā (*mohr*), a prayer rug, prayer beads (*tasbīh*), or fabrics for sewing clothes.

Socio-political aspects of pilgrimage

Embarking on a pilgrimage, both within and outside one's place of residence, has become very popular among middle-class and business families, especially to destinations such as *ziārat* and *hajj*. These have increasingly become the focal point for Islamic cultural innovation and the Islamic policy of nation-building. Such journeys are now being organised by travel agencies on a large scale, and the programmes may also include visits to new shrines. Through modern technology, and in the context of the new political economy, the journey to Mecca has been reduced from several months to two or three weeks.[81]

Before a restriction was put on Iranian pilgrimages to Mecca in 1987,[82] an increasing number of well-to-do women of various ages travelled in small groups, led either by female preachers (see details in Chapter 4), male spiritual leaders, or semi-government agencies.[83] Today, as the number of pilgrims has increased considerably due to the use of modern transportation, the state

[81]I was told that it took six months in 1960, three months in 1970, and two weeks in 1989.

[82]In a demonstration during the annual pilgrimage to Mecca in 1987, 400 pilgrims were killed, 300 of whom were Iranian. The demonstrations were apparently organised from Iran under the control of the prominent *'ulama* in Iran and the Shi'ī school in Madineh. The Iranian pilgrimage was abandoned for two years, and during my second period of fieldwork it was under the direct organisation of Ahmad Khomeini (son of Imām Khomeini). The number of obligatory pilgrims had by 1994 increased to half a million, with the closing date for applications being several years in advance.

[83]Such group travelling to Mecca is not new. The earliest cases were noted some 25 years ago.

arranges pilgrimages to Mecca twice a year.[84] Due to the political changes after the revolution, travelling to other Muslim countries on pilgrimages has increased. Going on a pilgrimage provides the people with a new political and social alternative. Meanwhile, the Islamic Iran encourages Islamic journeys of large scale while dismissing some of the customary rituals of visiting holy trees and the like as an incorrect practice of Islam. For example, a local house believed to be spiritually efficacious was closed by the local Islamic guards following the Iranian revolution in order to prevent the blessing of a tree and its mediation. This practice was perceived by the revolutionary regime as a kind of animism, and thus contrary to the Islamic belief in God as a single entity. The house was a place where female visitors came from near and far to cook a meal in the yard and to tie a piece of fabric as a sign of a vow. The tree was known among the traditional Muslim-oriented women in Shiraz as a blessing tree that produced miracles and mediated one's wishes.[85] Such visits were common among lower middle-class urban women. In contrast, it is possible to travel cheaply to a country such as Syria. Such journeys have been facilitated by both Islamic state and semi-private travel agencies, and must be booked at least one year in advance due to the large number of applicants.

The official state policy of purifying Islam from 'popular' and 'false' elements has affected some of the customary practices. Popular Islamic practice has been encouraged more towards the public religious places and mosques, where rituals of worship are in the charge of learned preachers and state authorities.

Economic aspects of pilgrimage

Some aspects and forms of rituals are distinctively practised by different socio-economic categories. This can be defined in terms of ritual economy, since certain practices such as pilgrimage and, as I mentioned earlier, distribution of big communal meal on holy days, are more accessible to the better-off than to the poor. Consider, for example, the cases of my two religious companions,

[84]During my fieldwork in Iran in 1994, the Islamic state started negotiations with the Saudi government to increase the journeys to Mecca to two or three times a year, with the help of the semi-private agencies.

[85]Since the revolution, such beliefs have been attacked as a passive form of Islam and in one case the place was closed by the Islamic police in Shiraz.

Shazdeh and Nezhat. The former believed it better to buy a place for *hajj* this year, rather than to wait for years in the hope that her name might come up in the ordinary waiting list. It cost her three times the normal price.[86] However, since the Iranian revolution of 1979, a new form of identity associated with participation in religious fora has emerged, so religious gatherings and sacred journeys have become a new type of enterprise and social involvement where various categories intermingle. This offers women of different social and class backgrounds an alternative opportunity to meet. The policy of the Iranian state plays an important role in discouraging people from travelling to formerly popular destinations such as Europe, in favour of the less expensive neighbouring countries. For a woman in 1989 it cost 10,000 tomans to travel to Syria, 70,000 tomans to Mecca (if a place is reserved a few years in advance), and 200,000 to Europe. The cost of a journey to Mecca doubled in 1994.

In 1989 my relative and religious companion, Shazdeh (55), together with her sister Gohar (50) and their sister's daughter, Narges (45), made a votive journey to the holy mosque Jamī, near the city of Isfahan. This is one of the places to which groups of female relatives and friends often travel at particular times of the year (such as the birth of the 12th Imām). Their purpose was to make a vow to the Shi'ī 12th Imām, who is said to fulfil many petitions. The journey may take 3 to 4 days, and the women may stay in the main hall of the mosque or in the guest room.[87] The three women were well-to-do, Shazdeh and Narges having sufficient savings and gold as part of their own property. They had on several occasions been to Europe, the USA, and some of the Arabic countries. Shazdeh had made a vow of a religious meal after she had sent her two unmarried sons and a daughter abroad to join their sister's family. She wished the children security on their journey abroad. Gohar had several wishes to make for her son who was doing his military service at the time, and for her daughter who was suffering from the bad temper of her husband. Narges sought a solution to her childlessness, hoping to change her husband's decision to remarry. They stayed

[86]The normal price was 100,000 tomans in 1989.

[87]Such a form of female Muslim pilgrimage has also been documented in many other Asian and African countries. See for example, the case of Morocco by Mernissi (1977: 102), the case of Turkey by Tapper (1987), the case of Iran by Hegland (1986: 18).

at the mosque a few nights and cooked votive meals in the backyard of the shrine. My religious companions told me that they had brought some basic utensils with them, the rest they borrowed from other pilgrims. While some women go to fulfil their vows, others go to initiate one. Belief in the spiritual power of a particular shrine was not always founded on personal experience, but on the evidence of others. Public features of a shrine, such as the crowds, the number of votive meals being distributed (cooked by women in the backyard of the shrine), the frequency of journeys, were described to me as evidence of its goodness.

My informants maintained that certain pilgrimages are particularly efficacious. Pure intention (*nīyat*) and true faith (*ʿaghideh*) are thought to be two powerful conditions for success in the process of making a religious vow.

The female space for worship and initiating vows is, however, not limited to public religious houses. As I have explained in a previous chapter, it also includes a cluster of religious meetings arranged in private homes to mark various religious events (see Chapter 2).

In Islamic Iran women of different social and class categories carry out religion in different forms, endowing it with particular meaning. For example, pilgrimages to Mashhad or Syria are a more common kind of religious activity among members of the middle class and entrepreneurial families, and working women, than the expensive journeys to Mecca. Such religious events (whether initiated by oneself or another), have multiple meanings for the participants, who not only share events of happiness and sadness, but also have a chance to initiate their own vows and fulfil their own duties. Embarking on religious journeys is not simply a spiritual performance, functioning as part of the religious orthodoxy, but are complex social, economic and politically influenced events.

Conclusion

By looking at women's performance and experience of *hajj* and *ziārat*, I have in this chapter elaborated their large religious participation and broad social mobility in religious spheres. Going to *ziārat* and *hajj* are preferred political, social and spiritual choices for women, being opportunities to move out of the domestic sphere of daily routine without being sanctioned traditionally and under the new Islamic state policy. These spiritual journeys mediate different forms of knowledge, both secular and religious.

It is also possible to see the impact of these religious journeys at higher levels of society, as Islamic authorities undergo religious intensification in line with traditional institutions and beliefs. It is considered a desirable form of mobility among the lower class, the middle class, and the religiously oriented higher-class women. Single, married and widowed women consider movements within the religious arena privileged and safe. They are able to move freely and carry out their religious missions without necessarily receiving the consent of their husbands, fathers or brothers.

Shahla Haeri (1989) argues, for example, that it is possible for Muslim Iranian women to bypass the rigid sexual segregation in Iranian society within the sphere of religion. Thus, one can presume that there is not a perfect fit between articulated Islamic precepts and everyday social and cultural practices. Social sanctioning is somewhat problematic and may be resisted and distorted within the religious domain and its social sphere. In my study women were more willing to define the negative attitude of their husbands towards their religious participation as 'typical male chauvinism', rather than as an expression of concern for them. In this way women from various backgrounds moving freely within the religious sphere can challenge their husbands' conservative views and create an alternative social movement.

By looking at the different forms of ritual experiences of *hajj* and *ziārat*, I challenge the perception that these Islamic activities are rigidly structured by class. My study indicates that the constant social boundary and religious involvement is not so decisively maintained and, as I described in detail in Chapters 2 and 3, traditional Iranian female ideals of family, kinship, network and friendship rise above class differences, and generate common religious experiences over time. In my view, women's practices and beliefs, as reflected in the rituals, reveal the flexibility of expression and the fact that Islam in practice is not a fixed point in the structure. The ideal of purity of intention (*nīyat*) as a common Islamic notion, is a common cultural value for fulfilling one's vow in the course of ritual. On the level of religious practice, class distinctions among Iranian families are less marked, particularly in post-revolutionary Iran, where participation in religious arenas has become more widespread across conventional social and class categories.

EIGHT

REPRODUCTION OF THE ISLAMIC SOCIAL ORDER AND DISORDER

Introduction

In this chapter I will look at the post-revolutionary ideological production and ethical aspects of Islamic knowledge. The primary focus of this chapter will be on the way in which Islamic tradition is mediated and perpetuated through: (a) the female preachers' Qur'ānic commentary (*tafsīr*) and religious lessons (*dars*), and (b) women's lessons of performing prayers (*masa'leh-e zanāneh*). The leader of the Qur'ānic meeting acts as a leader of prayer, a story-teller, and a reminder of one's rights and duties. I view these as discourses in which sets of metaphors from distinctive domains of life – e.g. ethical, political, theological, ritual, etc. – as interacting to produce and reproduce religious meaning. These aspects of women's religious rituals function thematically and symbolically as educational and ideological learning.

My findings on the nature of Qur'ānic commentary and religious lessons contradict those of Richard Antoun (1989). In his study of religious transmission among villagers in Jordan, he maintains that the speeches of the male preachers are predominantly ethical and not political. Furthermore, he holds that theological and ritual obligations are central features of the relations between the participants and the preacher (Antoun 1989: 94). I maintain that political themes, either related to leadership, political parties or social control, are essential aspects at communal rituals in Islamic Iran, along with ethical themes on justice, equality, power and empowerment.

Ethical and political aspects of Islamic rituals

Victor Turner indicates that a ritual symbol may stand for many things at the same time (Turner 1967). By this he means that one must consider the informant's explanation of the socio-structural implication of the treatment and usage of ritual objects in performance, as well as the spatial and hierarchical positioning of ritual objects independent of exegesis and usage. At the women's Qur'ānic meetings, the female preacher often went into great detail to clarify the complexity of various issues and examples. She played an important role, not only in teaching women the correct performance of prayers and Islamic rules, but also in teaching how to understand surrounding political events.

Diversity among preachers

The degrees of political involvement and political rhetoric of preachers were distinguished both symbolically and through actual request. This can be deduced from the distinctive personal, social, and political views expressed in the context of sermons and the participant definition.

It was not unusual to find that a ritual was performed and interpreted by different preachers in a slightly different manner, depending on the political and educational background of the preachers. For example, in two separate *rowżeh* meetings, I saw two distinct forms of reading the Qur'ānic verse of *sājdeh* (prostration).[88] On the first occasion, in Ramaẓān 1989, I was in a *rowżeh* meeting where the preacher Mostafi, who was known as a *ḥezbullāhi* (member of the party of God),[89] was in charge. A woman volunteer started distributing *mohr*[90] (the clay of *Karbelā*) to each participant, and as the reading approached the verses requiring the performance of the two units of *sājdeh*, we laid our foreheads on the assumed clay of Karbalā, and repeated the verse read by the preacher loudly. The preacher asked those who were

[88]The ritual of two prostrations is said to be required in at least ten places in the reading of the Qur'ān.

[89]Today this idiom is often used to refer to anyone preaching/practising strict religious behaviour.

[90]Used only by the Shi'ī sect of Islam at the time of prayer. This is assumed to be made of clay of Karbalā which has historic and religious significance to the Shi'ī, and is the symbolic object of the memory of Imām Husain and his honourable fight against the O'maied dynasty in the early Islamic period.

menstruating to leave the meeting and stay outside where they could not hear the sound of the verses. This created an unpleasant situation for those women who were obliged to leave the room, and some preferred to leave the meeting altogether. On the second occasion I was in a meeting led by the preacher Zaki, who was recognised as a 'populist' (*mardomī*) among lower and middle-class families of the same area. As we reached the same verse (the two units of *sājdeh*) the preacher said that those who were menstruating, or who had not abluted (*dast-nemāz*), should avoid touching the Qur'ānic text, avert their eyes from it, and try not to hear the verse. But they were not asked, and did not find it necessary to leave the meeting, despite the sacredness of the verses being read. I noticed that some apparently menstruating, and thus 'impure' women turned their faces from the Qur'ān which was laid open on the floor, while another left the meeting and did not return. Such a break with normal ritual practice was commented upon by a few participants, who expressed their doubts loudly as to whether it would be more correct to stay or to leave the room in order to avoid an act that was forbidden (*ḥarām*). The less politically oriented preacher placed the emphasis on the person and her original intention to avoid the conventional bodily acts. She was more liberal and did not enforce the rules as strictly as the *ḥezbullāhi* preacher. The exegesis of the preacher was identified by the participants in terms of its political liberalism or conservatism by participants.

This example highlights the individual interpretation of norms in Islam in its conventional and moderate forms. There are explicit differences in the flexibility of a preacher's interpretations and views regarding women's act of purity and veiling. First it is a matter of social and ritual obedience, and secondly it is a matter of ritual in its cognitive sense, and not a problem of a social nature.

In several meetings it became clear that the *ḥezbullāhi* preacher was distinguished by the participants as one who made repetitive and restrictive references to women's rigid veiling and conventional behaviour. This was contrasted by the modesty of the politically neutral preacher (*bi-taraf*), who took a more moderate view. Some meetings were conservative, as judged by factors such as the number of women wearing head-scarves under their *chādor*, the content of the Qur'ānic commentary given by the female preacher, and the repetitive offering of the blessing (*ṣalvāt*) to Imām Khomeini; and his successor, and president Rafsanjani.

The negative term *monāfeqin*, which means conspiracy, is a strong multivocal symbol conveying various messages and contrasting attributes concerning a series of illegitimate social and political divisions. *Monāfeqin* may refer not only simply to good and evil, but also to state political norms, such as the Iranian case of women who are poorly veiled, as well as to any act of political resistance.

Qur'ānic commentary and religious lessons

On the 3rd day of Ramaẓān, March 1989, the Qur'ān verse of *al'omrān* (Qur'ān: sūreh 3) was read in the meeting I participated in. As is usual in such a Qur'ānic meeting, there were frequent pauses for commentary, most often initiated by the preacher herself whenever she thought it necessary to elaborate on the meaning of a verse. Sometimes the preacher was asked to explain the meaning of some verses which were considered to be ambiguous and that had not yet been elaborated on.

Ideological content of Qur'ānic commentary

A suppressor husband The preacher Zaki usually stopped reciting after every short verse (*āyeh*) to offer a commentary. She was one of the preachers who thought it better not to continue before ensuring that the participants had a proper understanding of what was being read. She translated the Qur'ānic meaning into a daily context, thereby making its realisation more practical for the participants, who were from various social categories (the majority being housewives and young schoolgirls). The preacher maintained that the kind of suppressions one could experience varied, and convincingly demonstrated this point by the use of metaphors. The reality of one's experience of 'suppression' was open to interpretation. On this occasion the effective terms were injustice and oppression (*zulm va setam*):

> An example of an act of *zulm* is whenever a newcomer joins a long queue to purchase food and stands in front of the others to be served first, ignoring the rights of others and acting 'cleverly' (*zerangi*). One of the participants who

> sat close to the preacher (a place often allocated for a religiously 'learned'), followed up this suggestion by putting it in another context, suggesting that it was also an act of *zulm* to give one's food coupons to a friend standing in the front of a long queue. (recorded Ramẓān/March 89)

Zaki continued further to clarify the Qur'ānic terms to her listeners. The image of the husband as a suppressor and the wife as victim continued among the participants, and the discussion became so heated that the preacher requested a greeting to Muhammad and his family (*ṣalvāt*), in order to change the topic in an orderly way, and to dampen the disagreement among members of the audience. She gave as another example the relation within a nuclear family:

> Some women disagreed, asked questions, and expressed their own views. Some commented more loudly than the others, addressing the preacher, or one another. One of the women said, 'How can a man treat them equally, as a man often likes the one who is new and younger best.' Another continued, 'A wife would rather see her husband dead in his grave, than in the arms of another woman. Who can tolerate watching her husband behave like that?'

Zaki excused herself to her students, by saying that they were short of time, and had to finish the rest of the Qur'ānic lesson without making any more *tafsīr* for that day.

According to the preacher Zaki Islamic suppression may be related both to the lack of juridical teachings concerning the rights of men and women and to being a good Muslim in practical terms according to legitimate Islamic codes. Public lessons on juridical matters were often brief, and in response to complicated questions the preachers might postpone answering to make further inquiries from a more learned religious person, such as a male or female *mujtāhed*.

A suppressor politician The metaphor of suppression continued on another level in another Qur'ānic meeting a few days later. This time it was raised by the preacher Mostafi, who defined suppression as acts of political tyranny, and as something that could be harmful to the whole Muslim community. She said,

> 'Leaders such as Rajavi[91] and Banisadr,[92] and Sadam Husain,[93] left many mothers sorrowful following the loss of their children. [The number of participants sending him *nefrīn* (misfortune) increased.] What the Indian (British) writer Salman Rushdie did to Islam was *zulm*.'

The *rowżeh* participants were familiar with the name of Salman Rushdie[94] and the Islamic state's political fight against him. He was understood to have committed an act of blasphemy by denying the existence of God and the legitimacy of Muhammad as his Prophet. I once witnessed the preacher Mostafi wishing him a misfortune (*nefrīn*), and punishment by hanging. Some of the attendants supported her statement by saying *āmen*.

The metaphorical references of suppression and the model of corrupt leadership were two on-going political themes in mass media. They were phrased according to the Islamic state dominant political view. However, on one occasion it was clear that the preacher lacked accurate knowledge of the international political situation, but was familiar with the Islamic state's political rhetoric. For example, on one occasion the preacher Mostafi referred to the both CIA (American Intelligence Service) and KGB (Soviet Intelligence Service) as the American secret service without anybody making any attempt to correct her. This did not prevent her from conveying the desired political message to her listeners, as she accused these international agencies of 'suppression', in their attempts to undermine the Iranian Revolution and its Islamic virtue.

A suppressor of poorly-veiled women The identities of 'poorly-veiled' (*bad-hejāb*) and 'non-veiled'[95] (*bi-hejāb*) despite their wearing Islamic suits (*manto*), have emerged in conservative

[91]Masuad Rajavi, the leader of the Mojāhedin political party, fled to France, and then to Iraq, following the revolution in 1979. He is still a popular leader among Iranian *mujtāhed* outside Iran.

[92]Abul Hasan Banisadr is one of the prominent ministers in the first Islamic state. He too was forced to seek refuge in France.

[93]Sadam Husain, the president of Iraq.

[94]Nobody I talked to had actually seen the book, or knew the exact story. Yet the local people often claimed to know that it was insulting to the Prophet and blasphemous (*shīrk*), informing matters such as the Indian ethnic origin of Imām Khomeini.

[95]It often defined a woman without wearing *chādor* by conservative Iranian Muslims.

political slogans, condemning the degree of immodesty among women. Posters covering streets walls, with slogans such as 'death to *bi-hejāb* and *bad-hejāb*', attach a negative label to women who neglect to veil themselves fully. 'Poorly-veiled' is a negative term applied to those whose appearance and social manner may be defined as fashionable, tempting and provocative; i.e to those wearing colourful scarves, light colours, fashionable styles, make-up, transparent stockings, etc. This is considered a political act of *monāfeqin*, and is generally applied on those who are believed to oppose and destroy Islamic values, instead invoking perversion (*fesād*).

The negative image of a poorly-veiled woman as a suppressor of the Islamic community has developed through religious speeches. This is further illustrated by the case of a widow who arranged the votive meeting of *anām*, in order to mark the annual remembrance ceremony for her husband. Close and distant relatives, as well as friends and local women, gathered for the meeting. The female preacher Mostafi frequently paused to interpret Qur'ānic recitations, and whenever she came to the term *monāfeqin* (conspirators), she explained it in terms of external and internal enemies of Islam. She also included women who wore thin stockings together with Islamic suits, for being 'provocative' and modern in style. Furthermore, she accused women who failed to dress properly of weakening the ideology of the revolution, and repeatedly saluted the martyrs (*shohadā*) and prisoners of war (*asiran*) with the verse of *ṣalvāt*. She unexpectedly addressed the married daughter of the house, a university lecturer who was serving tea to the attendants, asking her to stop serving to allow the audience to concentrate on the sermon. After the ceremony some participants believed the preacher had become cross with her on account of the way she was dressed. The initiator of the *rowżeh* complained that she was very disappointed, and that the memorial ceremony for her husband had been used for political ends, which was an insult to his memory. She regretted not having invited another female preacher whom she knew herself, rather than this one who had been recommended by her religiously 'orthodox' sister.

A suppressor shopkeeper Continuing, the preacher Zaki utilised Qur'ānic *zulm* placing it within an everyday social and economic context. She took an example from women's daily affairs to illustrate a cause of *zulm*:

> 'A shopkeeper wants to sell to you cloth for a *chādor*. He pretends to sell the last piece and at a cheaper price to you, as if you were a special customer. Then, having completed your purchase, you visit other shops and find that others sell it much cheaper.'

As an another example of being an Islamic conspirator, the preacher Zaki cited shopkeepers, who would hoard goods (*ahtekar*) and sell things at inflated prices. Economic gains at the expense of those Muslim customers who are in a financially difficult situation was considered an unmeritful act during their life of permanent economic well-being. Such undertakings were categorised as illegitimate (*ḥarām*), because the aim was solely to accumulate capital. Despite hoarding being described in official terms as acts of immorality and corruption, businessmen increasingly adopted it as a new avenue for economic success.

These Islamic lessons not only suggest the moral identity of authority at the level of family, community and state, but the way they can be corrupted and distract communal social order.

Disagreement was expressed among attendants in private religious meetings either as defenders or against the preacher. Although women seemed reluctant to counter the Islamic state policy directly, they often did so metaphorically. They often felt more free to express themselves outside the religious meetings when talking to a friend, to me, or to relatives.

Once, in the month of Ramaẓān in 1989, and during a regular lesson concerning the performance of prayer, an older participant interrupted the preacher Mostafi and asked the following question: 'I wonder how it can be an act of *halāl* (permission) to perform the prayers of *namāz* on the floor of a house, which has been a forcefully confiscated property (*qaṣbī*)?' This was not simply a ritual question, but had numerous connotations for me and other participants, who could clearly explain the political issue the questioner had in mind.[96] This created a funny situation, and some smiled slightly at the preacher who could not give a

[96]The Islamic state confiscated large properties of those loyal to the earlier regime who were resident abroad.

proper answer, and thus postponed it in order to make further inquiries.

On another occasion, also at a meeting held by preacher Mostafi, and following the month of Ramaẓān, a participant expressed her disagreement on the ethical lesson concerning a Muslim duty, saying: 'I wonder how it can be a sinful act to ask why the price of potatoes has increased so rapidly?' The preacher had repeatedly said that in order not to disturb the ongoing operation of the Islamic state, we should avoid any kind of criticism.

A politically reserved attitude, and a symbolic mode of expression, are more common than ever before in Iranian everyday culture, due to the social and political burden. Thus, in the meeting of *rowżeh,* some of the preachers, either as a matter of personal loyalty to the state, or as a way of avoiding politically sensitive issues, may fail to answer 'improper' questions, and cut them short with a *ṣalvaī.*

The contradiction between the actual political economy of Islamic states and Qur'ānic notion of *zulm* gives a false representation of ideal religious values. Some middle-class and educated participants were more sensitive to speaking up, and expressing such a distortion. The political opposition between questioner and preacher could be stated metaphorically.

In response to the direct and critical political questions, which a preacher could accept as reasonable, she may excuse herself from answering by giving the impression of not being bothered with such issues. I often noticed that she might request her listeners to recite a *ṣalvāt* so to avoid answering the question before inviting the participants to continue the ritual of reading the Qur'ānic verse for the day or before resuming her *tafsīr.*

The political overtone of the male preacher at the mosque was even more direct, and covered broader political and social matters to a larger audience. I was told of a case (July 1989) that had occurred in a mosque. A big crowd had gathered to pray and to listen to the sermon of a high-ranking male preacher who had come from Tehran. The sermon was held to commemorate the night of the death of the 3rd Shi'ī Imām. Narges, my religious companion's 45-year-old daughter, decided to go together with her husband. The next day she told us how disappointing it had been, because the preacher had only given a short speech on the Imām Husain's heroism and death. Instead he had spent a lot of time praising Rafsanjani, who was one of the two candidates for presidency in 1989. The martyrdom of the Imām Husain and his memorial service had been reduced to an election campaign, and only at the end was there a short sorrowful song (*noḥeh*), which made the audience cry a little. The experience left both her and her husband disappointed, since they had high expectations of hearing sorrow songs as well as having a vow (*nazr*) to initiate on the holy night.

Some considered that the political link to rituals would reduce the 'true' value of Islam. For this reason some hosts were reluctant to listen to or invite, any preacher. The Qur'ānic term of *efrat-va-tafrit* (too much and too little), is often used by disappointed religious participants, such as Narges, about situations where local events overlap political and religious commitments. Political intrusion is frequently given as the reason for the loss of one's former religious belief, and the loss of sacred traditional religious symbols in general. My religious companion Nezhat, a regular religious participant at private meetings, felt disturbed by the political overload in everyday religious activities. She found the regular Qur'ānic recording from our neighbouring mosque loudspeaker disturbing and tiresome. She telephoned anonymously, asking the authorities to turn down the volume of the loudspeaker because she had a sick relative at home.

Women as a cause of natural disorder

The connection between the ethical conduct of women's daily behaviour and the entire order of nature was often an element in the Islamic speeches of the preacher. The negative publicity given to unveiled women in the religious arena by male and female preachers was often the cause of public ideological conflict.

In an anthropological study of a Muslim community in Tunisia, the rain ritual at the time of drought is described as an act of penance and a rite of reconciliation by which the members of the community are 'purified' and reincorporated (Abu-Zahra 1988). However, in the context of the urban Shirazi, misfortunes or natural disorder are not only defined as a basis for community solidarity, but also as a metaphor for disagreement and political hostility between social categories, e.g. between the Islamic conservatism and the more liberal middle-class Muslim believers. In day-to-day social situations ideological differences have become aspects of individuals' social identities, frequently leading to conflict, and in extreme cases to public violence such as in 1989.

The concept of *mosibat* or *balā* denotes misfortune as a result of too much sin (*gonāh*). Sin is destructive to individual well-being and is believed to create social and ecological disorder, with drought as a consequence. The idea is that God is angered by ingratitude, arrogance, immoral behaviour, and particularly by non-veiling. Heavy rain and drought are both believed to be caused by social disaster (*balā*), bringing negative consequences to the whole community.

In March 1989, in daily Ramaẓān lessons, the preacher Zaki raised the unveiling question as usual. This time an attendant supported her view and defined it as a cause of a recent natural misfortune. She told the following story.

> The other day I went directly from the *rowżeh* meeting to buy bread for my meal of *eftār*. I was waiting in a long queue next to a woman who was *bi-hejāb* [women without proper cover]. She accused me, and others like me, such as *ḥezbullāhi*, of causing most of the current problems in life. I responded sharply and said that, on the contrary, it was the *bi-hejāb* women who were causing misfortunes, such as the recent heavy rain,[97] and the snakes which sprang from the earth in the town of Dezfol,[98] as well as the shortage of goods (*qahtī*).

Reproduction of Islamic order in ongoing political, social, and economic life has produced a new form of cultural complexity which is acted out in various social arenas such as religious meetings.

Women's prayer lessons

In addition to the reciting of the Qur'ān and its commentary, there is also reading from the book of *Tawzih al-Masā'il*[99] (clarifying ritual problems) and the giving of prayer instructions at the religious meetings. The *Tawzih al-Masā'il*, in Persian, is the

[97]Which destroyed crops south of Shiraz in February 1989.
[98]A western Iranian town.
[99]Also called *halol-masā'il*. The edition used was written by Ayatollah Sayyed Ruhollah Musavi Khomeini.

kind of book which may be found in the home of a student in a Qur'ānic class.

The women's lessons of prayers (*mas'aleh-go'i*) is central to each Qur'ānic meeting, and is often performed by a leader of the Qur'ānic seminaries or a preacher. The preacher will spend approximately 15 minutes out of the 2–4 hour meeting on instructions. The instructions are most often performed in the beginning, but sometimes also at the end. The female preacher, her assistant, or the religiously 'learned' give the instructions to the participants. Some of the participants use the free minutes in the middle or at the end of the *rowżeh* meeting to put their personal questions to the preacher, being ashamed to speak about some family and sexual matters in the presence of others. I frequently observed that the preacher, or ritual expert, referred a question to the local male preacher, or postponed her answer, as she herself was in doubt about the correct answer.

The lessons concerning the performance of prayers deal with questions closely related to the women's need to carry out the ritual as it is generally prescribed, particularly in the month of Ramaẓān. The dominant themes are the fast, the purification for prayers, alternative and compensation prayers, alms, and various forms of ablution (such as for death, *namāz-e mayet*). The other themes are compensation for prayers neglected or not performed for physical reasons such as menstruation, of *ṣīgheh*, of *mahram* and non-*mahram*, of *zakāt* (religious tax), of abortion (*seght-e jenīn*), and of illegitimate property (*mal-e ḥarām*). The lessons of prayers are largely concerned with ethical and personal matters.

The question of the prayers (*namāz*) and the matters which could lead to its break, e.g. praying in a house, or touching objects classified as unlawful property (*qasbī*), were dominant themes in the religious lessons.

The lesson of prayers is not simply about giving and taking. More importantly it provides an atmosphere for the preacher, ritual experts and audience to expound the prayers and the interpersonal norms of Islam, as well as its theology and sociology, in an informal manner (see also Fischer and Abedi 1989, Antoun 1993: 610).

Ablution

In course of the lessons on ritual purity and impurity (*najes and ṭāher*), obligatory prayers (*vājeb*), merciful acts (*mostahab*), and illegitimate objects or acts (*ḥarām*), the preacher would often go into detail about the social, sexual and psychological problems women might experience. The aim was to instruct and correct their rituals of prayer. The female preacher often went into great detail to clarify the complexity of questions, by reading to the participants from the book of *Tawzih al-Masā'il*, as well as quoting stories, telling a relevant narrative (*ḥadīth*), and citing examples from day-to-day social and political life.

The extent of an individual's sin and religious debt is emphasised in social and psychological terms with reference to whether the act could be considered intentional (*amdan*) or unintentional (*sahvan*). These are two central Islamic juridical concepts that determine performing a correct religious duty. The quality of an individual's ritual is evaluated in terms of impure (*najes*) and pure objects (*tāher*), and permitted (*halāl*) and forbidden acts (*harām*).

Unintentional neglect of obligatory prayers is not considered the fault of person and is thought to be excused by God. For example, failure to comply with the ritual prayer is said to be acceptable if the reason is humanitarian, such as saving a child. Menstruation, pregnancy and childbirth are considered arbitrary and natural causes, and are thus considered as legitimate reasons for not performing ritual prayers, but the women are still expected to undertake some form of compensation prayers (*ghazā*) at another time. This debt of prayers may be performed during one's lifetime, or they can remain a personal duty of another family member after a person's death. These are ritual services that may be purchased, that is, a spiritual man (*seyyid*) is paid to perform prayers on behalf of a dead relative. The living are obliged to perform the neglected ritual in the form of a substitute prayer (*namāz-e qażā*), or in the form of fasting, when they have recovered.

When water is not available for performing ablution it may be replaced by earth and sand (*tayamom*). Dust is substituted for water to allow flexibility and continuity in the praying ritual.[100]

[100]Religious women on long journeys may carry some dust in a cloth for *tayamom* if they will be in an airplane or car for the next prayer.

In this case the prayer performed is incomplete, or so-called 'half performed' (*shekasteh*), and is made in a sitting position. This also applies for very sick people who remain in bed. Such alternatives are not considered appropriate for a healthy person, but are most common among people who travel a lot and who therefore are unable to perform their prayer in the prescribed form.

The religious meetings often place a high priority on women's debt to God and after-life (*ākhirat*). For example, women who fast are advised not to submit to their husband's sexual demands. Sexual abstinence signifies a purity of one's obligatory prayers over the sexual desires of the husband.

Very often the subject concerning the ritual ethic is raised as an important condition to its performance. For example, the act of praying is said not to gain full merit (*savāb*) if the worshipper refrains from wearing 'pure' and proper clothing, or if the ritual is not performed on a lawfully owned property. The interpretation of correct prayers does not ignore the present lifestyle and economic situation. For example, once a question was raised as to how one could perform the ritual of daily prayer on the airplane, or while travelling from one town to another. Another example concerns the intentional or unintentional act of consuming food when this is prohibited. The former state applies when one is tempted to eat in secrecy, forgetting that God is a witness; the latter applies when one's health is threatened and requires the breaking of the fast. Those guilty of ignoring such a moral issue and ignoring God as witness not only lose merit, but also perform sin.

In fact, some particularly orthodox women may practise the ritual of fasting to an extent where they begin to suffer physically, and the doctor may suggest that they should avoid fasting. This is considered by the young and more liberal middle-class as 'madness', and by elderly women as a 'true' personal faith. These women believe that fasting reflects the value of hardship. The ideal is that the harder the prayers, the more merit will be gained. Furthermore, fasting to the point of physical suffering is considered as an act of *ḥarām* by the ritual experts. Once my religious companion's daughter warned her mother that it would be her own responsibility if she fell ill. The mother appreciated the concern her daughter expressed for her general health, but she believed that her daughter was not fully aware of the reality of after-life. She thought that nobody would be able to perform the required ritual for her, thus she had better do it herself. In her view an act of merit in this world (*donyā*), meant an investment of piety in the next. Thus, for religiously oriented women, achievement for after-life depends upon properly performed rituals, and the sanctioning of behaviour considered immoral. For my religious companion it is better to enter the world of after-life with 'full hands' (a metaphor for sets of meritorious acts which gave her confidence and reduce the fear of death), rather than to be materially well-off in one's lifetime.

Generally, women have more knowledge about the ritual instructions for prayers, as well as about visiting shrines and alms-giving, than the average male. This is largely due to a more regular attendance by women at ritual occasions concerning the family. I observed several cases in which a husband asked his wife about the correct way of performing a particular prayer. For example, once my religious companion was asked by her elderly *hajji* husband, whom I had expected to have sufficient religious knowledge himself, about the correct numbers and form of the prayers in the feast at the end of Ramaẓān (*ʿaid-e fetr*). She was far more engaged in alms-giving, meal offerings and Qur'ānic meetings than her husband who only went to the mosque on Fridays. He defended his lack of commitment to praying with reference to the political distortion of those in charge of the mosque.

Political content of prayers

Political views were not only expressed in the Qur'ānic language of *ḥezbullāhī* preachers, nor only in the atmosphere of the religious meetings, but were also brought into internal political metaphors, such as in communal religious and poetic songs, and chanting.

Performance of *ṣalvāt*

In this section I will first elaborate on the performance of rituals of salutation (*ṣalvāt*), before discussing the political metaphors. In salutations to the Prophet Muhammad and his family (*allahoma-sale-ʿalā-mohamad va āleh mohamad*), the Qur'ānic reader not only asks for her own merit, but also for the merit of her parents, or for the happiness of her dead mother's soul and those of other recently dead relatives. Men are seldom the recipients of salutations at women's religious meetings, unless recognised as being highly religious learned (*mujtāhed*), dead or war martyrs. Salutation signifies the women's position with strength and faith (*zane-bā imān*), and the reader is honoured as a mediator through whom a salutation is offered to the Prophet Muhammad and his family.

The arrival of the preacher, for example, is often highlighted by the offering of a *ṣalvāt*, which may be initiated by loyal followers, who then expect others to join in on the chanting of the welcome chant. Any disorder, such as whispering or signs of disagreement among the women, and any interruption to the reading of the Qur'ān, may induce a participant to request a *ṣalvāt*.

The average participant views the recitation of the blessing verses as an instrument to gain merit. Preachers and hostesses receive most of the salutations: the former for her religious performance, and the latter because she sponsored the rituals. Salutations may be addressed to the preacher herself, to her mother's soul, or occasionally to her husband. The mother–daughter relation, which is identified with the transmission of religious and ritual knowledge, is very often honoured by offering a salutation to the daughter, and to the soul of her dead or absent mother. Offering salutions to a martyr, or to the mothers or sisters of martyrs, are also important, as the latter represent new and prestigious categories within Islam.

This practice is not limited to ritual meetings alone, and such salutations may also be recited to indicate a miracle, or whenever one feels lost or confused in daily matters.

> *Case 1* One day during the Qur'ānic ritual in the month of Ramaẓān, the verse to be recited was the Qur'ānic chapter of Yusaf. The preacher elaborated on the familiar story as part of her commentary. The story was about Yusaf, the son of prophet Y'aghob, and the love offered by the Eqyptian woman Zolykhā. The prophet Y'aghob had six sons and Yusaf was the youngest and the most dear to him. One day the brothers planned to kill him, in order to inherit the father's property. They took Yusaf to town, and on the

> way back through the desert they dropped him into a well and bloodied his shirt, to prove to their blind father that he was dead.
>
> Joseph was, however, rescued by the servants of Zolykhā who were crossing the desert. As soon as she saw him she fell in love with him. She assigned him as a servant in her palace and attempted to seduce him, but this disappointed him and made him resistant to her beauty. In revenge, she accused him of making sexual advances towards her, hence ordering that he be sent to prison, where he remained for seven years. Then a drought struck the whole region, and he was assigned the duty of distributing food to needy people. One day he saw one of his brothers among the people waiting to receive food. When it was his brother's turn Yusaf left the golden scales in his bag and accused him of theft. He put his brother in prison and promised to call their father to him. As the father approached town he felt he was getting closer to his lost son Yusaf, noticing his smell. When he met Yusaf he recognised him, and so son and father were finally reunited.

This is a story about father-son affection, conflict with authority, unsuccessful conspiracy, the struggle against untamed temptation (*nafs*), and the triumph of truth and spiritual power over physical and political power. It includes themes relevant to everyday experiences of the average reader. It is a highly emotional story, often leaving the listeners with wet eyes, in spite of their different life experiences. In a particular case a woman expressed her emotion by showing her neighbour her hands, on which her hair stood at end, thus expressing her feeling of excitement. Often one of the women would offer a rousing salutation, which was then taken up by the others, even though the story was known to them. Some also whispered 'God is great' (*allaho-akbar*) to one another in their excitement.

At the end of text the preacher Zaki raised her hand, and wished that the mothers of the sons that had disappeared, or had been taken prisoners of war, would soon be reunited with them as the holy Jacob and his son Joseph had been reunited. The image of a miracle, and the wish for the return of prisoners of war, raised the voices of the audience in *ṣalvāt*.

The ability to work miracles is considered a personal quality of the Prophet. However, a person with a given religious status of *nażr-kardeh* (having been chosen by a holy prophet or holy Imām); or a spiritual person (*moqadas*) who displays the notion of holiness; or who claims to be able to mediate between worldly reality and spiritual life, or to have met the Prophet or someone of his blessed lineage (*omol-athār*) can claim to have the ability to perform miracles.

Changes to the prayers

Changes in the wider political sphere influence to some extent the verbal and non-verbal symbols referred to in the course of the Islamic meetings.

As a further example of how actual political reality and its changes influence everyday local events and create new meaning, I refer to the post-revolutionary religious poetry and propaganda songs that played an important role in the spread of political propaganda. In this we see how old idioms emerged in a new context. I have explored this as it is reflected in the text of salutation recited during and at the end of the religious meetings. For example, the preacher stopped offering salutation to Ayatollah Montazeri as soon as he was removed from his position as the successor to Imām Khomeni in June 1989. Likewise, the idea of offering salutation three times as a tribute to Imām Khomeini, and only once to the Prophet Muhammad, is not only uncommon, but is openly objected to by those with oppositional political views. The latter argued that it was an act of blasphemy (*kofr/shīrk*) to decrease the salutation of the Prophet to one and instead offer it three times to servants of God like Imām Khomeini.

A text of *ṣalvāt* prayer at *rowżeh* in 1989

The following examples illustrate the implications of the surrounding politico-religious ideas for rituals, the poetic speeches and *ṣalvat* performance.

ʿajl farjahom va ahlek ʿedovohom	give us all relief and comfort
va āyyad Imam al-khomeni	praise be to Khomeni
rahbareh nehzateh hosainī	the leader of Husain's revolt

va ensār al moslemin	the leader of the Muslims
allah-o akbar, allah-o akbar, khomeni rahbar	God is great, God is great, Khomeni is a leader.
Marg- bar zed-e velāyāt-e-faqīh	death to those who oppose *velāyāt-e-faqīh*
dorod-bar razmandegan-e islām	salutations to the fighters of Islam
salām-bar shahīdān	greeting martyrs

And finally a political slogan which was flexible in its use in 1989, such as

khodayā khodayā, tā enqelab-e mehdi	God, God, until the Mehdi Revolution the resurrection day.
khomeynī -rā negah dār	protect Khomeni's life
az ʿumreh mā bekāh	cut years from our life
be ʿumreh o beyafsāh	add that to his lifetime
razmandegan-e ma rā noṣrat ʿenāyat befarmā.	grant our fighters victory

or sometimes made it short and repeated:

razmandegān-e islām pīruz bāyad kardan	the fighters of Islam should be victorious
doshmanān islām nabod bāyad kardan	the enemies of Islam should be destroyed
sạleh ʿallā mohamad-va-ālleh mohamad	greetings to Muhammad greeting to Muhammad

The dominant themes at the end of the each religious meeting were the salutations to martyrs and Islamic fighters (*razmandegān-e islām*) in the war zone, and the condemnation of conspiracy (*monāfeqin*). However, the practice differs between different categories of preacher and participants.

Conclusion

In this chapter I have focused on the perpetuation and transmission of ideology and Islamic ethics in the offering of Qur'ānic commentary, preacher sermons, giving prayer instructions as understood in accordance with the Shi'ī school. To me, in order to understand the dominant Islamic ideology, one needs to examine the way in which ideological beliefs and perspective operates at the everyday level. These ideological beliefs serve in religious meetings as instruments for communication and for the transmission of Islamic knowledge and embodied political meanings of different kinds. As I have tried to illustrate, the content of Qur'ānic commentary and other religious lessons are a field of discourse associated with ethical, emotional and wider socio-political issues.

NINE

HEJĀB: ISLAMIC MODESTY AND VEILING

Introduction: **hejāb** *as discourse*

The Muslim woman's veil has functioned as a significant theme for Western researchers and travellers for decades (Marbro 1991; Ahmad 1992: 166) and much has been written about the veil as a cultural idiom of Islam and a symbol of the suppression of women. For early Western missionaries the custom of veiling among Muslims became a proof of the inferiority of Islam (Zwemer 1926). Religious modesty and veiling was often understood as an inherent core of Muslim women's seclusion and oppression. *Hejāb* does not only refer to the mode of the Islamic covering garment, but implies modest behaviour more generally, being important to an individual's identity as a Muslim woman. In the case of Iran, *hejāb* is often interpreted by native Iranian feminists as an overt symbol of social backwardness, sexual and political oppression, and of male religious-political hegemony (Neshat 1983; Afshar 1982; Tabari 1982; Azari 1983). The abovementioned authors, in line with other Muslim writers (Mernissi 1975), agree that Islam with the veil as a key metaphor is the main obstacle for the emancipation of woman. Furthermore, several feminist anthropologists miss completely the religious meaning of the veil and Muslim women's covering garments, as exemplified by Wikan's writings (1982).

Anderson's (1982) study among the Pakthuns in Afghanistan suggest that we should distinguish between seclusion and segregation in veiling. Seclusion by veiling is not synonymous with social and political segregation, it rather resolves the problem of interaction across gender boundaries (1982:401). Veiling denotes the Afghani man's and woman's cultural pride, his or her self-image, and allows for free social mobility across social spheres. Anderson (1982), Wikan (1982) and Altorki (1977) all suggest that the veil may define a cultural definition of sexual seclusion, without necessarily implying segregation and oppression of Muslim women in everyday reality.

The discourse to be assessed here is composed of a variety of situations, with social, religious and political as well as sexual connotations. I use the term discourse not in a strictly linguistic sense, but rather in the broader meaning of Foucault's (1972) terminology. I seek to understand the metaphors and cultural idioms associated with religious modesty and veiling, by studying them within the more extensive political, social and religious context. A decade after the Iranian revolution, the discourse of veiling is not a question of to veil or not to veil; nor is it a question of being secular or religious, as was the case during the 1978 revolution and the following years. Rather, it is a question of how and where to veil and which veil to adopt.

Veiling, modernisation and revolution

The social and economic modernity in several Middle Eastern countries in the 1970s became synonymous with the unveiling of women (R. and E. Fernea 1979). In the context of the social and economic modernity under the Pahlavi Iranian state, unveiling has often been associated with revolutionary acts, bravery, liberation, emancipation, and empowerment in the women's political and social movement. Two historical acts may illustrate such an image. (1) Upon the death of the famous mystic Mansur Hallaj in AD 922 his sister appeared in public unveiled to challenge men. (2) The story that a famous woman of the Bahai religion, Qurratu'l Ayn, in 1949 removed her veil to signal the equality of women and men (see also Fischer 1979).

In Iran, the veil was negatively identified in the course of the economic modernity and social reforms that started with the Pahlavi regime and extended under the former Shāh's regime in the early 1970s. This led to a compulsory unveiling law in 1936 and the importing of French-style clothes and hats for both men and women. The 1936 law meant a prohibition of wearing the veil at public places such as schools, the workplace, and outside on the street.

Kashfeh-hejāb was one of the important socio-political reforms of the Reza-Shāh (the father of the former king), who attacked whatever he considered to be the vestiges of backwardness, i.e. the *chādor*. *Chādori* women of that period told me they had to hide in corners when they were in the street, or their *chādor* would be forcefully removed by the police. See also Hooglund (1982), Fischer (1979), Najmabadi (1990).

The Iranian tradition of wearing a *chādor* (full-length veil) is customarily understood by the average people to symbolise cultural authenticity. Recent historical studies of the veiling of Middle Eastern women support the idea that Islam did not invent the full-length veil and instead identify it with the urban lifestyle phenomenon of pre-Islamic Iran (Rahnavard 1978; Ahmad 1992; Keddie 1991:3).

However, the emergence of veiling as a 'true' tradition and a central aspect of the Muslim identity during the revolutionary movement (1977–9), was associated with Islamic tradition. During the revolution, the wearing of a full-length veil by women became a symbolic weapon against the Shāh's regime and his Western alliances. The full-length veil in post-revolutionary time-represents the victory of the Islamic state and the repression of other secular political ideologies.

Veiling in the Islamic state

The *chādor* (full-length veil) covers the wearer from the top of her head to her wrists and ankles. During the Iranian revolution it has been correctly explained by many writers as a response to pre-revolutionary secular life experiences (see also Hegland 1986:18; Beck 1980:10, Fischer 1980:226; Thaiss 1978). As a revival of their identity many educated women, who previously only occasionally wore the full-length veil when visiting shrines, mosques or attending a funeral, began to wear a full-length veil in order to express solidarity with religious and lower-class women. A full-length veil signals a cumulative identity of religious and social integrity and the authenticity of women's political protest.

The practice of veiling in the ideology of the Islamic state and its local conservative agencies pertains to head and full-body cover, gender interaction and a range of bodily boundaries. The political ideology of the Islamic state views men as the weaker partner and in need of protection to control their sexual desire.

In other words, women tempt men, and thus endanger the social order and national political stability. The sexual danger of the woman in its invisible and visible forms is believed to be so powerful and impulsive that it can lead to the moral corruption of men and society. Hence, Muslim society such as Iran can remain socially ordered, harmonious, and healthy only if the women control themselves and avoid acts of exhibitionism.

Many public notices put on the walls of shops, state offices and buildings warn women who do not comply with the ideal that they will not be served as proper customers. For example *'hejāb-e-islāmi-ra'yat-shavad, vagarn-e az ānjāmeh-kar-e shomā jelogirī mīshavad'* (the veil should be observed, otherwise you will not be served as a customer). Thus, to receive proper service, women have to cover their heads completely, exhibiting no part of their forehead and wearing no make-up. Women's covering garment metaphorically produces political meaning, and failure to comply was often identified as an act of political protest and therefore a reason for punishment.

In post-revolutionary Iran, the full-length veil is not the only Islamic dress to receive public recognition. The common legitimate Islamic dress worn by the average urban woman consists of a long-sleeved, high-necked dress that stretches below the knees, a large head-scarf, trousers (not jeans) and thick dark-coloured stockings. Public control of women is dominated by *ḥezbullāhi* men and women. There are new jobs for controllers in airports, offices, academic institutions and public places, and recruitment is on the basis of positive attitudes to the new social rules and Islamic knowlege. They function effectively and restrictively.

On one occasion I was stopped at the entrance to the Shiraz University by a male guard for not wearing trousers, being dressed in an Islamic suit, a large head-scarf and thick stockings. He explained that he was powerless in this matter and if he allowed me to enter the '*ḥezbullāhi* sisters' in charge would turn me out. I left and returned the day after wearing trousers. The wimple head-scarf (*maqna'eh*) and trousers are the elaborate and dominant forms of *hejāb*, as conceived by the elite intellectuals of the 'Islamic institutions'.

The wimple head-scarf: from private praying cloth to public uniform

The wimple head-scarf (*maghnaʿh*) was traditionally worn as a praying cloth by elderly religious women in private prayers, and represented a private marginalised code of piety. Since the revolution it has been transformed from being a private sign of piety into an ideal Islamic dress that must be worn by women in nurseries, schools, universities, workplaces and government buildings. It is recognised by the Islamic experts and the educational authorities as the ideal form of veiling and an 'appropriate' public Islamic symbol. The wimple head-scarf should cover most of the hair on a woman's head, as well as the forehead, shoulders, neck and breast. Only an opening the size of the face should remain.

At school trousers like American Lee jeans were prohibited, as being symbolic of the political and cultural influences of American Imperialism. At the age of 9 girls are expected to start complying with a series of religious norms, and to make the transition from childhood to adult. Transforming the former secular educational system by means of religious knowledge, political consciousness and ideological forces has been one of the prime concerns of the Islamic Republic since the political turmoil in 1979. Today schoolgirls, university students and state employees are expected to practise full veiling and participate in the regular and obligatory prayers and fasts. Workplaces enforce the new restrictive head and body cover for women employees under the supervision of the Islamic association (*anjoman-e islami*). In schools and at the workplace this control has sometimes developed into violation in the name of religious duty in directing others to what is lawful (*amr-be mʿarūf*) and to what is not lawful (*nahī-āz-monker*).[101] In fulfilling this duty one is considered to be constructing the personal identity of a dutiful Muslim. The familiar religious and cultural terms *amre-be-mʿarūf* and *nahī-āz-monker* have served as a platform for the process of censorship and social control in the post-revolutionary period.

The new Islamic control at workplaces, universities and schools is part of the state administrative policy based on the new Islamic teachings and practices, and the enforcement system.

[101]For further discussion of the emergence of such religious norms as everyday forms of social and political control, see Chapter 5.

The mode of regulation is through the religio-political reforms in workplaces and the recruitment criteria set up for government positions. Religious training and the acquisition of 'correct' prayer and correct Islamic appearance at school and at the work-place have become important elements in the Islamic education of girls and boys.

Educational institutions were threatened with prosecution and closure if they did not enforce full veiling on their female students and employees, and female teachers, school administrators and female students were threatened by the Minister of Education with dismissal if they did not oblige (see also Paidar 1995:315). The Islamic state mandate on veiling at schools and workplaces has created stress and feelings of distrust. For some, not to have a proper veiling involved dramatic consequences, such as physical attacks or a few hours in detention.[102] This strict control of the full veil in particular led to violence against women during the period of war between Iran and Iraq (1981–8). At that time women were defined as the vehicle of social disorder and political instability. The less colourful and decorative appearance of women in public represented a strong image of solidarity, an expression of sorrow to families with casualties, and community solidarity. I personally experienced fewer street disturbances in 1994 than during my first fieldwork in 1989, when moderate veiling was not tolerated.

Public control of people's behaviour in the name of Islamic authority was not an uncommon practice in day-to-day interaction, particularly in 1989. The women's Islamic police (*Khahrān-e zynab*) could, for example, order a woman to fully cover her head and pull the scarf down to her forehead, and a religious oriented man passing by might remind you of your religious duty of being fully covered. I was asked several times by both men and women to pull my scarf down when I was outside in the park, on the street, at the airport, etc.

[102] A few years later such a detention was changed to a religious lesson (*ershād*) in which *ḥezbullah* women instruct other 'sisters' on Islamic morality and the general consequences of neglect of the veil.

Ḥezbullāhi and veiling control

Conservative Muslim (*ḥezbullāhi*) men and women have redefined the veil as 'true' Islamic norms that should be observed both in public and in private family gatherings. The family of *ḥezbullāhi*'s may adopt a stricter sexual segregation than the average urban family. For example, I was told of a wedding of a *ḥezbullāhi* bride and a groom where the bride wore a white religious scarf and appeared without make-up, thus expressing both simplicity and lack of ostentation and luxury. The wedding celebration took place in two houses located some distance apart, one of which was for the male and the other for the female guests. There was no music and the female guests were told to keep their full-length veils on after arrival, contrary to their expectations. The male guests went to attend the public prayers at the nearby mosque. These restrictions were completely new to the bride's uncle (a *seyyid* businessman) and his wife (a well dressed *hajji* woman), who were my informants.

According to the conservative Islamic category (*ḥezbullāhi*) a single hair may be as sinful as exposing all the hair. Strict religious women wear a full-length veil only exposing their eyes. Every single sexual interaction is considered important in itself for the record of one's behaviour on the day of judgment. The preacher Mostafi further discouraged women from shaking hands and instead encouraged them to call each other a religious 'sister' or 'brother'. The popular terms of address used by strangers outside in streets are *khahar* (sister) and *bradar* (brother), *ḥajkhānum* (female *ḥajjih*) and *hajagha* (male *hajji*). Furthermore, religious modesty was understood as a total cultural behaviour. For them, the nature of modesty should pervade all aspects of gender and social interaction. When encountering men (even agnatic relatives), a degree of distance and modesty should be observed according to orthodox practices.

During my fieldwork in 1989 I visited an Islamic bookshop with a female friend on an evening walk. There I met a woman who was confused by a series of new veiling rules. She asked the shopkeeper, a former imām of the mosque, whether she should practise veiling in the presence of her young son-in-law. The son-in-law, a Sunni man, had apparently requested that she should do so. Both the woman and I thought that the answer would be no, but the religious shopkeeper pointed out that there had always existed dress regulations *vis-à-vis* close kin as well as distant relatives. Women were expected not to display their legs above their knees, or to appear in sleeveless dresses. He maintained that the important issue was the possibility of arousing sexual feelings (*hayajan*), and if such feelings were present, then a full veil was necessary no matter if the man was a *maḥram* (brother or son-in-law) or not.

This view was confirmed a few days later by the preacher Zaki at a Ramaẓān meeting. She asked the participants to take greater care in covering themselves, even when in private homes and in the presence of close male relatives, such as a grown-up son, a son-in-law, or an unmarried brother (*ʿazāb*). She quoted a letter sent to her anonymously by a religiously oriented man, who accused his mother of unIslamic behaviour since she wore a loose veil at home. This offended him and his understanding of Islām. He pleaded with the preacher to tell his mother to practise proper veiling, both for her own sake and for the sake of others. The preacher Zaki, with reference to this example, insisted that the youth were full of passion since economic conditions prevented them from getting married and having legitimate sexual relations. Hence, modest behaviour is considered desirable even in relations with male relatives, despite the fact that they are traditionally classified as *maḥram* (legitimate kin). As such the idea of being a 'true' Muslim woman, as instructed by conservative religious authorities, went beyond the common practice.

The religious conservative men believe that the religious status of their women increases if they wear the traditional full-length veil. A man whose wife I knew well rejected the modern Islamic suit as a proper veil for his wife. He worked in the Islamic state organisation *Jihād-e Sāzandegī* (Reconstruction Holy War) and came from an orthodox family. His 22-year-old wife Vahideh wore a full-length veil to conform with her conservative religious husband's wishes, despite the fact that she, like other women, found it impractical. She kept complaining that it was very problematic to wear a full-length veil when she had to carry her child, push the pram, or carry a shopping bag.

Zohreh, a young divorcee, is another case. She is a hairdresser who has adopted the modern style of dress and a light make-up. She has a brother who worked as an Islamic policeman (*pāsdār*), and whenever she came to visit my sister she was anxious to return home quickly, or her brother might become suspicious, perhaps suspecting that she was out with men. She talked about her suffering to my sister in *dard-e dels* (the genre of telling one's troubles), and even claimed that her brother had threatened her with a gun on several occasions.

There are different degrees of veiling, not only among women, but also among different Islamic categories. Both of the above cases reflect typical sources and patterns of family conflicts and the control of women for male Islamic ideological purposes.

However, for some conservative Islamic authorities the public definition of what is a proper Islamic covering is more than simply wearing a full-length veil. Wearing trousers is also required. This can be illustrated by the following example. I once stood in a queue to enter a park formerly called the House of Ghavam, now the offices of the *pāsdār* and the legal department. A woman friend and I were conservatively dressed in a *manto* and large head-scarf, which we considered to be fully acceptable. To our surprise we were not allowed to enter and were told to dress 'properly' in trousers, or to borrow a *chādor* in the reception. As we left to borrow a full-length veil, I noticed that an older woman who was wearing what appeared to me to be a proper veiling was also refused entry. Her husband, who stood next to her, became angry; no one had ever insulted his wife in such a manner. He claimed that she had worn a full-length veil most of her life and had always been identified as fully 'veiled'.

In the post-revolutionary period, the Islamic political authorities encouraged the masses to watch over their family members, neighbours and relatives, in order to discourage them from committing non-Islamic acts. There are stories of the effects this had on the emotional relations and authoritative roles between family members. One party in a conflict could always claim the other was committing acts socially and politically endangering the stability of Islamic state.

According to the view of the religious authorities, what constituted immodest behaviour of women refers not only to the public display of the female body, but uncontrolled social interactions. Religious modesty and veiling in its broader social context remain a pertinent ideology of Muslim women's femininity.

Veiling and respect for the martyr

In 1989 the controversy surrounding the practice of women's modesty and veiling was of concern for at least five categories of organisations. On the institutional level the following organisations were involved: the Islamic police (*pāsdār*), who seek to eliminate and punish 'incorrect' Islamic acts; the agencies of the moderate Rafsanjani government, who seek to moderate public rules by recognising different forms of covering garments; and the Islamic elite women's organisation (*anjoman-e islamī*), which is powerful in educational and work establishments, controlling behaviour in accordance with the new images of male and female roles as prescribed in the school text books. The fourth group is represented in general by the female Islamic experts in the local area. The final category is the *ḥezbullāhi* women, who like the Islamic elite utilise the wimple head-scarf, but in addition insist on the Iranian tradition of a full-length veil.

The *ḥezbullāhi* women's demonstration against poorly-veiled women was used by the Islamic police authority to tighten up the veiling rules. The pro-veiling slogans continued to be supportive of the revolutionary police in 1989. The street slogans in the post Iran–Iraq war period addressed whether *bi-hejāb* (non-veiled) and *bad-hejāb* (poorly-veiled) women should feel ashamed in the presence of mothers of martyrs. By wearing dark colours and not wearing jewellery, particularly gold bracelets and necklaces that signify a higher socio-economic status, women express sympathy and solidarity towards the mothers of martyrs, both in the neighbourhood and the community at large.

On one side of this controversy are the relatives of the martyrs who identify themselves as first-class Muslim citizens of the post-war Iran period, on the grounds of having sacrificed family members on behalf of the Islamic state and community. On the other side of the controversy are the average urban middle- and higher-class women with very few martyrs in their families. They challenge the enforced Islamic dress by changing it to fashionable Islamic suits. In contrast, during the post-war period (since the Iran–Iraq war in 1988), the emphasis on the full-length veil has been maintained and manipulated locally by the *ḥezbullāhis*, their argument being that it is the only 'true' form of veiling. This kind of development strengthens the existing opinion between those directly or indirectly related to martyrs and those who are not.

This duality has caused considerable confusion. The term *bi-hejābī*, with its negative implications, has been applied by the local preacher to women wearing the *manto*, although this is officially recognised by the state and is a dominant veil among upper- and middle-class urban women. Housewives busy with extra-domestic tasks such as purchasing household goods and attending to family matters associated with public life also find the Islamic suit more convenient than the full length veil. They are, for example, able to hold shopping bags in one hand and children in the other, something which is difficult when wearing the full-length veil. Hence, among the middle-class women the tradition of veiling is impractical in their modern social and economic lifestyle, which includes a wide range of extra household activities.

The fact that middle-class women distance themselves from the traditional religious garment of the full-length veil has given rise to numerous demonstrations in Tehran, where conservative forces demand a greater control over the implementation of the Islamic suit and scarf. For example, when president Rafsanjani (July 1989) recognized the loose fitting suit, the *ḥezbullāhi* and the family of martyrs reacted immediately with a demonstration, condemning any act of bad veiling. The participants in the July 1989 demonstrations opposed the wearing of colourful scarves and stylish Islamic suits, arguing that it dishonoured martyrs and undermined the attempts to sustain a revolutionary ideology against Western influences and the search for an Islamic authenticity. Hence, to the mothers of martyrs, the *manto* and the new style of thin stockings represent a pre-revolutionary women's clothing that indicates a lack of solidarity with their suffering.

An example of a more liberal attitude of the post-war period in June 1989 was the resumption of the traditional marriage ceremony, characterised by public music and the custom of driving the bride and groom around the town while blowing the car horn. This custom had, like many other communal celebrations, been strictly forbidden during the war between Iran and Iraq, when the emphasis was on communal mourning and national expressions of grief and solidarity to families of martyrs.

Another sign of the return to normal life was the increased presence of tribal women in towns, the latter traditionally being less veiled than their urban counterparts. They come to town to sell their handiwork and crafts, including local musical instruments, at the market in Shiraz. Their colourful shirts strongly contrast with the dark colours and veils worn by the *ḥezbullāhi* women.

This normalization of a colourful bāzār life after eight years of the Iran–Iraq war excited the average person. The day after I witnessed the tribal women at the city market, I went to my regular Ramaẓān religious meeting at the house of Zaki. There the preacher Zaki addressed the topic of netting stockings as an attempt to bring about a change in the 'true' meaning of the veil. A participant added that some women wear netting stockings even at one of the popular local shrines, Asoneh.[103] Another participant whispered surprised that such behaviour was contradictory to a 'true' pilgrim, that it was an insult of a holy place. Another woman, a mother of a martyr, sadly referred to the tribal women selling musical instruments at town markets. She demanded that this ought to be stopped since the dust on her son's grave was not yet dry.

Modesty and sexual taboos

The religious conservatives' aim is to prohibit acts which they consider sexually provocative and socially destructive. Mary Douglas made a link between the rational behaviour of primitives and taboo-thinking. In her view taboo turns out not to be incomprehensible, but is an intelligible concern to protect society from behaviour that threatens its order (1992:25).

When conservative Islamists demand that both Muslim men and women should uphold community values through a series of restricted modesty and bodily boundaries, the aim is not only to moralise, but also to politicise Iranian society. Although the official veiling on bodily boundaries includes both men and women, women often are most blamed for jeopardising revolutionary society.

To look into the eyes, or touch the hand of a member of the opposite sex, whatever the relationship may be, is thought to

[103]This shrine is believed to be the grave of the 13-year-old brother of the 8th Shi'i Imām, Imām Reza, and Tuesday is believed to be his particular merit day to initiate vows (*vakham*).

lead to sexual temptation, and is therefore – outside of marriage – considered a provocative act. The idea of having 'pure' eyes, a modest gaze and a plain voice, even in encounters between an adult brother and sister, is identical with *ḥezbullāhi's* moralisation plan for Iranian society.

Preacher Mostafi, who is considered a *ḥezbullāhi* and supporter of the Islamic regime, repeatedly warned her listeners at the fast month meetings against seductive body movement. She argued that not only would such behaviour devalue their prayers, but severe punishment would wait them on the day of judgment (*ākherat*): 'One's body might be hanged by the breast, or by the single hair that has been displayed vulgarly in this world, and the offending part of the body might be burned.' She described the uncovered head (*sar-bāz*) and open-necked shirt (*syneh-bāz*) as immodest and contradictory to 'true' Muslim morality. The female breast and buttocks, the neck, foot and particularly the ankle, as well as the heel and arms are among the taboo parts of the body. They are often referred to with feelings of passion (*hayajān*), and therefore are deemed seductive and detrimental to the maintenance of morality and political stability. High-heel shoes are blamed as a metaphor for seductive sexual behaviour. Such a negative view of women's clothing developed publicly and was adopted by the university Islamic 'sisters', who issued a long list of clothing rules for female students and private and state employees.

Such an ideology is adopted by various categories such as schoolgirls, university students, religiously oriented women, ritual experts, students of religious schools, certified religious leaders, etc. They commonly moralise and politicise women's bodily movements in religious vocabulary and request official control.

Male modesty

Anderson (1982) is one of the few scholars who has developed an argument about men and veiling, i.e. veiling among Pakthun men in Afghanistan. He suggests that male veiling is the core of their politeness and modesty, paralleling the modest behaviour of women. Although recognising male modesty as an important aspect of Muslim men's identity, it seems to me that the consequences of lack of modesty are more serious for women than for men.

The Islamic state policy of sexual control of all its citizens does place some sanctions on male behaviour. Offensive remarks made by youths to women on the street have been discouraged by the Islamic police as being an insult to an Islamic sister. A man wearing a short-sleeved shirt with an open collar in public is also considered sinful. In the post-revolutionary period there were several cases where youths were arrested if dressed in a Western teenage style, i.e. tight trousers and colourful patterned shirts.

The fear of political repercussions, and of being arrested, has led many parents to increase their sanctions on the social activities of their children, and especially their daughters.[104] The Islamic Republic was determined to moralise public social appearances by replacing whatever they believed to be an influence of Western culture (*tāghoti*). Hence, a T-shirt displaying a picture of a film star signified a careless identity of stereotyped manners, contrasting with the devoted Islamic youths (*basījī*), who were sent to fight against the Iraqi troops on the front line during 1981–8.

On one occasion I went with my father to visit one of his friends, an expert in the Islamic art of calligraphy, at his workshop in the bāzār. I have known him as a friend of my father since my childhood. After a few hours' friendly talk about his work we took our leave. I stretched out my hand to shake in farewell, and to my surprise he responded only orally. I felt ashamed that I had not realised that he had recently become very active in the mosque, and being a religious man he had to avoid the courtesy of touching the hand of a woman. My father later explained that he had become man of faith (*bā-imān*), arranging rituals at the mosque, and that he had recently returned with a group of pilgrims from the shrine of the Imām Khomeini in the holy city of Qum.

On another occasion I and my religious companion met my cousin in her house on a regular family visit. She told me that she was hoping to obtain some news about the disappearance

[104]Common explanations as to why middle-class parents send their children out of Iran as refugees are fear that the youths would be sent into the army or behave in a way that would put them in political danger.

of her sister's son from the war zone in 1989. Soon she came to the point of how close they had been and also how his manners had changed in relation with other people after becoming an official member of the Islamic police. She said:

> 'I noticed that he stopped looking into my face and that he lowered his gaze; he wouldn't stay alone in a room with me. Then I knew that something had happened to him. As he continued his training to become *pāsdār* he began to turn his face away or look down whenever he met me or other women in the family. I had once been even closer to him than his mother, since he had often consulted me about personal matters. Soon he joined the armed forces as a voluntary soldier (*basījī*) and some time later he became missing in action.'

According to the conservative ideology men are considered the weaker part when it comes to controlling their sexual passion. Thus when enforcing social rules, some of the forbidden acts of men may be easily forgiven, as these are believed to be caused by the sexual powers of women.

Hejāb ***as a strategic behaviour***

Despite a conservative ideological view on veiling, the veiling practice among women is far from uniform. Women have become more creative and fashion-conscious, constantly attempting to subvert the blandness of the conventional veil. They have adopted various Islamic covering garments that play with colours, fabrics and design.

Although a person's Muslim identity is defined according to the correct performance of daily prayers, veiling and modesty, women in everyday practice largely adopt a complex cultural and religious repertoire of behaviour, where a pure state of intention (*nīyat*) takes a priority over rigid appearance. To the majority, having faith is not necessarily a matter of adhering to the static norms, but a pure state of intention.

Resistance of the middle-class women

Using different forms of veil to fit different social situations is an important aspect of one's identity among middle-class women.

In July 1989 I witnessed a family party where several of my relatives participated, including my religious companion Shazdeh, a *hajji* from a well-to-do business family. She, like some other female guests, wore an elegant foreign dress and a transparent scarf. The next morning I sat beside her at the Qur'ānic meeting held on the occasion of the month of Muharam. We talked less than usual at the *rowẓeh* meeting in order to pay respect and maintain order during the Qu'rānic reading. She did not wear any jewellery, nor the elegant foreign dress and transparent white scarf from the day before. Instead she had put on a simple dress, thick stockings, and a black full-length veil. Later on she told me that she wanted to buy some gloves recently to be found in the city market, to cover her wrists and arms, because the other day a preacher had said it was sinful to expose one's arms in short-sleeved blouses.

Shazdeh's strategic veiling was once observed by the preacher Mumeni. Shazdeh replaced her full-length veil with a scarf while sitting in her car on her way back from a religious meeting. Seeing this, Mumeni warned her against this forbidden act (*fele ḥarām*), arguing that her fast would be broken due to her face and the backs of her hands being visible. Shazdeh replied that the full-length veil disturbed her when driving and that it was too warm. These reasons were not accepted by Mumeni, who continued to warn her of the flames of hell and the day of judgment. This disappointed Shazdeh, and she told me that she would no longer attend any of Mumeni's meetings. She did, however, continue to attend religious seminaries led by recent Islamic graduate preachers on the grounds that they were more liberal.

Despite being a devoted Muslim, the norms demanded by the preacher Mumeni were not compatible with everyday life. After all, she argued, on her two pilgrimages to Mecca, when the contact with God is especially strong, and when the seven times ritual walk between the holy places Safā and Marvah is performed[105] by both men and women, it is not forbidden to display the oval face and the backs of the hands. In the opinion of Shazdeh the norms advocated by Mumeni on the 'true' veil make

[105]Safā and Marvah are local holy places in Mecca where pilgrims walk back and forth seven times (see Eickelman 1987, part 3). The two local holy places are associated with the story of Abraham and Hagar, who ran seven times back and forth in search of water for the infant Ism'il (Fischer and Abedi 1990:162).

religion static and difficult to practise on a daily basis, even for women like herself who strongly believe in women's modesty, the ritual of vow-making and the obligatory prayers, as well as in the importance of religious meetings.

The decision of what veil to choose for a specific occasion is situational and reflects the realisation of a broader social and political relation. Some middle-class women use the full-length veil only at religious meetings as a shared code, and remove it once they are in the street and out of sight of other religious friends. Ideally, a woman wearing a black full-length veil of heavy-quality cloth is identified by other religious friends as a woman deserving strong respect (*bā-shakhsyat*). The use of a thick-quality full-length veil during religious gatherings reflects religious prestige and a strong moral identity.

The religiously oriented middle class, in contrast to the religiously conservative women, may at smaller gatherings of friends from a Qur'ānic course or, as I several times witnessed, at wedding parties, change from a thick-quality full-length veil to one thinner and lighter in colour. Such a change can often be explained as a matter of personal comfort, informality and pressure from other relatives. The type of full-length veil worn may signify the degree of one's religious affiliation, personal strength and the religious occasion. For example, a full-length veil may be used at annual religious meetings by the more well-educated, modern working women, and a lighter, flowery one for happy occasions, such as the votive meal services where religious meetings develop into a feast. While women may dress elegantly at family visits and parties, the opposite may be the case at religious meetings where it is important to signify a pious identity. Thus a woman's good character is not only defined in terms of her relations with her male partner encountered in the public sphere, but also in terms of the moral identity sought in relations with other women.

The full veil at religious occasions

The privacy of religious meetings does not mean that participants are less reserved in their veiling, and women are seldom poorly-veiled in the presence of each other at religious meetings, the possible exception being religious meal feasts such as *eftāri* (the meal ending a fast), or when attending a less popular Qur'ānic course with very close co-seminary friends. Some women may use the dress as a religious device to signal special events by changing the colour and style of veil. For example, to mark celebrations such as the birth of the Prophet, or the death of the 'Umar,[106] women may wear dresses that are more colourful and elegant under their full-length veil.

Having a head-scarf under their full-length veil, women are more willing to lower their veil to their shoulders at the religious meetings since the wimple was officially defined as a proper and fully acceptable veil as it hung down to the shoulders, covering neck and chest. Women who remove their head cover and/or display a golden necklace or bracelet may be criticised by others as exhibitionists. Such a display of a new style of dress or jewellery is often believed by female preachers to lead to jealousy and competition.

The preacher Mostafi usually raised the theme of the veil in her speeches, whether in public religious halls or at private homes. Through story-telling she sought to illustrate the Islamic ideals and frameworks of meaning. I will use as an example a story she claimed had happened locally, in order to emphasise the importance of genuine moral rather than static religion.

> The night following the death of a young man, the *azān-go* (prayer-caller) in a mosque, [one of his close relatives who had known him well] dreamt of him. The relative asked

[106]Shirazi traditionally had a ceremony of *umari*, where local children made cotton dolls on sticks which they burned to mark their happiness over the death of 'Umar. (Umar was the second *khalif* of the Muslims.) On this occasion, some women wear exotic red dresses and red lipstick as a sign of celebration. This is offensive to the Sunni Muslims. Likewise, on the day traditionally called *umari*, red dresses may be worn in defiance, to display happiness in the face of other people's sadness. According to Shi'ī believers, 'Umar is believed to have insulted the Prophet's family by not accepting Imām Ali, the son-in-law, as the Prophet's successor (this early Islamic conflict explains the origins of the emergence of Muslim factions, as Sunni believe in Muhammad, Abu-Bakar, 'Umar, Usman's followers and 12 Imāmi while Shi'ī Iranians believe in Muhammad, Imām Ali, Hasan, Husain, Zaynu'l-Ābidīn, Muhammad-e Bāgir, Ja'far-e Sādegh, Musā-Kāzim, Ali-ibn Mūsā Reza, Muhammad-e Tagi, Muhammad-e Nagi, Hasan-e Askarī and Imām Mahdi). I learned, after my fieldwork, that such expressive religious devices were discouraged by Islamic authorities as insulting to Sunni brothers, and they have suggested a Muslim solidarity. However, this different historical understanding is marked in different manners of praying such as in the annual ritual of *hajj* to Mecca. As a *hajji* woman put it to me, the Shi'ī pilgrims to Mecca (male and female) avoid paying tribute similar to the Sunni pilgrims at the tomb of 'Umar.

> about his own prospects in the world of *ākhirat*. The *azān-go* burst into tears and nodded his head sadly, indicating that to his great regret and pain he was a man full of *gonāh* (sin).

This story was told to teach women various lessons on behaving like a 'true' Muslim. After pointing out that constant worship and 'pious' work was not in itself evidence, the preacher continued to warn women against dressing in thin clothing and gossiping, both of which were said to threaten the piety (*ṣavāb*) of personal prayers.

Mostafi repeatedly suggested that the importance of modesty today was connected to judgment in the after-life, and she asked if the women were taking seriously the responsibility of their own behaviour and that of others. She warned the women present of the possibility of committing a sinful act of incorrect prayers without being aware of it, despite being a religiously learned person. Furthermore, she listed the most sinful acts often committed by women, two of which were appearing poorly veiled and gossiping.

Similar moral lessons were followed up by the preacher Zaki in another Ramaẓān meeting a few days later. She pointed out that some participants had been seen wearing the full-length veil at religious meetings, while dressing elegantly with colourful scarves on other occasions. Then she told the participants that to obtain the world of *ākhirat* they must act with piety in spite of all the counter-forces.

The preacher Mumeni, like others in her rank, remained conventional when implementing the rules of Islamic modesty and veiling to her audience. A woman who has made the obligatory pilgrimage to Mecca is expected to display greater modesty and adopt a more restricted veil than before going to pilgrimage. *Hajji*[107] women from middle-class families who have made the obligatory pilgrimage to Mecca do not always wear the full-length veil. In their eyes those who observe a restricted Islamic garment are old fashioned.

Thus, a full-length veil is seldom removed in the presence of

[107]*Hajji-khānum* is the popular title for a woman who has made a compulsory *tamatoh-hajj* to Mecca. Those who have travelled to the holy towns of Karbalā or Mashhad may occasionally be called *Karbali* or *Mashhadi* indicating their sacred journey.

a female preacher unless the women are wearing head-scarves and are fully covered underneath. This indicates the women's expectations towards each other, their identity of piety. A 'pious' veiling is valued as a means of ensuring merit in the life hereafter, and it symbolises the individual's strong belief and personality. As a religiously oriented woman put it to me, 'strict dress over worldly attraction'. Thus she wears both head-scarf and a full-length veil, a double-Islamic dress for religious conservatism.

From *chādor* to Islamic suit

Changing one's traditional full-length veil to an Islamic suit has become a common practical solution among the old and the lower middle-class women. This has distorted the rigid ideology of the conservative *ḥezbullāhi* Muslims, who argue that a full-length veil is important to one's cultural and religious authenticity.

Being aware of the distorted practice and untraditional changes among women, the preacher Mostafi repeatedly warned her audience not to follow suit. Her remarks were directed at the strategic behaviour of the participants who changed their veil according to place and occasion. Such inconsistency in veiling is considered worldly (*donyavī*) and is associated with a kind of behaviour classified as 'dolly' (*arosaki*); i.e. behaviour considered artificial and Westernised, and that should be avoided even in the private sphere of family and friends. According to the preacher Mostafi women wearing a full-length veil, despite the heat and discomfort, display the firmness of their faith and their superiority in worldly matters. Although wearing a full veil might not seem attractive in the present, it will give rewards in the after-life.

Nezhat, my other religious companion with two pilgrimages to Mecca, was among the elderly women who used to wear the new Islamic suit (*manto*) outside on the street, while carrying a full-length veil in her bag in case she wanted to enter a religious place. She was an active religious participant and played a conservative role *vis-à-vis* other religious friends, who identified her as a woman of strong faith. She was seen without a full-length veil several times by her Qur'ānic colleagues and this left her with a feeling of embarrassment.

In an attempt to avoid standardisation some girls change the wimple head-scarves of the school uniform, sewing an additional chin or forehead piece to make it resemble a hat. This is considered to be more attractive and makes the mandatory veil more tolerable. Some prefer a black wimple head-scarf on the grounds that it matches their black eyes, which they accentuate slightly with make-up. A fringe of curled or dyed hair displayed on the forehead was adopted along with the Islamic suit by middle-class urban women, who insisted on looking fashionable in their adopted Islamic suits. This signified opposition and seemed to be a form of resistance and political protest,[108] since the women risked being stopped in the street and warned by Islamic police, and even fired from their jobs or arrested.

These examples illustrate that the veil is not uniform and in practice it remains subject to identity management. Despite the enforced veiling and the official warning against transforming the veil to a more decorative style, the authorities are not able to control such practices. Once a male clergy expressed his disappointment at a Friday sermon in 1989: 'We allowed women to wear a scarf, but this does not mean a shiny one like a *shab-chiragh*, a "night torch".' Such issues have become the focal point of controversies and power struggles involving the Islamic conservatives, the martyrs' organisations and the moderate authorities. The harassment and negative talk of women's behaviour was slightly reduced during my second visit in 1994.

Conclusion

In this chapter I have explored the ideology of mandatory veiling, gender boundaries and women's symbolic action and actual behaviour (not to mention my own experiences). I have explored Islamic veiling and modesty as a multi-metaphoric system of present-day Iranian society. Furthermore, I have argued that the religious practice and ideology of veiling in Iran is not only related to the static veiling rules which define the female segregated sphere of movement, but also relates to public rites and opportunity across gender boundaries.

First of all I can conclude, as I suggested in the beginning of this chapter, that the wearing of the veil does not have the same

[108] This may be viewed in terms of the infrapolitics of the powerless; resistance as defined by Scott (1990).

meaning to all social and religious categories of women. It is not merely a sign of oppression. The symbolic politics of women adopting the veil has changed in nature since the Iranian revolution; it has changed from a matter of veiling or not-veiling to different ways of veiling. It is clear that the production of meaning on the issue of religious modesty and veiling not only emphasises the normative aspects of Islamic dressing and the Muslim identity, but has also created new forms of social and ideological discourses across gender, class and generation boundaries. The contemporary veiling practice serves to identify a woman's personal qualities, her various Islamic identities, and her religious and political leaning.

Contemporary Islam and the debate surrounding its 'ideal' practice is not only used to produce political meaning and generate discourses, but charge and counter-charge as political competitors subject it to political expediency (see also Piscatori 1989: 9). This view has also been forward by Eickelman (1985) who states that 'Islamic tradition is continuously undergoing an internal dialectic of adaptation and self renewal'. Women in Iran neither abandon the cultural authenticity of modesty, nor completely adopt the state mandatory ideals. Meanwhile, women's bodily movement is a supreme symbol and index of the Islamic state's attempt to contain and control its citizens. However, women, by maintaining their religious modesty, generate Islamic discourses and multi-Islamic identity.

Secondly, the new Islamic cultural politics does not simply emerge from its tradition and create a new cultural consensus among its citizens. Bowen correctly states that in all Muslim discourses there is an 'other' against which a version of proper religion is figured (1993: 330). Opposing ideas have emerged between various social categories with different Islamic views in the local community as to what is 'true' or 'false' Islamic practice. Many aspects of the present official veiling rules are distorted and are considered by some to be contrary to what the state authorities impose as the traditional, 'true' Islam. The traditional Islamic issue of modesty and veiling in the socio-religious context of Iranian society has become a locus for political and ideological manoeuvre, implying a religious multivocality and condensation of symbols which are both unified and diversified. The ideology of the new Islamic veiling appears to be a rhetorical feature in a discursive struggle producing certain effects for political purposes, sustaining or challenging the social and political order (Eagleton 1991: 11). Thus it is not adequate to define the meaning of Islamic modesty as a static pattern of behaviour.

Islamist academic intellectuals recommend wimple head-scarves; and local religious experts recommend the full-length veil. Those who are in favour of both the wimple head-scarf and full-length veil at the same time represent the Islamic intellectuals. The female Islamist, through educational institutions and social activity, takes part in the dissemination of the Islamic state ideology along with other Muslim sisters and brothers. To the middle-class women the mandatory veil has in practice been distorted to a fashion phenomen and prioritises one's moral intention. The symbolism of the diversity of veiling is indeed a manifestation of different ways of acting as a Muslim. The restricted veil is accommodated as a politicised key symbol for entering into the public male-dominated area. Thus the veil not only reflects Islamic identity and signals membership in Islamic revivalist groups, but has risen as an alternative metaphor for female public rites, making possible free movement across gender boundaries.

The practice of the veil has, therefore, become a set of statements, verbal and non-verbal expressions and discourses in Foucault's (1972) sense. In this perspective, verbal and non-verbal expressions of social reality are fractions of knowledge with varying degree of power in the structure of society.

TEN

FAMILY MANAGEMENT IN THE CONTEXT OF CHANGE

Introduction

Sweeping economic developments occurred in Iran in the post-revolutionary period such as: (1) the ration method of purchasing domestic goods; (2) the Islamic religio-political identity and knowledge for recruitment to jobs and benefit of public services; (3) the emergence of a new 'niche' for small and large market enterprises within the free market system; (4) the internal relationship of households to the market economy. These developments were directly and indirectly responsible for changes in household compositions and in the viability of various forms of urban households.

In the following section I will outline a series of transformations which have taken place in Iranian family composition, economic adaptations in the context of larger political development, and the extra-domestic work of women in the turbulent social and political system of post-revolutionary Iran. I will explore the relationship between the household, the person, and the large-scale economic and social processes, and institutions. My intention is to define the position of women in the organisation and production of the family economic unit (Sharma 1980), as well as to outline the way the general economic and ideological situation may subvert the family economy.

It would be impossible to study the household entity and individuals' life cycle (Grønhaug 1976:44; Barth 1991), without describing the various empirical systems, which in their macro-social extensions produce and channel people's life courses in specific directions. In the Iranian family of today there is a connection between the intimate life of families and their members, the organisation of the growing free market economy, the ideology of the Islamic state, and the emergence of new institutions under the process of change. The Iranian family formation and its viability is as much an integral part of the political and economic structures of society as it is a reproductive unit.[109] I believe the internal lives of families must be understood in the context of the links between different levels of social life: e.g. household, state, religion, ideology and women's roles.

Household management: micro-macro economics and ideological concerns

I argue the importance of the large-scale ideological and economic factors in the everyday life situation of the individual, and the way in which this ideology has opened up the possibility of divergent adaptations and a new household economy. Moreover, the burden that economic changes place on adult males (who still are the main providers in most families), as well as career married women, has increased. This has complicated and intensified the tradition of child-rearing, cooking, washing, cleaning the house, taking care of the family and social networks, as well as the time spent on purchasing goods and supervising children after school.

How can we understand the domestic dimension of the life of Iranian families in general, and women in particular, without excluding it from the larger public, economic, and ideological flow? The large-scale economic reforms, and the new household economy, have affected the life of family members in different ways. The form and the rituals of household activities in everyday life are central themes in the following section. I will illustrate some of the above issues in the life histories of individuals and families.

Below I present an extended case study that exemplifies the process of social and economic changes for the Iranian middle-class family during my first and second periods of fieldwork.

[109]See also Yanagisako 1979.

Mahry and her family's decision to migrate

Mahry (30) and her husband (34) and their two school-age children moved out of Iran a short while after I left in 1989. At the time many of her relatives lived abroad (ten of her parents' close relatives, and one of Mahry's older sisters). I met other members of Mahry's family during my second period of fieldwork. Mahry's younger sister was also planning to leave Iran as soon as she married her fiancé.

I was a co-resident with Mahry and her family in 1989. She was a housewife and her husband worked part-time at a privately owned factory near Shiraz. Her husband's family were originally from the northern Azari Turkish city of Tabriz. Mahry's father was a retired teacher who worked the evenings as a shopkeeper for one of their better-off relatives. Mahry married before the Islamic revolution and moved to Tehran where her husband had just established a business with a mortgage from the bank. His business was small and production was low, due to the scarcity of raw materials. Soon after the revolution, and as a result of the increasing prices of goods and shortages in their supplies, he went bankrupt.[110] He was left with a large debt. They decided to return to Shiraz in order to be closer to her parents, from whom she could receive substantial financial support.

They moved to the house of Mahry's parents, hoping to settle there, but found that the first floor of the house was already occupied by her newly-wed brother, who also was experiencing economic problems. Mahry's grandmother helped them get a few rooms in the house of her *hajji* uncle (her mother's brother). Her husband found some daily waged work. He was paid daily according to the number of paper clips he could manufacture at a private factory. But his income also depended upon other economic and political conditions such as, for example, the unreliable electricity supply in Shiraz. During the war, when power cuts were frequent, the limited supply of electricity would reduce his daily production.

Mahry, who found her husband's income insufficient to meet

[110]Scarcity of raw materials for industry due to a series of import restrictions and closures of the large factories, along with the dramatic rise in prices of these materials, were the reasons given for bankruptcy of small businesses. See also Behdad 1989.

the household expenses, started to sew and knit in order to make some extra money. She even started to work for cash (*puli*) for close relatives. She was ashamed of demanding money for her services to close relatives and her sister-in-law, and said that before she used to do it free of charge.

However, Mahry's mother supported her economically with children's clothing, and by bringing her extra rationed goods. Events common to her better-off relatives, such as weddings and family parties (*doreh*), improved her chances of earning money during the summer of 1989. She spent much of her time on household affairs and sewing, a situation that her husband viewed unfavourably, as he thought the heavy work-load made her lose her sense of humour, as well as reducing her time with him. Mahry sometimes sent her son to his grandmother's house for several days, in order to get more time for sewing. The money earned by sewing was often said to be spent on herself, or to meet the social expenses of the family (*barj*) (such as children's clothing). Repaying family visits or meal services, buying gifts for relatives who were getting married or giving birth, welcoming a relative or visiting their new house, were among other social commitments.

Once Mahry wanted to give a family party (*mehmānī*) in honour of her brother and his wife who were visiting Shiraz. At first her husband objected, arguing that such a party was the last thing they could afford. *Mehmānīs* are popular family gatherings where women can mark a special occasion, or honour a relative, and where they can raise support and reclaim social debts. Mahry's husband thought, however, that before staging an expensive family gathering they should first carefully consider their economic situation. He argued this point both in private and in front of other female relatives. To Mahry, however, such a meal service was critical to her reputation *vis-à-vis* her sisters and brothers, who had already done their duties. Financially she was less well-off than her sisters and brothers, but she wanted to be seen as their equal. Mahry thought it necessary to give dinner parties, so as to maintain the culturally expected social relations. To her, as to housewives in general, such a large family party meant extra housework, sometimes taking a few months to prepare, as well as a few days to clear up. It also meant the collective participation of other women. Mahry and her husband argued about such issues, both in private and in the presence of other relatives, asking for further advice. Mahry insisted on arranging the party despite its economic burden. To her, neglected duty meant social isolation, exclusion from the female network, and loss of honour in the eyes of her own relatives. Finally her husband agreed, and they went together to the market to purchase the necessary items.

Mahry's husband decided to move to America or Canada, where his friends were residents. Mahry also planned to leave Iran in a similar manner as her older sister, who had fled to India when the war between Iran and Iraq threatened the central city of Shiraz in 1983. To Mahry, the move from Iran was part of a plan to provide a better future for her two children. I often heard similar views expressed by other Iranian refugee families I interviewed abroad. As an immigrant mother I could share some of her thoughts. However, to move from Iran would mean the loss of her social network, such as her parents and other relatives with whom she met daily.

After I had completed my fieldwork, Mahry and her family, due to their continued economic problems and anxiety regarding the future of their children, left Iran. They went to Senegal and were hoping to be sent to a third country as refugees. Then, due to the high cost requested by the middleman they changed their mind and remained there. Five years later when I visited Iran, Mahry's mother had recently come back from visiting her two daughters abroad. I met her other brothers and sisters during this second period of fieldwork. Mahry's youngest sister had recently graduated from a private university in Iran, but her qualification was not recognised as equal to that of the state university. She was engaged to an engineer, and was planning a marriage ceremony as soon as her fiancé could obtain sufficient funding. They lived separately, as is customary before officially marrying, meeting only in her father's house, or when going out together. The parents were worried, arguing that such a contact cannot be continued indefinitely, and that soon a marriage ceremony should be arranged. Having graduated from a private university, she faced a job discrimination, as she could not pass the Islamic test requested for all state employees.

Summing up

The life history of Mahry's family reveals an integrative chain of the social, economic and political in everyday life. Mahry's life history illuminates a typical development of the middle-class and young urban families that I met at home in Iran, and those young, semi-educated refugees that I interviewed abroad in my earlier studies. She and her younger married sister have increasingly become economically dependent on their parents, finding themselves in tight economic and social conditions, despite their working husbands and their relatively high education. This has added a new burden to their middle-class parents, whose business and source of income has been affected by inflation and the constant increase of prices. As in the Iran of the 1970s, when social and economic enterprise in the larger city was a route for higher social and economic mobility, contemporary Iran is not able to fulfil the rising expectations of the middle-class population in the cities. Political pressure and social insecurity made many families think twice about staying, some leaving home before the insecure political situation could hinder their departure. Islamic knowledge remained an important criterion for job interviews and university entrance examinations in the education and job sector. Those with poor Islamic knowledge were subsequently at risk of being prejudiced. Such a flow of interest among school and university students to learn Islamic science, was confirmed by a preacher acting as a Qu'rānic teacher both in school and in private homes. Mahry's sister also started learning the Qur'ān because of job application requirements. She hoped to become fluent in reading the Qur'ān.

Life of lower- and middle-class families

The economic crises of the Islamic state and the new ideological demands have incurred cumulative and overlapping perspectives. This has left a narrow range of options for young and ambitious couples, forcing them to seek opportunities outside the home country, as exemplified by Mahry's extended family.

Marriage and higher education has traditionally served as a passage for social and economic independence, although it has often been the case that newly-weds stay in the house of the wife's or husband's father for a while, before establishing an independent household. For ten years Halimeh, a 44-year-old female school teacher, shared a residence with her sister-in-law before she and her husband could save enough money to buy one of the two-room flats offered to school employees. Marriage has always been an economic security for the wife, and the husband is traditionally responsible for the economic security of the family.

The reality of the current socio-economic situation for the average lower- and middle-class category, is such that extra economic support is necessary, either from the wife – particularly in the case of young married couples – or from parents. The wife, as in the case of Mahry, was involved in home waged work, thus bringing her family some extra money. Even her university-educated sister chose home wage labour, by doing some computer work for her fiancé's employer. To these young families living costs were reduced by remaining part of extended households, and their income rose by the wife taking home waged work.

A young family's economic independence and higher social status, such as in the case of Mahry and her siblings, depends upon occupation and further education. Mahry and her family had less chance of obtaining higher education because of the increased number of applicants,[111] and also because of new Islamic ideological criteria for the selection of religiously active candidates. A new mode of adaptation, and a new economic niche, has emerged for family members who are able to take on additional roles. As a result of constant price increases on household goods, the consequences of these economic niches have affected males and females differently.

Managing the household economy is difficult in lower- and middle-class families, even when the breadwinner (often the man), has previous work experience, or higher education.[112] Families are dependent on a single income from employment in the public sector, such as teacher or office work jobs.

[111]The number of applicants to Iranian universities and colleges was 500,000 in 1988 and 700,000 in 1989 and of these, 40–50,000 passed the entrance exams. Approximately 20 per cent of the places are reserved for family members of martyrs and voluntary soldiers (*basīj*) of the war.

[112]As in many of the middle-class and lower-class family members I met.

Parents as main supporter

Grown-up children, despite their higher education, are economically dependent on their parents, as in the case of my religious companion's son, who returned home from abroad during the Iranian revolution in 1978. This dependency may be permanent for some, thus placing a burden on the parents.[113]

In post-revolutionary Iran, large numbers of urban middle- and higher-class Iranians left home. According to my random inquiries in 30 extended families, each had at least one adult member between the ages of 18 and 40 resident abroad. However, two distinctive, significant and completely new household structures emerged in post-revolutionary Iran. These were: (a) the extended household composed of parents and married children who shared a residence, and (b) the households consisting of elderly couples who remained in Iran, while their children left home and took permanent residence abroad. The former household composition is common among families where a majority of the members stayed in Iran, and only a few moved abroad. The latter household composition consisted of elderly couples who voluntarily lived alone at home, visiting their children only once in a while abroad. These are often better-off couples, contrasting dramatically with the lower- and middle-class extended household, where parents accommodate a married daughter or son and their families. Of the 30 young middle-class families with whom I had close contact, only a few of the couples, who had been married for 10–15 years, lived in their own homes. Those who lived on their own had either inherited their homes following the death of their parents; or had prior to 1980 purchased a small plot of land or a flat from the former state housing project, when special low-interest mortgages were available for government employees.

To maintain the economy of daily life many young educated men started a business of their own, or with another male relatives. The inevitable solution for lower- and middle-class families was to have two members of the family in employment. Alternatively the breadwinner of the family would take two jobs, one in the official sector and another in the private sector. In the case

[113]In many cases I met young refugee families who expressed a feeling of not having had the opportunity to maintain their own families, and of being a burden to their parents when living in Iran.

of Mahry, close and distant male relatives were employed as civil servants, teachers, low-ranking army officers, social health personnel, etc. Due to the high cost of living they worked in their spare time as independent taxi drivers, as salesmen buying and selling land, as dealers in foreign currencies or rationed goods, or as shop assistants. In comparison women were either housewives or, as is the case among a few middle-aged women, they were employed as nursery teachers, computer assistants, students, social health workers or, like Mahry, they worked with sewing and embroidery.

Most of the young families in the community of my research either rented rooms that cost them half of their salary as state employees, or they shared a residence with their parents or a close relative in order to save money. Many were also dependent on others for economic support, directly or indirectly, in the form of cash, household subsistence, and goods. Such socio-economic insecurity, along with the poor educational opportunities for themselves and the problems facing their children, as well as the general political harassment, has led many of these middle-class families to join the flow of migrants of the 1980s.

Housework intensity

Household work is not only a distinctive personalised domain, but is also a part of the larger economic and post-revolutionary ideological development, as well as being a locus of change. Domestic work in post-revolutionary Iran involved a series of new tasks and more intensive work schedules for women. Adaptability of household members to changing conditions depended on the availability of facilities and resources. A married woman explained that due to the intensive work schedule and, for example, the lack of communal facilities, she had to do the laundry at night when water was more easily available, and the shopping before sunrise so as to be able to prepare the midday meal for the family. This example illustrates how the mode of work among women mainly concerned with 'domestic' tasks has intensified due to broader political and economic conditions.

One could hardly escape the daily observation of lower- and middle-class women (often mothers), accompanied by small children, waiting impatiently for several hours in queues, in order to purchase hygienic supplies of milk,[114] foods, and other 'domestic' items, at a more reasonable price than in the open market. Commonly they were worried about the daily household routines; for example, one waiting in such a queue told me how worried she was at being delayed in preparing the noon meal for her husband and children coming home from work and school.

Foreign goods, such as electrical appliances, were very expensive and considered as luxury items by lower middle-class families. Moreover, these items provided a new form of enterprise for well-off families. My religious companion Shazdeh and her businessman husband made regular visits to foreign countries for *ziārat*, for holidays or for visiting their children, and when returning they brought foreign goods to sell in the home market. Being able to sell foreign goods in the home market greatly boosted the income of such well-off families.

The extended household has to some extent solved the problem of married children who are not able to establish an independent household without economic support from their parents. High prices of household equipment and house rent made it impossible for young families with average economic means to establish an economically independent household. However, such an intensive relation and extended household dependency has increased family conflicts dramatically, particularly in already controversial relationships such as between daughter-in-law and mother-in-law.

Open market and petty trading

Career options are limited for young members of lower-class families. Petty trading seems to be an acceptable strategy for boys. Wheeler-dealers (*dast-forosh*), and street vendors (*shoghl-e āzād*), are two forms of economic activity adopted by recent school-leavers. *Bazar-e azād* activity has opened a series of channels through which household items rationed by the state flow into the black market. Such enterprises, and the extra income earned, are often considered insecure, illegal, not quite respectable and even immoral. Middlemen, such as wheeler-dealers,

[114] The milk ration for each child was two boxes of milk powder weekly and two bottles of fresh milk daily in 1989.

after spending long hours in queues, buying goods such as cigarettes and eggs from the co-operatives shops, and then selling them at black-market prices. This type of occupation may serve as a source of income for young and middle-aged male members of low-income families.

For families with low incomes, daily petty trading is not a permanent enterprise. Self-employment yields more income than a low-paid permanent job (*rasmī*). Establishing a business requires both economic and social capital, without which it is difficult to obtain goods to sell, or to rent a shop. When renting a shop a deposit is paid. The price has increased with inflation from around 50 thousand tomans in 1979 to an average of one million tomans in 1990.[115] This means that it is virtually impossible to establish a permanent business. It also means that large profits can be made from letting shops, houses, flats and rooms. Those who have parents with a large capital may set up a small business. Alternatively, while the father is still alive, they will be allowed to enter the family business as part of their eventual inheritance.

The street-corner traders (*dast-forosh*) sell items such as dollars, cigarettes, rationed foods, and stockings. *Dast-forosh* is an enterprise open to even those with little capital, and is often a second source of income for individuals such as a grown-up son, or a head of a household. Any form of self-employment (*shoghl-e āzād*) to supplement the limited household income, is justified on the grounds that multiple sources of income are necessary. Since a single-income job in the public sector cannot meet all of the household's real expenditures, the idea of a second job (*kar-e āzād*) has become widely accepted. Resourceful entrepreneurs will be able to provide for family consumption, as well as accumulate considerable wealth.

In contrast, permanent business activities are generally open only to better-off middle-class merchants and craftsmen, and other traditionally independent producers and distributors. These are often co-operative family businesses jointly owned by close male relatives, such as a father and his sons, brothers, cousins and in-laws. This contrasts with the petty trader who sets up his business independently. Recently, because of restrictions, male shopkeepers are forbidden to sell female lingerie, or

[115]For shops not situated in the best market area.

to open female hair-dressing salons. As a consequence, female shopkeepers and co-partnership with a female relative has increased.

The open market makes non-rationed items available to the public, such as electrical appliances, clothing, and domestic goods, as well as scarce medicines. The scarcity and long queues have forced many people to purchase items in the black market. My religious companion, Nezhat, told me that when she could not find blood pressure tablets for her elderly husband in the town pharmacies, she could go to the black market. In the old bāzār in the crowded part of the city she would find a boy selling them, hiding the tablets under the cushion of his chair, and showing them only to his customers. Moreover, basic commodities such as rice, meat, vegetables, beans, oil, sugar cubes, tea, and sugar, are rationed by coupons, and the supplies were limited in 1989. In 1994 many of these basic goods existed only in open markets. Furthermore, the goods in high demand were available only two or three times a year, and then only in small quantities. Thus people relied upon the free market for staples as well.

The rise in prices of local commodities may be explained by: (a) the government extra export policy for earning foreign currencies; (b) the rise in the exchange rate for dollars; and (c) the two devaluations of the rial (see also Behdad 1988). Devaluation of Iranian currency has been of particular importance for the family household economy, since family incomes are in the form of rials. Subsequently they are the hardest hit by inflation, exchange rates, and the black market policy of the state.

Broad structural and economical changes, such as the rationing system for the distribution of goods, has encouraged the development of a new transactional pseudo-occupation niche. Some of these new enterprises are considered immoral, in terms of their transactional and insecure nature. Self-employment and free-enterprise activities are considered to offer greater opportunities for meeting the daily increases of expenditures. Government employees, who are particularly well educated, and with fixed low wages, have become very disappointed with the monthly income of their permanent jobs. It is not adequate to cover their household expenses, such as rent. The difference in the earnings of these well-qualified government employees, and those whose main source of income is selling dollars in the black market, has marginalised the former category both socially and economically.

Wages for average civil servants and employees in official sectors, such as education, have remained relatively the same as they were before the revolution. According to a study by Behdad (1989), in 1980 there had been an increase in the official minimum wage and a change in the rate of income tax to 12 per cent. This corresponds to my own data of 1994, where a teacher told me about the rise of her wages of a few thousands tomans. Most workers were affected by the new law stipulating minimum wages, the exception being urban workers in large firms. It must be keep in mind that family economic viability in post-revolutionary Iran is a problem for most government employees, hence the interest in free business and double waged jobs.

The most profitable enterprises involve trading in foreign currencies and goods, such as dollars, pounds, gold, household items and land, and money lending (*nozol-khor*). Thus, the families that had invested capital in such commodities as land, houses, cars, gold, shops, etc. prior to the outbreak of the war between Iran and Iraq in 1980 are now in an advantageous position. Expansion of the black market has further benefited those who have access to foreign currencies, imported goods, and are able to travel abroad frequently.

Households and families with more capital: economic mobility

The 37-year-old son of my religious companion Shazdeh returned to Iran with his family (wife 35 years old and son) in 1979. Both husband and wife have a masters degree, the former being qualified as an engineer, while the latter graduated as a political scientist from a university in Iran before the 1979 Iranian revolution. She neither continued her studies, nor made use of her qualification during her stay in England, due to the family's poor economic situation.

When they returned to Iran, the husband found a job as a manager of a small textile factory in Tehran, where they stayed for three years. However, following their return from England, his father had continually supported them economically by sending them cash and household goods. Political pressures at his workplace, as well as household economic pressures, forced him to leave his job. Subsequently he joined his father's business in Shiraz. In Shiraz he and his family stayed with his parents and received one fifth of the total income of his father's business.

After a few years he reluctantly accepted that his higher education was no longer a viable channel for social and economic mobility.

This family had a high rate of migration. Their economic and social position had risen from lower middle class to upper middle class over the last three decades. The educated son was the first member to travel abroad to get an education (in 1977). Following his return, his two brothers aged 30 and 22, as well as his two sisters aged 25 and 33, left Iran. Three of them had obtained refugee status and are residents abroad, and the fourth went to a Gulf state. First the older sister left Iran to join her husband's sister abroad, then the youngest brother and sister joined her in 1990. The third brother left for the Gulf states to start a business as an employee of a native resident. His business was to buy goods in the Gulf state and sell them in the local market in Shiraz.

The economic prospect for the foreign-educated son has improved since he started at his father's business. He was soon able to buy a house and lead a more desirable lifestyle. The stories of successful persons and enterprises reveal some essential features of the leading economic system. The high income from the exchange of foreign goods and currencies easily outshadowed even the highest incomes in the official sectors. Profit was also associated with free market transaction of properties.

Land transaction

Land ownership has always been an important source of local identity and power in Iran. After the revolution, long-term investment in land has more than ever become an important form of capital, as well as a strategy for rapidly accumulating wealth. The dramatic rise in land prices since 1980 has applied even to the purchase of the isolated land outside the city limit (*kharej āz mahdodeh*), which is not even supplied with electricity and water. An example of rapid social mobility through land ownership is the case of an educated civil engineer. He qualified in England in the 1970s. He and his family returned to Iran shortly after the Iranian revolution in 1980. He started to work for his former employer, where he had previously been employed in a junior position. Due to his high foreign qualification he was soon offered jobs in different cities, including one in a province where he received high wages due to the difficult geographical conditions. Shortly after he returned home from England he bought a piece of land at a low price. The land was on the non-residential periphery of a town without electricity and water supplies. It cost him 60 tomans per square metre in 1980. However, inflation increased its value to 5,000/6,000 tomans per square metre in 1989.

In the long term ownership of land is highly beneficial, the rapid increase in value making it a secure investment. The demand for land has particularly increased as a result of demographic changes. These can be explained as follows: (a) rapid population growth;[116] (b) the continuous migration from small towns and nearby villages to large towns.[117] The rapid expansion of towns toward the city limits increased the value of cheap and isolated land from 20–60 tomans per square metre in 1979, to 6,000 tomans per square metre in 1989–90. Such land could not, however, be used for building a house until it had been included within the town's official boundaries.[118] The profit from land ownership was greater than from the ownership of fruit gardens, the latter providing only a small annual income for urban middle-class and business families. This was the common enterprise that led to the serious destruction of the famous orchard land in Shiraz. The grape and apple farms changed into building sites, thereby bringing a high profit to their owners. It would be interesting to evaluate the impact on agricultural production.

Land confiscated during the revolution has been sold cheap to religio-politically privileged community members, such as war veterans (*razmandegān*), employees of the Islamic institution for rehabilitation (*Jihād-e Sāzandegī*), and to families of martyrs or hostages. In recent years government supporters have been favoured for the redistribution of economic and social opportunities, such as obtaining employment, education, rationed goods and land. Special allocations (*sahmyeh*) have been given as the rewards for their support.[119] Thus, economic advancement has been possible not only for those who have accumulated capital under the former regime, but also for those who have gained

[116]The population growth rate is 3.55 per cent annually in 1988.
[117]C.f. Hooglund 1982; Paydarfar 1974.
[118]If a house is built without permission one may risk its demolition.
[119]For more on Islamic education policy see Habibi 1989.

high status as first-class citizens in the Islamic regime, whatever their class background may have been.

Gold as gifts to brides

Gifts of gold signify sets of kinship relations and are part of large chains of acts distinguishing close relatives, high-ranking guests and close friends. The value of gold is both an objective and a subjective cultural phenomenon, and concerns the relations between people on various levels. Soon after arriving in Shiraz I was invited to the wedding of one of my sisters-in-law. I thought that since I was in Iran on 'work', I had an adequate excuse, and would not be expected to offer an expensive gift. Later someone told me that it would have been wise to bring some electrical appliances with me. As the ritual of *aqad* proceeded my mother-in-law, who had noticed my anxiety, and apparently felt that the honour of her daughter and her absent son was at stake, brought a gold necklace and put it in the palm of my hand. I was suprised by this act. However, when the time came to give gifts to the bride, I felt very relaxed at having something respectable to offer. The gift of the necklace was announced in my name, and its honour went to my husband's parents.

Gold has always been associated with prestige and high status and is often exchanged as valuable gifts among Iranians. There is a strong tendency for women to own some gold, receiving and giving in accordance with expectations. The saving and management roles women play within the family in this context is considered to be related to their orientation toward the future. Gold functions for women both as prestigious ornaments (*zinat*), and as a status symbol. Gifts of gold signify a 'proper' bride and provide capital for the family and her husband.

While purchasing land has remained the principal investment and economic transaction for men, gold has played a similar role for women. The constant rise in the value of gold, along with inflation, has meant that its importance not only as solid capital, but also as a status symbol, has grown. I was not surprised to hear that the preacher repeatedly discouraged her female listeners from wearing ornaments, a practice that was believed to misrepresent Islam and Muslims. Such a luxury was believed to be the root of jealousy and conflicts among families.

I was accompanied by female friends and relatives on my frequent evening walk to the commercial part of the city, in order to spend some time studying the prices of bracelets, necklaces and rings. The most popular and busiest city streets were those where shops selling gold and clothes were located next to each other in large numbers. I was also tempted to see how much money I would get for my own gold bracelet, which I had bought a few years ago. In this regard, middle-class women are acting as entrepreneurs, following daily changes in gold prices until the market is favourable for purchasing or selling.

The common strategy is to buy as many articles of gold as possible when the prices are low, and then sell or exchange these items when the prices have gone up. My close female relatives considered it unwise to sell my gold articles for cash, unless it was absolutely necessary. Accumulation of gold is considered a wise policy, both from the point of view of the individual and the family.

Gold is a significant gift requested by the bride. The amount to be received is often agreed upon at the time of engagement. Gold jewellery, or a number of gold coins, may be agreed upon as being a part of, or the entire *mahryeh*. The increasing tendency among middle-class brides to have *mahryeh* in gold coins than rials is because gold is more stable in price and more likely to rise in value than fall.

I attended four marriage ceremonies of my close and distant relatives in 1989, and was invited to another one in 1994. They were all arranged before or after the two months of Muharam and Safar, which the Shiī Iranians consider as months of prayers and sorrow, rather than celebrating. At the marriage ceremony the bride's mother and father, and the groom's parents and sisters, are among the immediate kin who may present gifts of gold to the bride, such as, for example, a pair of bracelets, earrings, or a necklace. The bride received gifts of gold while seated on the wedding cloth (*sofreh-aqad*). The quantity of gold received as wedding presents depends on how wealthy the relatives are, and the number of guests. Such gifts may also be given on other significant occasions, such as at the birth of a child, during the first pregnancy, upon obtaining a higher degree, or on the Iranian New Year (*noruz*) in March.

A lesson of mother to married daughter

The young married women were considered inexperienced, and were constantly advised by their mothers and sisters about future relations with their husbands and their families. Planning a secure future, I often heard the mothers advising their daughters to buy gold instead of toys and decorative items, and to be concerned about the future. Such issues have become important lessons given by mothers to their married daughters.

The importance of the gift of gold as capital is revealed at times of family crises. It is increasingly common for married women to give their savings to their desperate husbands to start a business or purchase property. Such a form of economic support brings extra recognition and respectability for the wife. The husband is often willing in return to register part, or whole, of the purchased property in her name.

On one occasion Farideh, a 30-year-old married housewife, proudly exclaimed how she sold all of her wedding jewellery and the children's gold to give 100,000 tomans to her husband, so he could purchase a piece of land that was especially offered to him at his place of work. Her husband in return registered the land in her name.

Another situation in which a woman's gold reserves may be vitally important to the whole family is exemplified by Mahtab, an elderly mother with a family of ten, who was forced to seek shelter in Shiraz during the Iraqi bombardment of Abadan in 1981. The only property they could bring with them was her gold (one kilogram). Soon she decided to sell it, despite the market rate being low, because she considered it was important to provide the necessary clothing and accommodation for her daughters, and to protect the family. The only thing she had been reluctant to sell was a ring that had once belonged to her mother.

A third example is that of a 55-year-old woman, who sold all of her gold jewellery and borrowed money from her oldest daughter, in order to visit two of her children living in Norway. To her the value of the visit was worth more than her gold. She thought, what would be the use of saving when she might never again have the chance to see her children and grandchildren? The distance, and the high cost of the journey, signified the importance of the visit and, and as she put it, 'it may be the only chance in my lifetime'. She had to insist on the importance of such a visit, since her old husband thought that it was more important to take care of the house, and was thus reluctant to give her any financial support. Finally she alone provided the money for her journey to visit her children. She frequently talked about this as an event to gain respect.

A fourth example is that of a couple educated abroad, who had recently returned home and needed to pay for the transport of their household goods from Germany to Iran. The wife, Shahla, decided to sell her own gold, as well as her daughter's, to pay the required sum. She considered the household items to be of equal value to the gold since these were enormously expensive and scarce in Iran. Her mother, Mahtab, proudly returned to this case, telling others how her daughter managed her family life, thus presenting her daughter as a good wife to a good husband.

Contributions to the family economy in times of crises will allow the wife to emphasise her honourable identity and enable her to negotiate with her husband. The latter may, as noted, often agree to reward his supportive wife by registering some property in her name. I came across several cases in which wives of educated middle-class and better-off businessmen had convinced their husband to register at least some of their properties – such as the house or a piece of land – in their name. Shazdeh, my religious companion, was among the lucky ones. This is a strategic role played by wives to gain influence *vis-à-vis* the husband. Such negotiations and sharing of property tends to change some of the static Islamic norms; for example, norms stipulating that only 20 per cent of the husband's property is the legitimate right of the wife.[120]

Some women insist on keeping some of the gifts of gold received through their own lineage by transferring it to their daughters or daughters-in-law, or to their mother's lineage (sister's daughter). Such a form of gold exchange signifies sets of kinship relations in which the wife competes with the husband's for support. Thus women often adopt far-sighted

[120]See also Fischer 1979; Motaheri, M. (1981) 'The Problems of Inheritance', in *The Order of Women's Rights in Islam (nezām-e-hoqoq-zan-dar-eslām)*, Sahāmi-ām press, Tehran, pp. 217–25; Khomeni, M. (1987) *The Economic Problems – Collection of Essays* (*masā'el-e eqtesādī*), translation by Shirazi, 'abdol Karim, The Islamic Culture Press, Tehran.

perspectives on the value of gold, a view that their husbands may not necessarily share, but from which they often benefit.

Inflation and dowry

Dowry and *mahr* are two important and integral parts of the Iranian marriage contract. Dowry consist of household goods that the bride will bring to her husband's house. *Mahr* is a sum of money or valuable items such as gold and land that the husband pledges to pay the bride upon marriage. This amount will be written as a legal document for the bride's security, and may become a legal debt upon the bride's request. These two forms of payment play important roles in the dynamics of the marital relation, giving a woman a high degree of security and also a deterrent for a divorce. It is generally assumed that the larger the dowry (i.e. consisting of kitchen utensils, carpets, bedroom furniture, etc.), the greater is the respect shown to the daughter and, thus, the greater is the prestige gained in the eyes of the husband's female relatives.

Due to the open market prices of dowry items people purchase presents through the newly established Islamic state marriage institution (*bonyād-e ezdevāj*), which offers a few items for those newly wed. These might include items such as a stove, a machine-made carpet, and an oil heater. Two or three items were sold to each newly married couple in 1989.

The better the daughter's education, job and appearance, the less pressure is placed on the parents to provide an expensive dowry (*jāhāzyeh*). This point of view was expressed by at least ten of the working women in my study, aged between 30–45, including 4 teachers (1 nursery, 2 school, 1 university), 3 hairdressers, 1 social worker, 1 accountant, 1 office worker. Of these two had resigned, one of whom was Narges (my religious companion's daughter), a 40-year-old woman and former accountant, the other being a teacher who had several times taken leave to avoid the political stress associated with her working conditions. Working women have often purchased household goods either through the co-operative institution where they worked, or when such goods were available at a special price. Six of them had been working before marriage. As part of their dowry (*jāhāziyeh*) they brought these goods to their husband's house without putting economic pressure on their parents. The average parent, with several marriageable children, may find themselves in serious economic difficulties, unable to provide a dowry for their daughters. However, some parents, in order to reduce these expectations, will give a little dowry to the daughter and in return agree for a simple wedding party and a smaller gift of gold.

In order to reduce the expenses of the groom a one-day celebration for the two phases of the wedding is the most usual form of marriage. The first phase of the wedding party starts with the *aqad* ceremony, in which the Muslim marriage contract will be written. At that time the close relatives of the bride and the groom are invited, and a warm meal will be served at the expense of the bride's family. In the afternoon the second phase of the celebration, known as the wedding party (*arosī*), will be held. Then dinner will be served to a large number of guests, including distant relatives, friends and close neighbours. This part will be held at the expense of the groom.[121] The wedding marks a recognition of the Muslim marriage contract. It is seldom the case that a bride moves to live with her husband before the second phase of the marriage celebration.

Devaluation of the rial brought a series of dramatic changes to families and the household economy. The reduced value of rials provided grounds for parents of brides to request higher *mahr*, to guarantee more security for women at the time of divorce. The average *mahr* requested by the bride's family increased from a few hundred thousands before the revolution, to 3 million for the average middle-class family in 1989, and to 10 million in 1994. Knowing the existence of such a threat causes the girl's family to request a higher amount of *mahr*.

The more educated the bride is, the less *mahr* is requested. The most extreme case I know of was that of a divorced nurse, Shohreh, who married before the revolution and divorced a few years later. I came in contact with her through my family, and took part in several of the religious meetings she had at her home. She was from a moderately religious family. When she married she had recently graduated from nursing school. She thought there was no need to make a traditional request on the

[121]The groom, or his father, will pay for the wedding party, including the wedding dress (bought or rented), the hairdressers, filming, dinner, sweets, drinks, and a gift of jewellery.

groom. Thus, the only thing she requested for *mahr* was a copy of the Qur'ān. She considered this to be a generous demand at the time. She regretted this later when she entered into a conflict with her husband and asked him for a divorce. She got her divorce without any payment from her ex-husband, but received custody of her daughters, who were only a few years old. Such demands are often made in the process of marriage negotiations.

In the past, the *mahr* was so low that initiating a divorce today has been easy for some husbands, being only a matter of paying an insignificant amount of cash to the wife. The predicament of a woman facing divorce due to low *mahr*, can be illustrated in the case of Narges. In 1970, when she married, her *mahr* was 100,000 tomans (a high sum at that time). When she divorced in 1989 the average *mahr* was 3–5 million tomans among the better educated and well-off families. Her husband thought it was an easy matter simply to give her the total amount of 100,000 tomans in cash, thus fulfilling the sole legal condition for a restricted third-degree divorce (*seh-talāgheh*).[122] For the husband this equalled the price of a pair of car tyres. The high amount of *mahr* today makes it impossible for husbands to pay it to their wives in case of divorce. However, to women the sum is more a matter of status, providing them with more power and ability to negotiate with the husband in case of divorce. Family insecurity and the increasing number of divorces on one hand, and the continuous devaluation of rials on the other, induces parents to increase their demands of *mahr*, thus hoping to guarantee greater security for their daughters in marriage.

Conclusion

I have outlined a series of economic and social transformations in the composition of middle-class households, as well as the economic adaptation of families in the context of micro life and the macro political and economic reforms in Islamic Iran. I will conclude on the following points. First, the revolutionary pro-

[122]The law of *talāgh* applies in three different degrees: first degree (*yek-talāgheh*) and second degree (*do-talāgheh*) allow a couple two and one more chance respectively to resume the marriage. The third degree (*seh-talāgheh*) leaves no chance of resuming the marriage, unless the wife first marry another man (either in a real marriage or as a formality, recruiting a man to act as *mohalel* (mediator husband)). Then after a divorce, she may remarry her ex-husband.

gramme proclaimed in 1979, which included the protection of the interests of suppressed social categories such as villagers, women, youths, urban poor, the working class and civil servants, was a failure. The central objectivities of the new form of family investment and enterprise, the irresistible socio-economic forces, and the upward economic mobility, occurred only among higher middle-class and business families. The families which had invested capital in land, houses, cars, gold, shops, etc., prior to the outbreak of the war between Iran and Iraq in 1980 were able to sustain their pre-revolutionary position. The families of militant Iranian Muslims were among those who were promoted into state functional and administrative positions, and thus remained part of a centralised state position.

Second, the increased investments in people's substantive resources, such as accommodation, food, medicine, household goods, private schools and universities, were a product of free-market conditions that became manifest in the household economy. On the way toward a free-market economy the Islamic moral economy of low interest rates, as well as sanctions on hoarding and equal distribution of welfare undermined the programme of restructuring the domestic economy.

Third, post-revolutionary socio-economic necessities have made women an important part of the labour force and the public sphere. This continues, despite Islamist trends (Keddie 1991:19). It is important not simply to confine the analysis of women and family to the functioning of the 'domestic sphere'. The economical and ideological situation of the Islamic state subvert the family economy, as well as the traditional role of women in the organisation and production of the family economy.

ELEVEN

CONCLUSION: WOMEN, ISLAM AND RITUAL

This study has represented Shirazi women's religious accounts, ritual performance, and Islamic revivalism. My main message is that the religious participation of these women is far from being marginal or muted. I argue that the Iranian Muslim women carry a religious load, that they have a religious 'work' to do, and that they are even more involved in religious and socio-ritual activity than the average male family member. In the different chapters I have tried to show women's modes of religious participation and their activity across religious, family, social and political spheres. Among my central issues have been: (1) how can we recognise women's mode of Islamic knowledge; (2) how can we better understand Muslim women's ritual exchanges and nature of morality; and (3) how can we come to grips with the contemporary rise of female Islamic identity, its pragmatic and ideological aspects as well as theoretical?

The religious arenas – *rowżeh* meetings, shrines, schools and mosques – have neither traditionally nor in the context of the contemporary Islamic revivalism hampered women's active participation as religious followers and as experts, but rather encouraged it. There is some disagreement and debate among the Iranian Islamic authorities on public female religious leadership with reference to the rules of *sharī'a*. The interpretation of Islam and its everyday practice generate discourses and also conflicts among social categories and between the Islamic state and society. The current political Islam produces a distinctive political culture of privileged and authoritarian categories with concomitant social and economic consequences. But this does not mean that women lack full participation in contemporary

Islam or that their religious activity has been merely a 'muted' voice, to use Ardener's term (1971).

Women may act as initiators, sponsors, assistants and participants with the aim to acquire benefits in this life or in after-life. Arranging a 'proper' ritual displays women's ability in using the traditional knowledge acquired through experiences within their local networks. Women have constructed cultural activities where important social issues and values are dealt with. The religious ritual is the forum in which women display spiritual orientations, personal engagement and concern for their authoritative role in the family.

In my view, the classical anthropological model of women's roles in Muslim societies denies them religious and political consciousness. As the Iranian case suggests, the state's expansion of religious education is more than merely a means of ideological control over the populace. Women do not act as a homogeneous category with unified political and Islamic objectives. One display of religious differences is in women's veiling, signalling not only cultural pride but also factions and counter-ideologies in religious discourse. The discourse of 'correct' and 'incorrect' Islamic veiling, as symbolised through the covering garments and women's bodily movements, carry connotations of importance for the implementing of official and unofficial views. At the same time, the notion of women's modesty and veiling represents a condensation of symbols and a religious multivocality.

In the introduction, I suggested that the study of Muslim women in general, and Iranian women in particular, often sidesteps the ways Islam provides meaning for women. Islam has by and large been studied as if it is predominantly a male culture; this is often the case in the ethnography of the Middle East (Fischer 1980, Thaiss 1978, Antoun 1989, to mention only a few), or presented in sociology as being mainly a constraint for women (Afshar 1982, Mernissi 1975). Islam has often been presented as a mode of repressing Muslim women, as a conservative force rather than a system of differentiated meanings and ideas with an activating and expanding potential also for women. The usual tendency in the literature has been to treat women as passive objects rather than as subjects actively involved in the movements of Islamic renewal.

As an example, the study of Qur'ānic lessons for girls has emphasised the role of male Islamic experts as the source of women's religious learning and knowledge. Some interesting observations of the range of Iranian women's religious activity have emerged in the work of female ethnographers (Betteridge 1983, Hegland 1983), but the accounts have considered the pre-Islamic state context only.

Muslim women use their family networks, as well as the networks created through religious meetings and local Islamic events, to advance their household economy and achieve spiritual and social goals. Women participate actively in the religious events of the Shi'ī Islamic calendar by activating their networks through family, friends and kin. Individually or as members of families, they circulate in a series of relations linking family – vows – religious duty – ritual exchanges – blessing – morality.

The religious life of women in this study is practice, culture and ideology displaying aspects of power and privilege (Keesing 1987). The wide range of their religious activities represent occasions for practising Islam, for acquiring and propagating Islamic knowledge. Women's practice and organisation of Islam should be viewed as important for two reasons. First as an *Islamic mode of representation* relating to the symbolic development of Islam in Iran. The ritual performances can be seen as the process by which new meaning is produced. I have emphasised how women's religious meetings and rituals are connected to day-to-day political changes, and I have particularly focused on the politicisation of rituals and emergence of 'Islamist women'. In order to understand how a dominant Islamic ideology functions, one needs to examine how ideological beliefs and perspective operates at the everyday level. Women's Islamic rituals are in different degrees associated to the pragmatic interest of political and Islamic authorities. Although the female religious meetings may not have changed in their elementary forms, there has been a clear change in the way these meetings have adopted ideas from current daily life. They have also changed in their functional capacity, in the sense that a large number of various social categories have become involved.

Second, women's Islamic rituals and practices should be viewed as a *mode of education* of a distinct mosque organisation with a particular religious experience. It includes a specific socialisation process in terms of Islamic education, moral order, daily and ritual practice and active mosque participation. Islamic Republic policy has resulted in the transformation and spread of religious knowledge through compulsory education at school, popular media, local, family religious events and Qur'ānic seminaries. The state has developed a series of formal and informal practices to include 'Islamic' women in the process of Islamic nationalism, by favouring access to resources for 'true' Muslim citizens. This has influenced the language of young female university graduates and religious students. It has also brought public recognition for the previously marginalised female ritual experts and Qur'ānic teachers, as knowledge of the Qur'ān today lies not only in recitation, but emphasises its interpretation and exegesis.

Thus, it is misleading to portray the religious beliefs of women as pre-Islamic, peripheral cults or belonging outside the structure of the 'valid' or standard Islam. As exemplified in studies with observations limited to spirit possession in Muslim societies (e.g. Lewis 1971), the religious life of women is often understood as countermodels or a response to hegemonic praxis and male ideology. We must recognise the 'Islamicity' of Muslim women's religious activities and the elements of its change. The religious rituals of today's Iranian women are a powerful mixture of Islamic tradition and existential experience, and they represent creative interpretations of texts and new social identities. A consideration of the religious role of women is vital for any analysis of how Iranian women maintain their sense of traditional and modern Islamic identity under the Islamic state.

In contemporary Muslim societies such as Iran, learning and knowing Islam are mass educational issues. The local Islamic events are important channels for the communication and transformation of traditional Islamic knowledge. The ideas of Islamic intellectuals and thinkers, and the textual tradition itself, are being adapted to practical and popular ways of thinking as well as for the school curriculum.

Today, ways of knowing and learning Islam are beyond the orthodoxy of scriptural knowledge, and also beyond the distinction of popular *vs* elite culture. The sociology of knowledge about Muslim societies of the past was based on assumptions about social divisions like class and generation (Kamalkhani 1992; Mannheim 1952). Today's freer access to Islamic texts across lands and peoples makes possible a considerable social and religious mobility. Contemporary Islamic knowledge is accessible to average citizens through modern communication systems; it intermingles with people's everyday experiences and it represents a particular brand of modernity within religious limits. Beliefs, actions and identity forms associated with Islam are a concern not only to male, but also to female students and intellectuals. Through religious 'work', many women are able to build religious careers and take part in Islamic discourse. This has particularly provided middle-class women with economic and social alternatives across gendered segregation lines.

There is an increasing number of women embracing Islamic orthodoxy and intellectualism. Contemporary Iranian women's orthodoxy is not a reaction against the social and moral order, but is part of a new religious practice and the creation of a new identity model among women. Women have taken advantage of expanded educational opportunities, building on their own informal, customary channels for religious learning. Women have created new spaces for debate about religious and political issues through the negotiation of relevant texts and scriptural traditions. The activity fields of Islamic women leaders also include social welfare and charity work. As women's knowledge of Islamic teaching increases, they are better versed in their general rights and duties as defined in Islam, and men's control of the relevant information can no longer remain exclusive to them.

The higher Islamic knowledge required from all Muslim citizens has especially had the consequence of spreading the right to and the competence of reciting, interpreting and reinterpreting the Islamic texts. This, and other features, like educational requirements for religious students to write theses (*resāleh*) and perform interpretation (*tafsīr*), will provide women with new and definitely authoritative roles. Indeed, the linkage between informal, customary religious learning and formal, state-sanctioned education has not only fortified the anti-imperialist movement among women since the 1978–9 revolution, but has also led to the reproduction of Muslim culture by women who are forging a new religious identity for themselves.

GLOSSARY

In the general use of the following words, I have attempted to preserve the Farsi pronunciation and Shirazi dialect. I used ch for چ , j for ج , gh for ق , h for ح , kh for خ , q for غ , sh for ش , zh for ض , h for ه , s for س , ṣ for ص , t for ة , ṭ for ط , z for ز , yi for ي , u for ع , o , e are used for Farsi short vowels. For long ا , ā and for ا , a and e.

'abā — Arabic type of cloak
āb-e-shafā — the blessed water
abjad — a term from astronomy
abuhamzeh — the chapter of *do'ā* in the book of *mafātieh*
'ādat — custom
adā-nakardan — unpaid debt
'aghideh — faith
ahl-el-byt — household members – in this text refers to the Prophet's household
aḥyā — all-night watch
'aid-e fetr — the feast breaking the fast on the last day of Ramaẓān
ājil-moshkel-goshā — nuts and candies common in ritual vows
ākhirat — the world after death; the after-life
akhūnd — lower-rank priest
al'af — forgiveness
al-ankabud — the spider, a Qur'ānic sūreh
Al-aqṣā — mosque in Jerusalem
'alem — man of knowledge
al-Qadar — Qur'ānic sūreh: 112, verse 3
al-qadr — day of destiny
al-Quds — the new Jerusalem
al-'ūd — a Qur'ānic sūreh
āl-zadeh — one possessed by the supernatural figure of 'āl'
'ām — people without noteworthy religious descent
amdan — on purpose, deliberate

GLOSSARY

ʿāmm	layman
amr-be- mʿarūf	directing others to what is lawful
amvāt	dead people
anām	sūreh Qurʾān: 6
aqad	wedding contract
ʿaqel	wisdom
arosī	wedding
āsh	stew
aṣnāf	shopkeepers
āsoneh	small local shrines where holy persons such as the distant kin to an Imām are buried
āyatollah	highest religious rank, chosen of God
āyeh	short passage from the Qurʾān
ʿazā	grief
ʿazab	unmarried men
ʿazādārī	emotional grief
azhān	call to prayer
az-khud-bī-khud-shodan	being out of oneself
bad-hejāb	poorly veiled
bā-imān	believers
bānī	initiator, sponsor
barakat	blessing, grace, religious power
barj	secondary initiator expenses
balā	unfortune
bandeh	servant
basījī	mobilisation force
bast	asylum in shrines
bāṭel	futile
bāzāreh-āzādor/ bāzareh-seyāh	black market
bāzārī	merchants
bāzār-yābī	accumulating
behesht	paradise
bī-hejāb	non-veiled
boht-zadegi	full shock
boʿż	spite
bonyād-e ezhdevāj	the institute for marriage
bot	idol
chādor	a round-shaped edged piece of cloth which covers the whole body from head to toe, a full-length veil
cheleh	40th day ritual marking a death
cheshm-e-shor	jealous eye
dāʿgh/dāʿgh-dīdeh	suffering from some misfortune
dallāl	go-between
dard-e del	the genre of telling one's troubles
dast forosh	pedlar's jobs

dast-namāz — minor washing before praying, minor ablution

dīn — religion

do'ā — prayer; invocation recited in blessing

doreh — periodical meeting; menstruation

donyavī — worldly

'ebādat — worship

efrāt-va-tafrīṭ — take an extreme course; too much or too little

eftārī — the meal breaking a fast

eghvā — temptation, seductive sexual behaviour

elāḥyāt — religious science

enyakād — verse of the Qur'ān

ershād — guidance

estekhāreh — speculating about one's intention in pursuing some act

eṣrāf — waste

fātaḥ — the blessing of the dead

fatwā — appeal, decision

feqh — Islamic legacy

feṭri-e-yeh — alms payment based on the value of the wheat consumed by the family during the year and paid at the end of the month of fasting

foqarāh — poor

gerogān — prisoner of war

ghaleh/kerayeh — rent

ghara'at — pronunciation

ghom-va khishi — kinsmen and relatives

'ghorbat — exile, land of strangers; any displacement from the natal home

ghorfeh — guest room for pilgrims to the shrine

ghosl — bathing ritual, religious washing, ablutions

golab — rose water

gonāh — sin

ḥadīth — tradition, the sayings of or about the Prophet Muhammad and his companions, one of the four sources of Islamic law

ḥafteh — 7th day ritual marking a death

hājat — wish, hope

hājj-āqā — man who has made the pilgrimage to Mecca

hajj-e-tamatto' — obligatory pilgrimage to Mecca

hajj-e-'mreh — temporary pilgrimage to Mecca

ḥājji-khānum — woman who has made the pilgrimage to Mecca

ḥalāl — approved

halol-masa'leh — solution to problems

ḥalvā — sweet made of sugar, oil and wheat flour

ham-jalese'i — co-participants in a religious meeting

ḥarām — forbidden, illegitimate

hei'at — religious group

hejāb	religious modesty and veiling
ḥeyż	menstruation
ḥezbullāhi	party of God, pro-Iranian state religious conservative
husyneh	halls of mourning and religious education
Ibn al-Monjam	one of the Prophet's friends whom Shi'ī Iranians believe killed Imām Ali at the time of praying
imān	religious faith
imām-e-jom'eh	preacher leading the Friday prayers
jādu	magic
jahannam	hell
jāhāziyeh	dowry; the gift that the bride brings into the marriage
jaleseh	religious meeting
janmāz	praying rug, the place of prayers
Jihād-e Sāzandegī	Construction Holy War/rehabilitation institute
jinn	an invisible creature mentioned in Qur'ān; spirit, literary; called: *az-mā behtarān* (better than a human being)
jira-Bandi	rationing system
Joshan-e kabir	a *do'ā* in the book of *mafātieh,* often read at *aḥyā* meetings
kafanī	winding sheets for the dead, shroud
Karbalā	the town in Iraq where the tomb of Imām Ali is located
khādem	servant of a shrine, or mosque
khāharān-e-Zaynab	(sisters of Hosain's sister Zaynab), the female Islamic police in the post-revolutionary period
khalīf	caliph
khānegāh	the sufi's house
khānom-e-jaleseh	participants at a religious meeting
khānum	ladies, Mrs
khārej-az-maḥdodeh	out of the city limit
kharjī	household wages or expenses paid to a wife
khāsegarī	seeking marriage
khaymeh	tent
khayr	pious
khelāfe- e-e'ffat	breach of modesty, immodest
khejālat-zhadeh	to shame
kheyrāt	goodness; meals offered to the dead; public donations

khobī	friendship
khums	'one-fifth'; the religious tax given to an āyatollāh, traditionally half earmarked for sayyids and half, called *sahm-e Imām* (the Imām's share), for the occulted 12th Imām. In the nineteenth century, the *sahm e-Imām* became an important resource for the clergy in creating a financial base independent of the state[123]
kofr	blasphemous
kumail	a chapter of *do'ā* in the book of *mafātieh*
kupanī	rationed goods
lahn	a stone laid under the head of the deceased
lavāt	incest
lebāseh-kāmel-e-islāmī	the complete Islamic suit
ma'alolīn	handicapped (soldiers)
ma'amorān	the authorities
ma'arefe-islāmi	Islamic science
mafqodīn	those lost (in the war)
mafātieh	book of *do'ā*
mahr / mahryeh	the money or the gold coins (*sekeh*) that the groom agrees to pay to the bride in the case of divorce or separation
maḥram	spouse and close kin with whom one cannot marry and before whom a woman need not veil
maḥżar-dā	a clergyman in charge of the Notary Public's office
makroh	disapproved; something best avoided
maktab	school
mas'aleh	problem
maqām	status
maqn 'eha	pieces of cloth sewn somewhat like a scarf, but with material under the chin to cover the neck; wimple, religious scarf
marja'-e taqlīd	'source of imitation', a supreme Usuli jurist whom the common Shi'ite folk follow
mashā'	undivided, collectively owned land
mazlom	innocent
mehmānī	family gathering
meyyet	corpse
minbar	podium; a high stair on which a preacher or seminary teacher sits
mobārezīn	fighters
mobalegh	missionary
mofasser	commentator
mohabat	affection
mohāfeż	protector

[123]Quoted partly from 'Glossary' in Fischer and Abedi (eds) (1990) *Debating Muslims*, Madison: The University of Wisconsin Press.

mohājerīn	refugees
mohr	the clay of Karbalā
mojizih	miracle
monāfeqin	conspirators, hypocrites
monājāt	conversation with God
mord	myrtle
morīd	followers
morshed	the sufi priest
mostahab	voluntary action, recommended for its merit
mostakbarīn	the rich and powerful
mostażafīn	the poor and powerless, needy people
motodyyen	civilised jurisprudence
muāfeq	to consent
Muharam	mourning month
muḥram	legitimate male relatives, with whom marriage is forbidden
mujtāhed	a person qualified to undertake a legal interpretation (Islamic)
nādel	regret
nafs	passion, temptation
nahi āz-monker	directing others to what is not lawful
nahs	object of misfortune
Najaf	holy Shi'ī town in Iraq
najes	religious terms for impurity
najīb	modest
nakīr	angel that comes after burial
ṇā-maḥram	'illegitimate' male relative, whom a woman could marry
namāz	prayer
nāmeh-a'amāl	record of one's deeds and behaviour
nażar-kardeh	reception of blessedness
nazr	vows
nazr-e-imām	ritual given in memory of the Imām
nazr-kardan	to vow
nefrīn	words wishing someone misfortune
ne 'mat	for God's benefit
nīyat	notion
nī ysān	rain in the month of spring
nodbeḥ	a *do'ā* in the book of *mafātich*
noḥeh	poetic song of grief, lament
noḥeh-khān	male and female religous singers who perform narrative songs and chants
noruz	New Year
nozol-khor	moneylender
omol	social backwardness, outmoded outlook
omol-athār	blessing lineage
punjtan	the five holy ones (Muhammad, Ali, Hasan, Hosain and Fatem-e Zahrā)
pāsdār	Islamic police

pīsh-namāz	the clergy who performs the prayers with others behind her
porseh	visiting the dead
qabr	the grave
qahr	anger
qaṣbī	confiscated, unlawful
qaẓā'	replacement ritual
qebleh/ka'abeh	direction of God's house
qirā'at	pronunciation
qiyāmat	the day of resurrection
qorbān	the day of sacrifice
qurān-khān	professional readers of the Qur'ān
Ramaẓān	the month of fasting
rasmī	permanent
razmandegān	participants in the fighting
re'īs-e jaleseh	female priest in charge of religious meetings
resāleh	book of solution to a problem
rezq	livelihood
rowżeh	religious meeting
rūh	spirit
rūpūsh	suit
rūsarī	scarf
rūz-e-qiyāmat	resurrection day
sadegi	simplicity
ṣadqeh	charitable donation; non-obligatory pious gift; alms
saḥarī	meal to start a fast
sāheb-e 'azā	the 'owner' of sorrow
sahmiyeh	special allocations
sahvan	accidentally
sājdeh	prostration
ṣalvāt	salutations of God upon the Prophet Muhammad and his relatives
sangeh-qaṣāb-khāneh	the place where the ritual washing of corpses takes place
saqā	one who gives water
saqa-khāneh	house of one who gives water
sarāb	deed
sar-bāz	unveiled head
sarqolfī	key-money, deposit
sar-sāl	annual mourning ceremony
ṣavāb	merit
sepah	Islamic police
sevvom	3rd day ritual following a death
seyneh-bāz	unveiled chest
s'yyid, sādāt	Prophet Muhammad's descendants
shabestān	large hall
shab-zendeh-dārī	whole night watch

shafā	curing
shahīd	martyr
shakhsyat	personality, character
Shām	Syria and its capital Damascus
sharī'a	the law of Islam
sheikh	certificated religious student
shekasteh	broken
sherkate-ta'āvonī	co-operative institution
shīrk	polytheism, dualism; blasphemy
shī'i	those who believe that after the Prophet's death leadership should have gone to Ali, the Prophet's son-in-law. The Shi'ites are further divided into groups; the majority in Iran are Twelvers (Ithnā asharī)
shoghl-e āzād	free enterprise, self-employed
shoghl-e kāzheb	false enterprise
shol-zard	a dish prepared from rice, sugar, saffron, almonds and cinnamon
ṣigheh	concubinage
sineh-zanī	flagellation
sūreh	chapter of the Qur'ān
tabarrok	blessed, holiness
tablīgh	proselytising
tābot	coffin
tafsīr	exegesis of Qur'ān
ṭāher	religiously pure
taḥrīm	prohibited by the law of shar'ī
takyeh	a public place where religious meeting such as *chelah* may be held and meals of *nazrī* are distributed
ṭalabīdan	paid attention by imām and saint
tasbīh	prayer beads
tashyīḥ-jenāzeh	funeral
Tāsoah va Ashorā	the days on which the Imām Hysain was stabbed and died
tavāẓ'o	humble
tayamom	alternative ablution; washing with dust or sand
ta'zīeh	passion play
ta-ẓāhor	ostentation
telesm	magic
torbat	'dust' of Karbalā where the prophet Hosain was martyred; is believed by Shi'ite folk to have healing power
tulabe	graduates of the religious school
'ulama	(singular 'alem) religious leaders, clergy
'Umar	believed to be the Prophet's father-in-law, married his daughter Hafsa, the second *khalif* of the Muslims (considered to be an illegitimate successor by Shi'ī Muslims)

vaqār	soberness
vaqf	religious endowment; properties endowed in perpetuity according to provisions of Shi'ī Islamic law for charitable or religious purposes (i.e. maintenance of mosques, shrines, and theological school premises)
vājeb	obligations, duties
vāseteh	middle man
velāyāt-e-faqīh	guardianship by the clergy; the supreme council made up of six theologians
wużū	ablutions
ya-ho	Allāh, God
zakāt	mandatory alms; tax on surplus production and wealth; charity tax
zamīn-mashā'e	the collective ownership of a piece of land
zekr-kardan	conversing with God
zinā'	sexual intercourse outside marriage and with non-marriageable relative
ziārat	pilgrimage
zulm	injustice, oppression

BIBLIOGRAPHY

Abu-Zahra, Nadia (1988) The rain rituals as rites of spiritual passage, *International Journal of Middle East Study*, vol. 20, no. 4: 507–29.

Afshar, Haleh (1982) Khomeini's teachings and their implications for Iranian women, in A. Tabari and N. Yaganeh (eds), *The Shadow of Islam*. London: Zed Press.

Ahmad, Lila (1992) *Women and Gender in Islam*. New Haven and London: Yale University Press.

Altorki, Soraya (1977) Family organization and women's power in urban Saudi Arabian society, *Journal of Anthropological Research*, vol. 33: 277–89.

Anderson, Jon W. (1982) Social structure and the veil: comportment and the composition of interaction in Afghanistan. Vienna: *Anthropos*, vol. 3–4: 397–420.

Antoun, Richard (1989) *Muslim Preacher in the Modern World: A Jordanian Case Study in Comparative Perspective*. Princeton: Princeton University Press.

Antoun, Richard (1993) Themes and symbols in the religious lesson: a Jordanian case study, *International Journal of Middle East Study*, vol. 25: 605–24.

Ardener, Edwin (1971) Belief and the problem of women, in J. S. La Fontaine (ed.), *The Interpretation of Ritual, Essays in Honour of A. I. Richards*. London: Tavistock.

Azari, Farah (ed.) (1983) *Women in Iran: The Conflict with Fundamentalist Islam*. London: Itacha Press.

Barth, Fredrik (1987) *Cosmologies in the Making*. Cambridge: Cambridge University Press.

Barth, Fredrik (1992) Towards greater naturalism in conceptualizing societies, in A. Kuper (ed.), *Conceptualizing Society*. London: Routledge.

Beck, Lois (1980) The religious lives of Muslim women, in Janet Smith (ed.), *Women in Contemporary Muslim Societies*. Lewisburg: Bucknell University Press.

Behdad, Sohrab (1988) Foreign exchange gap, structural constraints, and the political economy of exchange rate determination in Iran, *International Journal of Middle-East Studies*, vol. 20: 1–12.

Behdad, Sohrab (1989) Winners and losers of the Iranian revolution: a study in income distribution, *International Journal of Middle East Studies*, vol. 21: 327–58.

Betteridge, Anne (1980) The controversial vows of urban Muslim women in Iran, in N. A. Falk and R. M. Gross (eds), *Unspoken Worlds: Women's Religious Lives in Non-Western Cultures*. New York: Harper & Row.

Betteridge, Anne (1983) To veil or not to veil: a matter of protest or policy, in G. Nashat (ed.), *Women and Revolution in Iran*. Colorado: Westview Press.

Betteridge, Anne (1993) Women and shrines in Shiraz, in D. L. Bowen and E. A. Early (eds), *Everyday Life in the Muslim Middle East*. Bloomington: Indiana University Press.

Bloch, Maurice (1982) Death, women and power, in M. Bloch and J. Parry (eds), *Death and the Regeneration of Life*. Cambridge: Cambridge University Press.

Bonine, Michael and Keddie, Nikki (eds) (1979) *Dialectic of Continuity and Change*. Albany: State University of New York Press.

Bourdieu, Pierre and Passeron J. C. (1977) *Reproduction in Education, Society and Culture*. London: Sage.

Bowen, John R. (1993) *Muslims through Discourse*. Princeton: Princeton University Press.

Buckly, Thomas and Gottlieb, Alima (1988) *Blood Magic: The Anthropology of Menstruation*. Berkeley: University of California Press.

Buitelaar, Marjo (1994) *Fasting and Feasting in Morocco: Women's Participation in Ramadan*. Oxford: Berg.

Bynum, Caroline Walker (1986) Introduction: the complexity of symbols, in C. W. Bynum, S. Harrell and P. Richman (eds), *Gender and Religion: On the Complexity of Symbols*. Boston: Beacon Press.

Clair, Vickery Brown (1982) Home production for use in the market economy, in B. Thorne and M. Yalom (eds), *Rethinking Family*. New York: Longman.

Constantinides, Pamela (1978) Women's spirit possession and urban adaptation in the Muslim northern Sudan, in P. Caplan and J. M. Bujra (eds), *Women United, Women Divided: Cross Cultural Perspective on Female Solidarity*. London: Tavistock.

Delaney, Carol (1990) The Hajj: sacred and secular, *American Ethnologist*, vol. 17, no. 3: 513–30.

Douglas, Mary (1992) *Risk and Blame;* Essays in Cultural Theory. London: Routledge.

Dubisch, Jill (1986) Culture enters through the kitchen: women, food and social boundaries in rural Greece, in J. Dubisch (ed.), *Gender and Power in Rural Greece*. New Jersey: Princeton University Press.

Dwyer, Daisy Hilse (1978) Women, sufism and decision-making in Moroccan Islam, in L. Beck and N. Keddie (eds), *Women in the Muslim World*. Cambridge MA: Harvard University Press.

Eagleton, Terry (1991) *Ideology; An Introduction*. London: Verso.

Early, Evelyn A. (1993) *Baladi Women of Cairo: Playing with an Egg and a Stone*. Boulder: The American University in Cairo Press.

Eickelman, Dale (1980) The art of memory: Islamic education and its social reproduction, *Comparative Studies in Society and History*, New York University, vol. 20: 485–516.

Eickelman, Dale (1981) *The Middle East; An Anthropological Approach*. Englewood Cliffs NJ: Prentice Hall.

Eickelman, Dale (1985) *Knowledge and Power in Morocco*. Princeton: Princeton University Press.

Eickelman, Dale (1987) Changing interpretations of Islamic movements, in; W. Roff (ed.), *Islam and the Political Economy of Meaning*. London: Croom Helm.

El-Zein, Abdul Hamid (1977) Beyond ideology and theology: The Search for the Anthropology of Islam, *Annual Review of Anthropology*, vol. 6: 227–54.

Fernea, Robert and Fernea, Elizabeth (1972) Variation in religious observance among Islamic women, in N. Keddie (ed.), *Scholars, Saints and Sufis*. Berkeley: California University Press.

Fernea, Robert and Fernea, Elizabeth (1979) A look behind the veil, *Human Nature*, Jan 1979: 72–77.

Firth, Raymond (1959) Problem and assumption in an anthropological study of religion, *Journal of the Royal Anthropological Institute*, vol. 90: 129–48.

Fischer, Michael (1979) On changing the concept and position of Persian women, in L. Beck and N. Keddie (eds), *Women in the Muslim World*. London: Harvard University Press.

Fischer, Michael (1980). *Iran: From Religious Dispute to Revolution*. Cambridge MA: Harvard University Press.

Fischer, Michael and Abedi, Mehdi (1989). Revolutionary posters and cultural signs. *Middle East Report*, vol. 19, no. 159: 29–32.

Fischer, Michael and Abedi, Mehdi (1990) *Debating Muslims*. Madison: The University of Wisconsin Press.

Foucault, Michel (1972) *Power/Knowledge*. New York: Harvester Wheatsheaf.

Friedl, Erika (1980) Islam and tribal women in a village in Iran, in N. A. Falk and R. M. Gross (eds), *Unspoken Worlds: Women's Religious Lives in Non-Western Cultures*. San Francisco: Harper & Row.

Friedl, Ernestine (1967) The position of women: appearance and reality, *Anthropology Quarterly*, no. 40: 97–108.

Geertz, Clifford (1959) Ritual and social change: A Javanese example, *American Anthropologist*, vol. 61: 991–1012.

Good, Mary and Good, Byron (1988) Ritual, the state, and the transformation of emotional discourse in Iranian society, in *Culture, Medicine and Psychiatry*, no. 12: 43–63.

Grønhaug, Reidar (1976). *Micro-Macro Relations*. Bergen: Bergen Studies in Social Anthropology, No. 7.

Habibi, Nader (1989) Allocation of education and occupational opportunities in the Islamic Republic of Iran: A Case Study in the Political Screening of Human Capital in the Islamic Republic of Iran, in *Journal of the Society for Iranian Studies*, vol. 22, no. 4: 19–46.

Haeri, Shahla (1989) *Law of Desire: Temporary Marriage in Iran*. London: I. B. Tauris.

Hegland, Mary Elaine (1983) Two images of Husain: accommodation and revolution in an Iranian village, in N. Keddie (ed.), *Religions and Politics in Iran*. New Haven: Yale University Press.

Hegland, Mary Elaine (1983) Aliabad women: revolution as religious activity, in G. Neshat (ed.), *Women and Revolution in Iran*. Colorado: Westview Press.

Hegland, Mary Elaine (1986) Political roles of Iranian village women, *Middle East Report*, no. 139: 14–19.

Higgins, Patricia J. (1985) Women in the Islamic Republic of Iran: legal, social, and ideological changes, *Signs: Journal of Women in Culture and Society*, vol. 10, no. 31: 477–94.

Holden, Pat (ed.) (1983) *Women's Religious Experience*. London: Croom Helm.

Holy, Ladislav (1988) Gender and ritual in an Islamic society, the Berti of Darfur, *Man*, vol. 23, no. 3: 469–87.

Holy, Ladislav (1991) *Religion and Custom in a Muslim Society, The Berti of Sudan*. Cambridge: Cambridge University Press

Hooglund, Eric (1982) *Land and Revolution in Iran 1960–1980*. Austin: University of Texas Press.

Hooglund (Hegland), Mary (1982) Religious ritual and political struggle in an Iranian village, *Middle East Report*, no. 12: 10–17.

Jamzadeh, Laal and Mills, Margaret, (1986) Iranian 'sofreh': from collective to female ritual, in C. W. Bynum, S. Harrell and P. Richman (eds), *Gender and Religion*. Boston: Beacon Press.

Kamalkhani, Zahra (1992) The sociology of knowledge; an understanding of ideology and religious knowledge in the writing of social scientists and indigenous intellectuals. Compulsory lecture on theory of science as part of the scheme for Dr.polit. degree, University of Bergen, Bergen.

Kamalkhani, Zahra (1993) Women's everyday religious discourse in Iran, in H. Afshar (ed.), *Women in the Middle East*. London: Macmillan Press.

Kamalkhani, Zahra (1994) Family and household economic management in the context of change: a case study in Shiraz, *International Journal of Comparative Family and Marriage*, vol. 1, no. 1: 125–33.

Kandiyoti, Daniz (ed.) (1991) *Women, Islam and the State*. London: Macmillan.

Karimi, Setareh (1986) Economic policies and structural changes since the revolution, in N. Keddie and E. Hooglund (eds), *The Iranian Revolution and the Islamic Republic*. New York: Syracuse University Press.

Keddie, Nikki R. (1991) Introduction: deciphering Middle Eastern women's history, in N. Keddie and B. Barron (eds), *Women in Middle Eastern History: Shifting Boundaries in Sex and Gender*. London: Yale University Press.

Keesig, Roger M. (1987) Anthropology as interpretive quest, *Current Anthropology*, vol. 28, no. 2: 161–9.

Keesing, Roger M. (1990) Theories of culture revisited, *Canberra Anthropology*. vol. 13, no. 2: 46–60.

Kopytoff, Igor (1986) The cultural biography of things: commodization as process, in A. Appadurai (ed.), *The Social Life of Things*. Cambridge: Cambridge University Press.

Kurin, Richard (1983) The structure of blessedness at a Muslim shrine in Pakistan, *Middle Eastern Studies*, vol. 19, no. 3: 313–24.

Lambek, Michael (1990) Certain knowledge, contestable authority: power and practice on the Islamic periphery, *Americal Ethnologist*, vol. 17: 23–40.

Lewis, Ioan M. (1971) *Ecstatic Religion*. Harmondsworth: Penguin Books.

Loeffler, Reinhold (1988) *Islam in Practice*. Albany: State University of New York.

Macleod, Arlene Elowe (1991) *Accommodating Protest: Working Women, the New Veiling, and Change in Cairo*. Egypt: The American University in Cairo Press.

Malinowski, Bronislaw (1954) *Magic, Science, and Religion and other Essays*. New York: Doubleday Anchor Books.

Mannheim, Karl (1952) *Essays in Sociology of Knowledge*. New York: Oxford University Press.

Mauss, Marcel (1954) *The Gift*. London: Routledge & Kegan Paul.

Mahdavi, Shireen (1984) The position of women in Shia Iran: views of the Ulama, in E. W. Fernea (ed.), *Women and the Family in the Middle East*. Austin, Texas: University of Texas.

Marbro, Judy (1991) *Veiled Half-Truths*. New York: Turis.

Mehran, Golnar (1991) Socialization of school children in the Islamic Republic of Iran, *Iranian Studies*, vol. XXII, no. 1: 35–59.

Mernissi, Fatimah (1975) *Beyond the Veil: Male Female Dynamics in a Modern Muslim Society*. Cambridge: Schenkman Publishing Company.

Mernissi, Fatimah (1977) Women, saints and sanctuaries, in the Wellesley Editorial, *Women and National Development: The Complexity of Change*. Chicago: The University of Chicago Press.

Mernissi, Fatimah (1991a) *The Veil and the Male Elite: A Feminist Interpretation of Women's Right in Islam*. Reading MA: Addison Wesley.

Mernissi Fatimah (1991b) *Women and Islam*. Oxford: Blackwell.

Mutahari, Morteza (1975) *Nezam-e Hoghoghe-Zan dar Islam*. Tehran: Sahami-ʿām.

Najmabadi, Afsaneh (1990) Hazards of modernity and morality: women and the state ideology in contemporary Iran, in D. Kandiyoti (ed.), *Women, Islam and the State*. London: Macmillan.

Nashat, Guity (1983) Women in the ideology of the Islamic Republic, in G. Nashat (ed.), *Women and Revolution in Iran*. Colorado: Westview Press.

Nelson, Cynthia (1974) Public and private politics: women in the Middle Eastern world, *American Ethnologist*, vol. 1, no. 2: 551–63.

Nelson, Cynthia (1991) Old wine, new bottles, in E. L. Sullivan and J. S. Ismael (eds), *The Contemporary Study of the Arab World*. Alberta: University of Alberta Press.

Obeyesekere, Gananath (1981) *Medusa's Hair: An Essay on Personal Symbols and Religious Experience*. Chicago: The University of Chicago Press.

Ortner, Sherry (1974) Is female to male as nature is to culture? in M. Z. Rosaldo and L. Lamphere (eds), *Women, Culture, and Society.* Stanford: Stanford University Press.

Ortner, Sherry (1989) *High Religion: A Cultural and Political History of Sherpa Buddhism.* Princeton: Princeton University Press.

Paidar, Parvin (1995) *Women and the Political Process in Twentieth-Century Iran.* Cambridge: Cambridge University Press.

Parry, Jonathan (1986) The gift, the Indian gift and the 'Indian gift', *Man,* vol. 21, no. 3: 453–73.

Paydarfar, Ali (1974) Differential life-styles between migrants and non-migrants: a case study of the city of Shiraz, Iran, *Demography,* vol. 11, no. 3.

Piscatori, James P. (1989) Introduction, in J. P. Piscatori (ed.), *Islam in the Political Process.* Cambridge: Cambridge University Press.

Piscatori, James P. and Eickelman, Dale F. (1990) Social theory in the study of Muslim societies, in D. F. Eickelman and J. P. Piscatori (eds), *Muslim Travellers, Pilgrimage, Migration, and the Religious Imagination.* Berkeley: University of California Press.

Rahnavard, Zahra (1978) *Payam hejāb Zan Mosalman* (in Persian). Tehran: Nashar Mahbubeh.

Rosaldo, Michel (1974) Women, culture and society: a theoretical overview, in M. Rosaldo & L. Lamphere (eds), *Women, Culture and Society.* Stanford: Stanford University Press.

Rosander, Eva Evers (1991) *Women in a Borderland: Managing Muslim Identity where Morocco meets Spain.* Stockholm: Stockholm Studies in Social Anthropology.

Scott, James C. (1990) The infrapolitics of subordinate groups, in Scott, J., *Domination and the Art of Resistance.* New Haven: Yale University Press.

Sharma, Ursula N. (1980) *Women, Work, and Property in North-West India.* London: Tavistock Publications.

Starr, Sered Susan (1992) *Women as Ritual Experts: The Religious Lives of Elderly Jewish Women in Jerusalem.* Oxford: Oxford University Press.

Stirrat, R. L. (1984) Sacred models, *Man,* vol. 19: 199–215.

Strathern, Marilyn (1980) No nature, no culture: the Hagen case, in C. P. Maccormack and M. Strathern (eds), *Nature, Culture and Gender.* Cambridge: Cambridge University Press.

Strathern, Marilyn (1987) An awkward relationship: the case of feminism and anthropology, *Signs: Journal of Women in Culture and Society,* vol. 12: 276–92.

Tabari, Azar (1982) The enigma of veiled Iranian women, *Merip Report.* 22–27 Feb.

Tapper, Nancy (1983) Gender and religion in a Turkish town: a comparison of two types of formal women's gatherings, in P. Holden (ed.), *Women's Religious Experience.* London, Croom Holm.

Tapper, Nancy (1990) Ziyarat: gender, movement, and exchange in a Turkish community, in D. J. Eickelman and J. P. Piscatori (eds), *Muslim Travellers.* Berkeley: University of California Press.

Tapper, Nancy and Tapper, Richard (1987) The birth of the Prophet; ritual and gender in Turkish Islam, *Man*, vol. 22, no. 1: 69–92.

Tambiah, Stanley Jeyaraja (1990) *Magic, Science, Religion, and the Scope of Rationality*. Cambridge: Cambridge University Press.

Tett, Gillian (1994) Guardians of the faith?: gender and religion in an (ex) Soviet Tajik village, in C. F. El-Solh and J. Mabro (eds), *Muslim Women's Choices*. Oxford: Berg.

Thaiss, Gustav (1976) The rhetoric of religious mediation in Iran, delivered at the 10th annual meeting of *Middle East Studies Association*.

Thaiss, Gustav (1977) Religious symbolism and social change: the drama of Husain, in N. Keddie (ed), *Scholars, Saints, and Sufis*. California: The California University Press.

Thaiss, Gustav (1978) The conceptualization of social change through metaphor, *Journal of Asian and African Studies*, vol. 8, no. 1–2: 1–13.

Tiffany, Sharon W. (1984) Models and the social anthropology of women: a preliminary assessment, in D. O'Brian and S. Tiffany (eds), *Rethinking Women's Roles: Perspectives from the Pacific*. Berkeley: University of California Press.

Turner, Bryan S. (1983) *Religion and Social Theory: A Materialistic Perspective*. London: Humanities Press.

Turner, Victor (1967) *The Forest of Symbols: Aspects of Ndembu Ritual*. Ithaca: Cornell University Press.

Turner, Victor (1969) *The Ritual Process*. Chicago: Aldine.

Turner, Victor (1974) *Dramas, Fields, and Metaphors; Symbolic Action in Human Society*, Ithaca: Cornell University Press.

Ustād-Malek, Fatemeh (1989) *Hejāb va Kashf-e-hejāb dar iran*. Tehran: ʿaṭaʾī Publications.

Weiner, Annette B. (1989) *Women of Value and Men of Renown*. Austin: University of Texas Press.

Wikan, Unni (1982) *Behind the Veil in Arabia: Women in Oman*. Baltimore: Johns Hopkins University Press.

Yanagisako, Sylvia J. (1979) Family and household: analysis of domestic groups. *Annual Review of Anthropology*, vol. 8: 161–205.

Zwemer, Samuel M. (1926) *Muslim Women. The Central Committee on the United Study of Foreign Missions*. Vermont: North Cambridge, Mass.

AUTHOR INDEX

AUTHOR INDEX

SUBJECT INDEX